MORE PRAISE FOR
Awakening Together

"A timely and essential offering, generous and brilliant. Larry Yang is acknowledged as a pioneer in insisting on the diversity and anti-racism work needed in many contemporary spiritual communities. What a gift this book is!"

—**GINA SHARPE**, cofounder of New York Insight Meditation Center

"Filled with love. As a seasoned and well-loved Dharma teacher, Larry Yang's long-awaited gift satisfies the soul that yearns to be seen."

—**ZENJU EARTHLYN MANUEL**, PhD, Zen Buddhist priest and author of *The Way of Tenderness*

"Like no other that I have encountered, *Awakening Together* offers a profound teaching of how to be inclusive and how to practice faith in community. This book is a real treasure, and a map to great awakenings in our worldwide sangha."

—**MYOKEI CAINE-BARRETT**, Shonin, resident priest of Myoken Temple in Houston

"In *Awakening Together*, Buddhist teacher and diversity/inclusivity activist Larry Yang invites us to extend our practice on the cushion into a collective practice of understanding and compassion. Inspiring, compelling and deeply wise, *Awakening Together* is essential reading as we seek to heal our own hearts, our communities, and our world."

—**TARA BRACH**, author of *Radical Acceptance*

"Larry Yang's voice, heart, and insight in *Awakening Together* can be both trusted and radically illuminating. We do indeed need each other for any of us to awaken to our true nature as human beings. Mindfulness practice has to be about inclusivity and diversity and justice if it is to be kind and compassionate and wise. If we truly 'inter-are' as Thich Nhat Hanh asserts, then, as this book shows, we have to widen our scope of what is worthy of our attention. Parts of this book may make some people in the greater mindfulness community uncomfortable. It certainly was true in my case. That is precisely why it is particularly valuable to read and reflect upon and learn from. We need trusted others to show us our blind spots, our tacit assumptions, and our ignorance. I highly recommend this elegant, highly personal, and hopefully profoundly influential book."
—**JON KABAT-ZINN**, author of *Full Catastrophe Living*

"Essential reading for anyone interested in building and sustaining a diverse, inclusive, empowered, wise, and compassionate community."
—**KITTISARO AND THANISSARA**, authors of *Listening to the Heart*

AWAKENING TOGETHER

The Spiritual Practice of Inclusivity and Community

Larry Yang

FOREWORD BY Jan Willis
FOREWORD BY Sylvia Boorstein

Wisdom Publications
132 Perry Street
New York, NY 10014 USA
wisdomexperience.org

Library of Congress Cataloging-in-Publication Data
Names: Yang, Larry, author.
Title: Awakening together: the spiritual practice of inclusivity and community / Larry Yang.
Description: Somerville, MA: Wisdom Publications, [2017] |
Identifiers: LCCN 2017003560 (print) | LCCN 2017013299 (ebook) | ISBN 9781614293699
    (ebook) | ISBN 1614293694 (ebook) | ISBN 9781614293514 (pbk.: acid-free paper) | ISBN
    1614293511 (pbk.: acid-free paper)
Subjects: LCSH: Spiritual life—Buddhism. | Spirituality—Buddhism. | Communities—
    Religious aspects—Buddhism.
Classification: LCC BQ5660 (ebook) | LCC BQ5660 .Y35 2017 (print) | DDC
    294.3/444—dc23
LC record available at https://lccn.loc.gov/2017003560

ISBN 978-1-61429-351-4   ebook ISBN 978-1-61429-369-9

26 25 24
6 5 4

Cover design by Jess Morphew.
Interior design by Gopa & Ted2, Inc. Set in Scala Pro 10.2/15.

Wisdom Publications' books are printed on acid-free paper and meet
the guidelines for permanence and durability of the Production Guidelines
for Book Longevity of the Council on Library Resources.

Printed in the United States of America.

Please visit fscus.org.

Contents

Foreword

By Jan Willis

All men [sic] are caught in an inescapable network of mutuality, tied in a single garment of destiny. Whatever affects one directly, affects all indirectly. I can never be what I ought to be until you are what you ought to be, and you can never be what you ought to be until I am what I ought to be. —Reverend Dr. Martin Luther King Jr.

The Reverend Dr. Martin Luther King Jr. recognized—as did the Buddha before him—the fact of our shared interdependent reality and the interrelated nature of all of reality itself. We do not exist in isolation—and neither does our enlightenment. Our personal liberation is tied up with our collective liberation; we cannot be fully liberated alone. This truth is the chief theme of this powerful and poetic book by Larry Yang—mindfulness practitioner and teacher, deep inclusivity activist, and diversity change-agent. It is a book about community building as spiritual practice, a book we need now more than ever.

This profound insight about our interdependence would seem, on the one hand, to be undeniable—yet for many, even those in Buddhist Dharma communities, it remains unrealized. This fact gives rise to two questions: First, how do we make visible the invisible systems of privilege that prevent realizations of interdependence, even as those systems are denied or held unconsciously? And second, how do we move through those systems, together, toward our mutual liberation?

You have in your hands a book that can undoubtedly help us do both of those things. *Awakening Together* is written by a wise and kindhearted man who wants Buddhism to be more widely accessible to people of color and other marginalized groups. It is part personal reflection, part guidebook, part manifesto, and part rich analysis of what ails our country and our Dharma communities. Ultimately, *Awakening Together* is a treasure-trove of insight and hands-on advice, gleaned from years of experience and offered with clarity, gentleness, and—most of all—love. It takes seriously the notion that, in Larry's words, the "Dharma is about being aware of the needs of all communities, not just our own." Larry explores here how we might all achieve our fullest potential, together—*in relationship with one another*—and he offers practical advice on how to make our awakening together a real possibility.

I have known Larry for many years. I have listened to and watched him teach in multicultural environments with sensitivity and with magnanimity. I have seen him handle potential crises with skillfulness, wisdom, and bodhisattvic aplomb. In short, I have witnessed him actually *practice* deep inclusivity. And Larry has experienced Buddhist *sangha*—even the ordained community (during his time as a monk in Thailand)—deeply, with all its saving graces.

Pragmatist that he was, the Buddha knew and described for us the type of community and organizational structure that would best suit the living of and promulgation of his teachings. One of his earliest activities was to establish the Buddhist sangha, or community. Strikingly radical amid the structures of his day, the community that the Buddha founded included a diversity of beings, accepting people from all castes—and accepting women. More than 2,500 years ago, the Buddha saw that the ideal community was one of diversity and deep inclusivity. Were this not so, he would not have established his sangha in this way. This fact reveals, as Larry tells us, that the Buddha "was inviting us to explore, as deeply as meditation itself, what it means to awaken together in community. He was inviting us to explore community itself as a practice of meditation or cultivation."

In the West, there are very few traditional Buddhist monasteries. Rather, here the containers for communal/community Buddhist practice are Buddhist centers or Dharma communities (this is especially so for us so-called convert Buddhists). One can reasonably ask whether such centers or communities still operate in as deeply inclusive a manner as did the Buddha's own sangha, or whether a different dynamic is at play in such contexts. *Awakening Together* not only raises this important question but offers us sound analysis of the underlying issues—as well as sage advice for addressing them. He writes, for example,

> Western cultural norms and inclinations have already influenced our own experience of the teachings. Even though we, in the Insight Meditation circles, acknowledge that sangha is a practice of being in community, we (as Western convert groups) do not place as much emphasis on this aspect as practitioners from traditionally Buddhist countries.

And he speaks of the difference in worldview and cultural archetypes between the West (where one emphasizes individual experience) and the East (where the collective experience is paramount), saying,

> Many of our Western Dharma communities, which are largely focused on European American values and norms, have yet to examine how the Dharma has been changed in its transition and transmission from interdependent cultures to an independent culture. Moreover, our own cultural reinterpretation of the Dharma is largely an unconscious, unexamined phenomenon.

I believe that these are appropriate critiques of convert-Buddhist sanghas in the West—and Larry points us to others as well.

For more than twenty years now I have been writing about my observations that Dharma centers and Dharma communities in the West are primarily homogeneous, being composed, generally speaking, of mostly white, middle- to upper-middle-class participants with very little diversity. Being African American and finding much that is of value to me in Buddhist Dharma, I want the Dharma to be accessible to other people of color and other culturally specific groups, and for Dharma communities to be more reflective of our richly diverse society. The benefits of inclusivity run both ways, and we can "wake up" in the best and only real way *together*. Larry Yang clearly gets this. He writes, for example,

I believe that if Dharma practice is meant to be comprehensive—that is, to leave nothing in life outside of its scope—then culture is not to be transcended or left behind. In fact, culture is something to be integrated into the very fabric of our spiritual practice, including the diverse facets of our behavior and identities.

Larry also knows how it feels to attempt to practice Buddhism in communities that are not welcoming. Describing one of his first "loving-kindness" retreats, he writes, "My predominant experience with spiritual and religious traditions that purported to teach unconditional regard was that they were typically unable, unwilling, or unskilled at directing love toward those aspects of life important to *me*, someone outside the dominant white, hetero-normative American culture." At that first retreat, he notes, "All I could focus on was that I was the only person of color out of about a hundred people—and how awkward, lonely, and even unsafe I felt." There was nothing inviting or safe about the space or the experience, and Larry began to feel that "I had to leave this part of my life—my experiences as a person of color, as a gay, queer man—outside the door." He adds, "The message I felt was that those aspects were not worthy of awareness and kindness, and by extrapolation, I myself was not worthy of this practice."

Especially in times like these, fraught on every side with threats from racist, xenophobic, misogynistic, and anti-queer bias, a welcoming and safe space for practice is the most kind and compassionate thing we can create for each other. If such issues are denied or go unacknowledged in Dharma settings, where can they be safely voiced and heard? If in Dharma settings people feel, in Larry's words, "unattended, unloved, unseen, and even harmed," where is the safety—the refuge—that sangha is meant to offer?

Fortunately for us, Larry's initial retreat experiences led him not to turn away from the Dharma but to truly embark upon the great challenge of making Dharma communities more inclusive and diverse. Alongside others, he began the project of creating the East Bay Meditation Center (EBMC)—one of the most deeply inclusive communites to be found anywhere in the United States. *Awakening Together* provides us with a detailed, step-by-step blueprint and history of the hard work involved in creating that community and, in doing so, shows us how we can begin and continue to build an inclusive sangha.

As important as that alone would be, Larry's greatest gift to all of us in the Dharma is his commitment to supporting the conditions for producing Dharma teachers of color and Dharma teachers from other culturally specific groups. If we truly want diversity in our sanghas, we must do more than simply pay lip service to the idea. Like me, Larry has argued that one of the primary ways of doing this is to have people of color and other culturally specific Dharma teachers *actually teaching* in our Dharma communities. But Larry has done even more. He has lobbied for the vital necessity of having a pipeline of such teachers for the future, and he has himself committed to *training* many of them. Since 2000, with the support of Spirit Rock, Larry has been training new people of color, LGBTIQ-identified people, and other culturally specific teachers. As he notes, such activity requires "awareness and involvement from all of us. This is how we are interrelated." This is the gift of our practice.

And so, dear reader, if you are ready to commit to the idea that we, as a diverse group of Buddhists, ought to be able to awaken *together*, and to honor and share all of what and who we are in the process, then take up this book, Larry's loving clarion call. Consciously, mindfully, read *Awakening Together* with openness and with joy.

JAN WILLIS is professor of religion emerita at Wesleyan University in Middletown, Connecticut, and visiting professor of religion at Agnes Scott College in Decatur, Georgia. She is the author of *Dreaming Me: Black, Baptist, and Buddhist—One Woman's Spiritual Journey.*

Foreword

BY SYLVIA BOORSTEIN

SOME YEARS AFTER I had begun practicing mindfulness meditation, I made an appointment to meet with Chagdud Rinpoche, a Tibetan Buddhist teacher renowned for his understanding of the altered states of consciousness associated with intense meditation practice. I needed his help.

My practice had led me to some genuinely liberating insights and some calming of my habitually anxious mind—both of which had been rewarding for me, and hoped for—but in addition I had begun to experience unusual energetic sensations that were intense and often uncomfortable. I felt energy running up and down my spine, I told him, and I felt alternately very hot and very cold. I described how I heard sounds that definitely were not part of my ambient experience, sounds like motors running in my head. I told him that my body, as I lay quietly on my bed concentrating on my breath, would leap suddenly into a yoga posture—seemingly on its own. And I also told him that when unusual experiences began to happen, I initially found them pleasant and was quite interested in them, but now they had become intense and uncomfortable, and so I sought help. I was also hoping, although I did not mention it to the Rinpoche, that he would be at least a little impressed with my ability to develop extraordinary attention.

Chagdud listened to all I'd said and asked me, "How much compassion practice do you do every day?"

I was surprised. I had expected him to give me a calming meditation instruction. I replied, "I'd understood that with concentration comes insight, with insight comes wisdom, and that the wise mind is spontaneously compassionate." This is a rather standard formulation of the purification of the mind through practice.

"No," he said. "How much compassion practice do you do every day."

"I don't know what you mean."

"How much do you go out into the world every day and look at how much people are suffering?"

For a brief moment I thought perhaps Chagdud Rinpoche was rebuking me, seeing my preoccupations as self-centered. His demeanor, though, was so kindly and his words so mild that I knew that this was not about me, that I could skip right over being embarrassed and hear what he was telling me.

And, of course, he was right.

He correctly added the awareness of life around me to the steadiness of mind I had been cultivating. The concentration I had developed enabled me to stay more open to the manifold instances of pain and suffering in my personal world, as well as in the world that I met through knowing the news. I could not look away from it or pretend it wasn't there. My heart, which could have missed it—being absorbed as it often was in self-preoccupation and lack of courage—was available to respond to the suffering. Letting my heart freely respond to others—whether in compassion when it meets sorrow, or joy when it meets instances of celebration—is a more enduring and trustworthy pleasure than my experiences of profound concentration (in which the world had disappeared) had ever been.

I heard years ago that Thich Nhat Hanh said, "The next Buddha will be the sangha." At the time, I thought perhaps that was a tribute that meant the greatness of the Buddha was such that only a group of people could measure up to his value. Now I think it quite literally means that we can learn from everyone and everything, that the teacher is the world around us waiting to be seen and deeply understood. We learn from each other, in relationship, the pain of being inevitably separated from what we love by old age, sickness, and death—and we come to know that we share this vulnerability with all human beings. Feeling at ease, in a community in which we experience the comfort of feeling seen, we discover our natural ability to feel empathy for others through the sharing of our individual challenges.

When I began my Buddhist meditation practice decades ago and heard about taking refuge in the Buddha, the Dharma, and the Sangha, I thought that my sangha included not only the people in the Buddhist groups I practiced with but my family as well, and the professional groups I am part of, and the synagogue community I belong to. I thought of all the people I had learned I could depend on to see me and support me. I've begun to think in more recent times that the sangha I hope to feel part of some day is the world, including and perhaps especially the parts that seem most different from me and difficult to feel at ease with, near and far away. In those moments, reflecting on how everyone in the world will suffer together from a deteriorating planet, I am able to think of everyone with compassion. And while at times I might feel sad, I do not feel alone.

Larry Yang has been my friend and teaching colleague for many years, and I have always admired his steadfast emphasis on inclusivity, his dedication to making the Dharma relevant to, and accessible to, the widest possible audience. The Buddha, in a society that was distinctly hierarchical, discarded class lines and insisted that his community be open to anyone who was willing to undertake a vowed life. "Teach the holy Dharma in the idiom of the people," are the instructions he gave to his disciples as they left his community to spread his liberating doctrine. His understanding was that wisdom and compassion were the antidotes to the universal experiences of grief and loss, which is certainly true in modern times just as it was in the time of the Buddha.

Awakening Together is being born into a world in which suffering caused by greed and hatred, on an individual and a global level, are part of an ongoing news cycle. Habits that are part of trying to cope with escalating life stressors make descriptions of a relaxed and grateful mind seem like quaint anachronisms. Now more than ever, I think, the need for an emerging self-aware group of people dedicated to developing wisdom on behalf of compassion is vital to address the strife and divisiveness of the people of the world and the perilous state of the planet. The new teachers of wisdom in the idiom of the people will not be recognizable by their robes but by their hearts. This book speaks to this need, and Larry's is such a heart.

SYLVIA BOORSTEIN is a founding teacher of Spirit Rock Meditation Center, and is the author of *It's Easier Than You Think: The Buddhist Way to Happiness*, as well as several other books.

Preface

Now More Than Ever

THIS BOOK IS my attempt to connect a personal spiritual path and journey with the larger course of our shared human experience.

When I was a much younger person, I kept searching for something that was elusive and seemingly beyond my reach—a way to be happy. The spiritual values of Unconditionality or Love I heard about so often that were elevated as goals seemed so far away from the limited experience of my small life. I kept seeing the particulars of my life to be too unique, too different, or even too difficult or painful to understand myself, let alone to be grasped by other people. I felt isolated, separated, and hopeless.

Little did I know at the time how commonplace in our world this feeling of separation can be.

I now see in hindsight that even when I did not follow an explicit spiritual faith tradition, there was still a motivation urging me toward living a life that was as fulfilled as was humanly possible. The realization began to emerge as I grew older—as I met more friends, lovers, business associates, acquaintances, and even enemies, and as I began to collect these people into my consciousness—that everyone was trying to live in the same way. Not to live the same life as I was, of course, but motivated by the same intentions of living the best life possible in the short time we have on this earth. In the midst of all the seeming differences, we were all seeking a way to be happy.

In that commonality of experience is a deep teaching.

We learn not only from our personal individual lives but also from the rich gathering together of our collective experiences. When we tread any path, start any project, embark on any journey, it is often easier to do it in the company of friends and associates than alone. We learn both individually and collectively. This is why the Buddha offered the teachings of Sangha, of Community: because there is both wisdom and freedom in exploring our collective experience. One of my intentions with this book is to explore our *awakening together* within the multiple experiences of community and communities, however we each choose to define them.

The experience of community brings with it complex issues of belonging: who is included, what power dynamics are involved, and how any community defines its collective identity through the individual identities that form it. I believe not only that the teachings of the Buddha help us navigate those complex issues but that such complexities are embedded in the Dharma itself.

Issues of identity emerged as an expansive theme early in my own personal practice. Outside the Asian cultures of origin of the Buddha's teachings, Western Buddhism has been most accessible to people who are middle to upper-middle class, white, heterosexual, and privileged. While there have been efforts to diversify and broaden the Dharma's reach, this profile still remains largely accurate. One current challenge is whether the Dharma can expand beyond appealing to dominant cultural interests into true relevance for the multiplicity of our human cultural diversity and inclusivity. Can the Dharma become truly meaningful for the global cultural dynamics that currently face us all?

For me, it is through the lenses of community and identity that I began to see how identity can be a door into Dharma practice and spiritual freedom. The beauty of the Dharma is that everything—*everything*, even all the particulars of identity—is integral to our spiritual practice. Accordingly, freedom is not just about transcending identity but embracing it until what is beyond the experience of identity reveals itself. And, as with much of our human existence, this is not always a linear process.

Especially within our society's current sociopolitical and cultural conditions, race, sexual orientation, and multiculturalism have never been more relevant to the evolution of our larger world. This relevance can be seen in many places: the overt inequities of the inordinate mass incarceration of and police violence toward African American men; the murders of transgender people, especially of color; the inability of people to find a sustainable livelihood in parallel to the increasingly extreme wealth of the few; the ever-growing economic disparities that marginalize afford-able housing; arrogant and mean-spirited policies toward immigration; the polarized screeching of our current political discourse; or even the intrusions upon people being able to perform intimate bodily functions without state intervention. Communities are aching for spiritual guid-ance on the most varied and difficult of social dilemmas.

Now more than ever, as the world's problems are increasing expo-nentially in complexity, we need to address these problems as people, communities, and nations. In this lifetime and in this modern age we are being asked to carry, manage, and navigate more and more people, places, things, activities, and issues, whether we face challenges in our personal life about changing the world, caregiving for our families, or surviving adverse personal circumstances. Some of the complexity may feel unresolvable—a family trying to make ends meet despite multiple stressors; inherent democratic values of our country being summarily dismissed by power without accountability; disparity, discrimination, and deception in a supposedly free society; terrorism with both its causes and impacts; justice when the needs and values underlying those intentions are increasingly complex in a more diverse society; or trying to find purpose and meaning in a world that might feel incomprehen-sible. Now more than ever we need our mindfulness practice. We need the Dharma.

We need the freedom into which mindfulness invites us—the free-dom to not have to follow the patterns of our unconsciousness, either individually or collectively. We do not have to follow the ways of the world simply because we have been taught them or because everyone else does. We do not have to be someone we are not, just because the world says that is who we should be. We need to remember that it is possible to notice deeply what is happening right now, and understand it with enough wis-dom, treat it with the compassion inherent in our humanity, and move into responses and actions that are of benefit as best as we are able. We are called by the voice in our collective hearts to move toward that which lessens suffering and creates more happiness, not just for us personally but for us as communities within a global society and collective world.

What we do on the meditation cushion—create clarity of mind, openness of heart, and mindfulness of thought, emotions, and actions—is not any different than the work we do in the world to create a better life for us all. As many spiritual masters and social activist elders have told us, "We must be the change we wish to see in the world." Mindfulness can be the practice that connects our individual spiritual path with the path of all beings.

Our paths toward freedom are the same—we are not separate from one another.

Now more than ever, we need to remember this.

A note about sources: Most of the Pali scriptural sources I cite in this book are translated by Thanissaro Bhikku and appear on the Access to Insight website (www.accesstoinsight.org), except where otherwise noted in the text.

Acknowledgments

WHATEVER BENEFIT that I have been able to share with others in this lifetime has been due to the care and love and guidance from my parents. They have been and are my most profound teachers. I offer my deepest bows and most tender hugs to them as their son.

My endless love and appreciation go to my husband, Stephen Pickard, without whom I could not do what I do, and without whom I could not be completely who I am. I do not have enough gratitude in this world to offer my dearest friend, Gina Sharpe, for always unconditionally holding my back, and standing by my side, and embracing me in front. I have felt completely supported by the expertise of my editor, Josh Bartok, and the skills of all the staff at Wisdom, who have been indispensible in offering this material. My boundless thanks go to Brandi Auset, who transcribed over a dozen of my Dharma talks, which helped me to begin this long process of writing.

And I would like to express my deepest respect and humility toward my multiple communities—Spirit Rock Meditation Center, East Bay Meditation Center, Insight Community of the Desert, and others with whom I have worked. I have grown, learned, and been transformed by the teachings of Dharma and Freedom; I received so much care and love; I have gotten so much joy and laughter; I have been offered generous support and kindness; and I have been repeatedly forgiven for my shortcomings. Thank you.

1

From Suffering into Freedom

O VER THE YEARS I have come to a deep commitment to and faith in the teachings of the Buddha. These are teachings that have fed and nurtured my spiritual needs and development as a human being. In this life that has been given me, the Dharma of the Buddha has been transformative.

It might be an easy assumption to make (or maybe a stereotype) that an Asian American, born to rather traditional parents who emigrated from the outskirts of Shanghai in northern China, would gravitate to a Buddhist spiritual practice. Indeed, my mother was raised in a household whose members were devotionally Buddhist, and my father, who was a Confucian Taoist, was not unfamiliar with Buddhist temples and practice. However, the cultural equation of connecting my own Asian heritage to the Buddhist tradition (or any spiritual tradition at all, for that matter) was not so direct or simple.

Much of my early childhood was spent in Levittown, Pennsylvania— the epitome of those postwar suburban developments of affordable, homogenous homes of the late 1950s and early 1960s, the ones that Pete Seeger sang about. For me at the time, though, Levittown did not seem to have the monotonous, uninspired uniformity Seeger's lyrics evoked. After all, it was the world of my childhood. And as for most children, even this most mundane environment was exciting and interesting.

Levittown was a place with a hill for shooting down on a bike whose weight and design would be embarrassing in today's sophisticated choices of racing, recumbent, mountain, touring, and BMX models: a "Schwinn-built" American Flyer. And in bright maroon, it was the coolest thing to show off on as a seven- or eight-year-old.

Levittown was a place with a creek—though English being my second language, I remember having trouble with whether the word should be pronounced "creek" or "crick." That creek provided an illusion of wilderness for a young, wide-eyed, mock scientist who dissected bugs, poked at frogs, and tried to catch minnows with awkward little fingers. My scientific methodology was undeveloped, but the intention of curiosity was already well into formation.

It was in Levittown on November 22, 1963, that I remember running up the front lawn (it wasn't that big, but to my short, stubby legs it seemed like a track field) telling my mother that President Kennedy had been shot. My mom had not been listening to the news that day, but I had been listening to the radio in the carpool coming home from my Quaker elementary school. I knew that it was an event that was really important and really sad. We sat in front of our RCA black-and-white TV set transfixed by the unfolding tragedy along with millions of other Americans that day.

And it was in Levittown where I had my first experience of racism.

I can remember running up the same lawn with different news for my mom. Instead of bursting inside without a care in the world, I carefully opened the screen door. I turned the brass knob of a front door painted as red as my Radio Flyer wagon, and let the screen door gently close without the typical crash that followed me.

I guess I didn't look too happy: my mom came up and knelt so that her face was at the same level as mine. We weren't a physically affectionate family; that hasn't been my experience of the Asian or Chinese way of doing things. Love and other emotions were shown through behavior, rather than gesture or verbal expression. But this time, she reached out to my shoulder, "What's the matter, Larry?"

I almost didn't want to answer.

"Ma, what does *chink* mean?"

My mother's prolonged pause reinforced what I already knew—that this, like the news of Kennedy's assassination, was a life experience that was really sad. It was a lightning bolt that illuminated for me how people perceive each other and treat each other badly based upon how different they seem. I didn't know the words *race*, *culture*, or *ethnicity*, but I could still feel the nausea and tension in my little body. It was one of those aha moments that children can have, and it came in a flash.

It wasn't an experience of *understanding*—as a kid, I couldn't understand what was happening—but I did recognize that it was something important. It simply was what it was: a moment of awareness—awareness of suffering in my life. And that is what my mother reflected back to me.

She said after a moment, "Sometimes that is just the way things are in the world."

It was an unsatisfactory response to the racism of which I was just beginning to become conscious. But it was also the best she could offer at the time in a world rife with the cultural complexities of post-McCarthyism and the Vietnam War. I was too young to grasp anything beyond the immediate experience of my own suffering and pain.

Much later in life I read a passage in James Baldwin's *Notes of a Native Son* that resonated very deeply with me. At the end of his description of the experience of being refused service at a diner because they didn't serve "Negroes" there, Baldwin writes, "And I felt, like a physical sensation, a click at the nape of my neck as though some interior string connecting my head to my body had been cut."

In hindsight of my own string being cut, I appreciate that I recognized some part of my experience as a moment when cultures intersect. I was fast-tracking out of childhood, and I was losing my innocence.

My childhood home was a place where my everyday companions and best friends were the kids of our immediate neighbors on both sides of our house. A pair of brothers, Steven and Burton, lived to the left of my house, and another pair of brothers, Buddy and Randy, lived to the right. There was about three years' difference between the two pairs, enough at that age to completely separate them into different interests and different preadolescent worlds. I was exactly in the middle age-wise, allowing me to hang out with either pair of boys.

It was a confusingly tender time for me—the naive simplicity of rolling down freshly mowed lawns, hiding from grownups in the hedges, and plotting not to be seen by the "nerdy" girls—because I was hiding one more secret from everyone else, a secret kept hidden in the safe recesses of my own mind where I thought I could control and manage it. My secret was that I was a boy who felt the need for more connection and relationship with other boys.

As with the racism I encountered, I didn't even have a word for this feeling, much less comprehend terms like *sexual orientation, homosexuality,* or *gay.* I just knew that I felt even more different from other kids around me, beyond my skin color, the shape of my eyes, and the details of my cultural background. I felt different from those whom I felt I belonged to—my family. And I knew almost as soon as I had the feelings, whatever it was called, that people did not treat it with acceptance, kindness, or love. The cultural worlds I found myself torn between began to expand in number.

In the balance of things, for me life usually felt more painful than not back then. There was tremendous pain in not knowing where I belonged and not feeling that I belonged anywhere with anyone. I imagine some version of this arises in many people during adolescence, regardless of culture, race, or sexual orientation, but those issues simply heightened the angst of a young person who had yet to develop any life skills that would be of guidance or support. And it created in me a tremendous desire to get rid of the pain and suffering. I became determined to become a person who I was not.

I lost interest in my language of origin, my cultural heritage, and some of the deep sources of my identity—even in my childhood friends who were Asian. Family history and lineage became quaint stories that I tolerated to humor my parents and relatives over holidays, but they did not concern me in my "real life" in the "real American" white world.

I measured myself against the achievements of others who looked as if they belonged to the American mainstream and who seemed successful in the dominant culture. I wanted to assimilate without condition— to be accepted by them. The feelings of unmitigated separation produced a craving for connection, a desperation to belong. In a determined exertion of willpower as I came of age, I remember having the fixed conviction that *if it is this difficult to be a racial minority in this world, there is* no way *that I will be gay*—thereby adding another padlock to an already hidden closet door.

But the locks wouldn't hold; the closet and the closet door were rotting from the inside out.

I was deeply unhappy even though I had no idea why. My attempts at assimilation into a white, heterosexual culture took me further away from my identity as a gay Chinese man. This gap between realities became deeper as the internal dissonance lengthened in duration. The void was filled repeatedly with excessive amounts of alcohol, drugs, caffeine, and nicotine—anything at all but the real feelings emerging from my experience with my life.

When I encountered the Buddha's teachings, I was a deeply tortured soul.

Though I might have had many elements in my life (including, at the time, a partner) that might have looked good from the outside, inside my psyche was ruptured. Even during my recovery from substance abuse, the pain did not abate.

When the Dharma entered my life, I realized that my life was deeply unhappy because I was turning away from who I was. I was trying to be who I was not. In turning toward all of the aspects of myself that I had denied and repressed earlier, I was beginning my path of mindfulness, of being aware of who is living this human life as "me."

I turned toward the familiar stranger within myself. I turned my attention to the pieces of my personality and history, my successes and failures, my dreams and depressions, I was afraid to get to know, much less become intimate with. I turned toward my sexual orientation and identity and my racial and cultural background.

This path of Dharma was the beginning of the healing process, of recovering who I saw myself to be in this world and who I could become. From that deeply tortured soul, this path has shown me greater and greater amounts of ease, peacefulness, and—dare I say—freedom. What more can I ask for? This path of Dharma has shown me where to start, where to continue, and how the path has no end to possibilities of freedom—even amid the myriad forms of suffering.

2

Finding a Spiritual Path

W E ARE all seekers.

We are seekers regardless of which spiritual tradition we affiliate with. We are seekers even if we do not espouse any religious faith at all. We all search for meaningful experiences, satisfying objects, compatible people, useful knowledge, fulfilling activities, well-being—and more. Seeking is part of our humanity. When we seek, inquire, and explore, we open up to our own life and to the world. This openness is a tender place for both our minds and hearts. From this tender place, we look for things that we hope will create more happiness and contentment for ourselves.

This begins so early in our precious lives.

We are on this earth for such a short period of time. It's no wonder that moments after we enter this life we start looking, learning, and seeking that which will make the best of this life. Even before we have any words to describe it, there is the message implicit in a baby's cry of "What will satisfy me?" "How do I get my mother's milk?" "What is that flashing color?" "Look at this thing that is a 'foot.' I don't even know the word *foot*, but look at what it can do!"

As we are parented, cared for, and nurtured, we reach further into the world, recognizing the pleasant sensations of a pillow or blanket or favorite stuffed animal, and, later, begin to wonder "why?"

Why is the sky blue?

I remember lying on the grass in the warmth of a sunny day—daydreaming or maybe day-wondering—simply staring into the sky with amazement and openness. I was content to watch the clouds, looking on as scenes and objects and beings appeared, dissolved, and reappeared amid the ever-shifting curves and wisps of white billowing puffs. Those early memories are the first time I had a sense of presence, of peace—even if it was fleeting, or not fully recognized by me in that moment. We all dream as children.

In the Buddhist tradition, there is a story of a prepubescent boy having a similar childhood experience. Even though the story is specifically set in a distant culture, in a distant time more than 2,500 years ago, in what is now northeastern India and southern Nepal, I feel a connection to the tenderness of this child—and indeed any child who is seeking. That boy was named Siddhartha and was the son of a local king. At the age of seven, Siddhartha attended a celebratory festival and party over which his father was presiding. His attendants (whom we would perhaps now call his daycare providers) got attracted to the party themselves and left the youth to his own resources in a vast field under a great tree.

As with many cultures and human traditions, the tree has tremendous significance in what it represents. Even in those times of ancient India, one association was the tree of life—the feet of which are anchored with roots deep into the earth with a summit reaching into the heavens in all directions. This image is embedded in our collective psyche, regardless of whether our cultural origins are from Asia, Africa, the Americas, or Europe. The Great Tree encompasses and shelters all experiences in our life, just like it was protecting the youthful Siddhartha. Indeed, that tree echoes Siddhartha's birth into the world beneath the boughs of another ancient tree and presages the Buddha's enlightenment sitting underneath the spreading limbs of the great bodhi tree.

As the boy sat in the field, a sense of stillness and peace cascaded into his awareness. He wondered, "As I am sitting in the shade of this tree, removed from the distractions of senses and difficult states of mind and heart, allowing the mind to settle into a natural joyousness, can this be the path that I am searching for?"

Whether we are totally conscious of it or not, our spiritual lives begin when we are children.

Our spirituality has always been with us, and the seeker has always been present.

I grew up in a family that had immigrated to the United States during difficult global and cultural times, encompassing situations not unlike the challenges facing many culturally displaced peoples today. My parents emigrated from China just at the ending of World War II and the resurgence of the Chinese Civil War. They settled into the American Midwest during the time of Joseph McCarthy in the turmoil and cultural xenophobia of the 1950s. Their survival strategy was to assimilate and acculturate as quickly as possible—always trying to not make waves and not to stand out or be noticed.

Part of their survival-by-assimilation involved letting go of many traditions they might have carried into a life in a new culture. I suspect that many immigrants must go through the painful process of trying to honor the ways of life supported by their culture of origin even as they try to assimilate into a new world with very different values and norms—trying to discern what must be given up when survival overrides comfort. At the time of my birth, the status of Asian immigrants was legally still tenuous because the Chinese Exclusion Act of 1880 was still nominally in force (not fully remedied until the Immigration and Nationality Act of 1965).

There was an instance when FBI agents in their classic black hats and trench coats visited my mother while my dad was at work. They wanted to know why our family was receiving Chinese language newspapers in the mail, and we all found the encounter intimidating and frightening. I don't know whether the explanation that my mom gave was satisfactory or not—but fear came into the house. My then twelve-year-old brother slept with a baseball bat when he went to sleep at night for the next several months.

I suspect my parents coped with that kind of fear by further assimilating our family into mainstream American culture. When I was growing up, I saw no culturally specific spiritual practices among my parents' families. As far as I knew, being Chinese meant eating delicious food that no one except my mom knew how to cook. That was the only distinction I could see.

I knew more what it felt like to be American than to be Chinese. I recall doing a report on China for my fifth grade class and not knowing that China had a communist government. I remember writing the report "as if" I were an "American" learning about a foreign land that I was not a part of. I didn't feel connected with my culture of origin or even particularly recognize it as my culture of origin. My report ended in the year 1948, one year before Mao Zedong took over the government—and I thought that things had continued to develop as they had before 1948.

I marvel now at the naivety no one in my family or school chose to correct.

When I was old enough, we went as a family to a local Baptist church, mimicking the suburban white dominant culture around us. We joined the congregation, which was more progressive in its attitudes than other Baptist groups. I remember our local church circulating a copy of the Black Manifesto for review by the general congregation and the heated conversations around the document. My family and I didn't have a sense of connection or resonance with the congregation—only a sense of obligation and a feeling of this-is-what-an-American-family-does.

This American Baptist church usually baptized children when they reached adolescence when it was viewed that they could be responsible for their own personal choices. By the time I was in my teens and approaching the conventional time for baptism, I had distanced my personal beliefs from anything religious. It was then the mid-1960s, and the secular culture and the sociopolitical revolution of the younger generation was the call with which I resonated. I was an atheist, or perhaps an agnostic (I wasn't sure)—but I was adamant that I didn't care about any religious faith or tradition.

When I declined my pastor's invitation to go through the baptismal rites of passage, I stopped going to church—and interestingly enough, when I did that my parents also stopped going. I realized they were only going for the benefit of my acculturation into American society. From my family, I felt the strong pull to assimilate, and from the pastor, I felt pressure to go through with the baptism. But I also saw it was possible to not accede to either pressure.

This was a baptism of sorts within my own internal experience.

I realized that I could act on my own set of beliefs and not be swayed by external demands. I realized I had a choice: I could pick what path I followed. But before I could make that decision, I had to become aware of my options.

I would rediscover the importance of this awareness, over and over again, much later on in my life, but in the meantime, I was making spiritual decisions, even as I eschewed anything spiritual or religious. We are all spiritual beings. Spirituality is hardwired in us—even when we negate it.

At times in my life I have been explicitly religious, spiritual, and existential; at times I have experimented lightly or devoted myself deeply. It is all part of a grander path. There is always a larger picture even if I cannot see the whole canvas in the moment. Even pushing away spirituality is a spiritual decision.

By the time I came into the lineage of the Buddha and found my spiritual home, I had begun to see in Buddha's teachings much that resonated with the way my parents had brought me up. While they shifted away from their culture of origin in many external ways, they could not and did not negate the inner cultural values with which they themselves were imbued from their own heritage. For this reason, as soon as I came into contact with the Buddhist tradition, I felt a kind of visceral recognition even before I made a cognitive connection. All I had to do was pay attention.

Of course not everyone will have a similar cultural story or related familial circumstances, but there may be aspects that others might recognize beyond the details of my personal experience: the seeking, the path even when there is uncertainty, and the support one feels in finding a spiritual home.

These are important components of awareness as a spiritual practice.

Recognizing the components of one's spiritual path and spirituality supports the path itself. Awareness that a spiritual path exists is a mindfulness practice itself. Awareness of a spiritual path offers options to deepen what works for us and to create more freedom around it or minimize what does not.

And awareness of our own paths is so very useful in determining how and where to meet others on a similar path. Walking together in communal support with mutual aspirations for living this life with more grace and more freedom is a beautiful way to grow and connect with others—to live in community and awaken together.

I feel that I have recognized many Christian values absorbed early in my childhood in those in my current Buddhist faith. Whereas unconditional kindness, compassion, patience, ethical integrity, and spiritual wisdom might be languaged differently in different cultures and different traditions, the living feeling is the same for them all. Across the amazing breadth and diversity of linguistic expression, cultural forms, and personal stories, there is still only one way to feel compassionate, there is still only one way to feel kind: the human way.

These days I feel more congruence than dissonance between religious faiths and spiritual traditions. While prayer is not ostensibly part of the Insight Meditation lineage to which I am currently connected, I nonetheless feel a resonance with this human form of expression. My understanding of prayer is that it comes ultimately from the root "to ask." Whether the request is made to God; to Allah; to named, unnamed, single, or multiple deities; to the Great Spirit or many spirits; or to the impersonal forces that come together to create life—prayer has been around since before recorded time. We can describe prayer as opening to the vulnerability of asking sacred questions, and meditation can be experienced as creating the tender, open, and humble space for receiving the sacred answer.

In receiving what life has to teach us, it helps not to be distracted by the multitude of pressures, obligations, information, and activities that all of us in our current society tend to multitask. Filling the mind does not allow the subtle nuance of life's teaching to reach us. Preoccupied with how we think we should live our lives and how life should be, we deny attention to how our life is already being lived. Often we are so compulsive and obsessive about finding answers rather than *learning from* the questions that we miss the reality: the answers we seek are not provided by any definitive resolution but by how we are asking the questions and by how we are relating to the questions themselves.

Rainer Maria Rilke describes this gracefully:

Don't search for the answers, which could not be given to you now, because you would not be able to live them. And the point is, to live everything. Live the questions now. Perhaps then, someday far in the future, you will gradually, without even noticing it, live your way into the answer.

The dance between inquiries and answers, between prayer and meditation, between what our cultural heritage offers to us and what we are able to create in this lifetime, between where we have been and what we are seeking—this dance is a place of incredible energy, opportunity, and richness.

Even if we have lived many years into our adulthood, it is useful to reflect and remember that we all have been seeking for the length of our lives. This is how we begin to be conscious and aware of our yearnings beyond material pleasures and beyond anything that is outside of us to give us satisfaction.

All great wisdom traditions speak to our own ability to have happiness and freedom. These experiences do not lie outside of ourselves. In this great diversity of spiritual paths, they all lead to the same mountaintop—from where the most expansive view of humanity is the same.

For Reflection

When did you become aware of your spiritual path?

When did the glimmer of the seeking become clearer for you?

What were the internal movements of your heart and mind that pointed you to goodness in the world and a sense of connection?

How did you recognize something larger than "yourself"?

In what ways do you currently feel your spirituality?

What are your current spiritual aspirations and what do you currently seek?

3

This Precious Life

MY FATHER was a small man of slight build, but he was always quite hardy and healthy.

I remember him forever mowing and tending the lawn of our suburban home by himself. He could rarely convince me to assist him—only those times when I noticed him working alone and my guilt about not helping rose up. He never hired anyone to do it for him, except when he was ill. Even in his late eighties he was puttering around in the garden beds of his assisted living facility, weeding, pruning, and parenting his outdoor plant-children.

A few years ago, when he reached the age of ninety-two, his lower back pain became unmanageable for this man who had had a tolerance of discomfort that would rival the fiercest ascetic. He was diagnosed with myeloma, a form of cancer that resided in his bones—particularly in the vertebrae of his lower spine. It seemed quite sudden, even though there were probably several unexamined symptoms leading up to it for several years. In the language of my father, a mathematician and engineer all his life, the number of undiagnosed symptoms was directly proportional to the level of pain that he had to tolerate. In the week after his cancer diagnosis, we almost lost him. My mother was in shock—they had, after all, been married for sixty-six years and together for sixty-nine. To this day, I still have no idea what it would be like to be connected so intimately with someone for longer than many people's lifespans. She always thought that she would leave this world first, but he was fading rapidly, getting weaker, unable to take care of his bodily functions, and lapsing in and out of consciousness.

Then, remarkably, the physicians gave him a certain drug combination that caused a surprising reversal. It was quite dramatic, sudden, and gave us all another chance to appreciate life—his life, but also all of our lives. Within another two weeks, he recovered most of his baseline functioning and could even return home to continue living the sixty-ninth year of his relationship with my mom.

We woke up a little more to the gift of life, as clichéd or sentimental as that sounds. Awareness is like that: it is awareness in the ordinary moments of living that makes it such an extraordinary practice for life. Awareness delivers messages that are often right before our faces, even if we are looking beyond what is currently present in our lives.

While we had two more years with my dad, his recovery did not last. Right before my fifty-fifth birthday, he journeyed into another semicomatose state after losing most of his communicative abilities. Over the course of the subsequent days, his ability to communicate in English left him first (even though he was as fluent as I am), then his speech in Chinese faded. For a short time, he could write a few words or characters in a sometimes shaky, indecipherable script on a small marker board we held in front of him, but then that escaped him too. We could sense he was letting go of everything that was outside himself. The veils separating the world of life and that which is after were beginning to reveal themselves more clearly. At times, his movements were restless in his coma-induced silence as if the body needed to express some residual tensions or anxieties. Those too subsided, as the only visible signs of movement became the rhythm of his breathing. It seemed "stable"—whatever that meant. Did we feel that he would live forever in this state? Of course not. But it is so curious that in the minds of all of us there still was a hope for "stability" and seeming certainty, even for a moment or two.

But it is his last hour that remains so poignantly seared into my memory . . .

It was getting toward dinnertime. My brother and I volunteered to go and get some takeout food for everyone else who was holding vigil—my mom, my husband, and my brother's partner. With my attention turning to taking care of others, almost as a casual gesture of courtesy rather than a real intention to connect, I said to my father, "We are going to get some food for dinner. We will be right back." As we began to walk out the door, my mom called us back. After several days of not moving or expressing himself, my dad was making an effort to communicate—unintelligible as it was.

We all now converged at his bedside.

My own awareness was heightened, and I found myself intentionally trying to stay with all the details of my experience and his. The only sounds in the room were his textured breaths as the air passed in and out of his open mouth. The rise and fall of his chest was getting slower. In that moment, I realized that it was all about the breath—life is all about the inhale and exhale. How can we be with these last precious moments of breath, of life? Is it possible to meet these moments with their simple arising and passing away without needing them to be any different than what they are?

In that moment, I sensed that there is peace in that ability; I sensed that there is ease in that process.

A memory flashed through my mind of my father coming to a daylong meditation retreat I was teaching for people of color ten years previously at Spirit Rock Meditation Center in Northern California. I had to smile with the remembrance because, in his life, he never identified himself as a person of color. It was a term that did not have much meaning for his generation, but he was aware of how the phrase resonated with me and others of my generation—an illustration of the complexity of how diverse we hold our identities even within one family.

And another memory arose for me, of my dad recounting how when he first arrived in the heartland of the American Midwest, there were public restrooms still segregated for "whites only" and for "colored people"— and he never could figure out which door he should go through. I could feel his awakening to the racial realities of this culture being as complex as my own awakening to my own realities. But in spite of not needing to identify or label himself, he came to Spirit Rock to see what I actually did when I taught meditation.

Dad was already hard of hearing and couldn't hear all of what was said in the meditation hall. When the schedule moved to walking meditation, he came up to me and said, "I think I got what you said about the breath—I actually can follow it. But I couldn't hear what you said about walking meditation. Can you teach me how to walk?"

How sacred is that tender question coming from one's own parent!

As our archetypal life roles reversed, I invited his awareness to simply be with the sensations of the lifting, moving, and placing of his feet— even if his gait was unsteady or slow—and encouraged him to use all the support he needed. He had a way of touching my shoulder while looking away, as if to moderate any expression of intimacy—he did that then and just said, "Thank you."

At his bedside I imagined he might be able to follow his own breath now, just as he said he could at the daylong retreat. Maybe that was a fantasy on my part, but it comforted me. The pause between the exhale and the inhale began to linger and then to extend from seconds to many seconds. Over the next thirty minutes, the pause between out-breath and in-breath first became thirty seconds, then forty, then a minute. Not only was the breath pausing, but it felt as if life for all of us was pausing reverently in the silence.

In those moments, I felt time, space, and life itself being transformed, even as impermanence was revealing itself in unrelenting detail.

In the pause between his breaths, in the stillness, my dad was giving us one last teaching: that it was possible to transition in peace. He was showing us how to die peacefully and, perhaps, how to die well. It is not an opportunity that everyone in this life has—and it may not even be an opportunity that is given to me—but in that moment my father was showing me that it is possible.

What an amazing gift to receive.

In the midst of the surrounding silence, each micro-moment was as precious as it was fleeting. We thought we had lost him when the pause between his breaths reached two and a quarter minutes, but the breath came back and life returned. As we reached the inevitable outcome when his inhale was nowhere to be seen, heard, or felt, it was my husband's voice that shifted the silence when he whispered, "He is gone."

I never would have thought I would say that my father's death was so precious and valuable, but I feel so blessed to have been offered every detail and every moment of that experience.

In the fourteenth century, Tsongkhapa, the founder of the Gelug School of Tibetan Buddhism and the lineage of His Holiness the Dalai Lama, wrote (as translated by Thubten Jigme Norbu):

> The human body at peace with itself
> is more precious than the rarest gem.
> Cherish your body:
> it is yours for this one time only.
> The human form is won with difficulty;
> it is easy to lose.
> All worldly things are brief,
> like lightning in the sky.
> This life you must know as
> the splash of a raindrop,
> A thing of beauty
> that disappears
> even as it comes into being.
> Therefore,
> Set your goal.
> Make use of
> every day and night to
> achieve it.

In the Dhammapada, an early collection of teaching verses from the Buddha, it is said that mindfulness practice is so precious that living a single day with its wisdom is better than living without it, even if we were to live a hundred years in this lifetime.

My father was not able to achieve centenary status before he died. Over 2,500 years ago on the Indian subcontinent, in the time before recorded history and when the average life expectancy was likely one-third at most of ours today, it was three times more difficult to reach the age of a centenarian. This chronological context makes this teaching all the more prominent. Translated into today's life expectancy, we could say that living a single day with mindfulness, moment to moment, is more precious than living three consecutive lifetimes.

Why are the mindfulness and awareness practices of the Buddha's teachings so valued, not just as a spiritual technique but as a way to live every day? It is not only that the practice yields such valuable benefits, although current psychological and neuroscientific research has identified tremendous cognitive, behavioral, psychological, and even professional benefits. It is also that life is precious itself. Awareness allows us to experience directly the *aliveness* of life with as much of our mind and heart present and available as possible.

Mindfulness allows us to actually experience life while we are living it. This is often called the "present moment," the "here and now." It is life. The irony is that we take so much for granted in this precious life that we can feel it is our entitlement to live on this planet. It is my "right" to live. However, when we are experiencing a severe illness or a close family member or friend passes away or a traumatic accident happens, we can feel how the description of *precious life* really means "delicately fragile life." It is fleeting and can leave us at any time. This precious life is worth our attention and our ever-expanding awareness—and so living life for a single day with mindfulness is precious.

A classic image in the Samyutta Nikaya (one of the collections that record the Buddha's teachings) describes this intrinsic value to our lives. The Buddha says that in the Great Ocean (a metaphor for the ocean of all life), there is a single ring-like wooden yoke that floats every which way, buffeted to and fro by the winds from all directions. In the depths of the Great Ocean resides an ancient, blind sea tortoise that needs to break the surface of the water only once every hundred years to get a breath of fresh air. The Buddha asks his followers what the chances are of that blind sea turtle coming to the surface once every one hundred years sticking its neck through that yoke. The reply by the gathering was, "It would be a sheer coincidence, lord, that the blind sea turtle, coming to the surface once every one hundred years, would stick his neck into the yoke." The Buddha goes on to teach that attaining a life in our human form is as rare, coincidental, and precious as the sea turtle poking his head through the yoke.

Our usual pattern of going through our lives is actually not to be aware of life unfolding as it happens. Sometimes we are caught in the multiplicity of how much there is to do, how much to be entertained by, how much to think about, and how much we are consumed by how our life should be, or could be, or would be, or is not. This preeminently multi-tasking culture we live in has also become global. It is the new normal to have several conversations going on at once, in person, on a smartphone, through email, through texts, on Instagram, and with tweets—not just in our culture but in most every culture of our world. Popular trends, behavioral patterns, information and knowledge—both useful and not useful—traverse spans of latitude and longitude in days, even minutes and seconds, rather than the months, years, or decades of previous generations. All this serves to emphasize our collective unconscious conditioning toward the state of mind called greed—that more is better. This is the view that accomplishing more tasks is better; more speed is better; more communication and connection are better; more things are better. Greed never leads to happiness, even though we so often believe, think, and feel that it does.

Beyond the motivations of unconscious greed, we are often not living the direct experience of life because we are always trying to change it. When there is minimal mindfulness, we are constantly acting on our desires for our life to be different than it actually is. Why? One of the classical teachings on mindfulness is that when we are not mindful we tend to do one of three things: (1) deny and get rid of things that we don't like; (2) try to get more of the things that we do like; or (3) simply not pay attention to or notice things that we are indifferent toward.

Mindfulness allows us to get familiar with and get real with our life and the full range of our experience, not just the portions we enjoy. From the teachings of Chuang Tzu, the Taoist master to whom my father would often refer, we learn each individual human existence has its share of the ten thousand joys and the ten thousand sorrows of this universe. As a child when I heard this, I thought, "Gee, ten thousand is a lot of anything," but then my dad told me that "ten thousand" is the numerical metaphor for "infinite" within Asian cultural traditions—so it was even more than I thought!

The extension of Chuang Tzu's teaching is that no individual life is only about sorrow (although we can think it is when we are caught in what feels to be interminable suffering), and no individual life is only about joy (although we would like to think that this is where life should be, or even that this is the purpose of life itself). Each life has an innumerably full spectrum of joys and sorrows. To only focus on either joy or sorrow—much less a single joy or sorrow—for whatever reason is to miss the wholeness of our existence. It is to be unaware of how broad and expansive our life really is.

We actually take most of life for granted. We take for granted that we should be able to push away, deny, repress, or get rid of things that we do not want. We take for granted that we deserve more of the things that we do want. We take for granted that when something is not a high or low, when something is not a peak or valley, when something is not "great" or "awful" that it is not even worth attending to. And so we miss so much of our life. We miss learning from difficult experiences because we are trying to get rid of them; we miss enjoying positive things because we are trying to get more of them; and we miss neutral things because we overlook them in boredom.

In the book *Darkness Sticks to Everything* the poet Tom Hennen vividly describes this tendency:

> Like people or dogs, each day is unique and has its own personality quirks which can easily be seen if you look closely. But there are so few days as compared to people, not to mention dogs, that it would be surprising if a day were not a hundred times more interesting than most people. But usually they just pass, mostly unnoticed, unless they are wildly nice, like autumn ones full of red maple leaves and hazy sunlight, or if they are grimly awful ones in a winter blizzard that kills the lost traveler and bunches of cattle. For some reason we like to see days pass, even though most of us claim we don't want to reach our last one for a long time. We examine each day before us with barely a glance and say, no, this isn't the one I've been looking for, and wait in a bored sort of way for the next, when, we are convinced, our lives will start for real. Meanwhile, this day is going by perfectly well-adjusted, as some days are, with the right amounts of sunlight and shade, and a light breeze

scented with a perfume made from the mixture of fallen apples, corn stubble, dry oak leaves, and the faint odor of last night's meandering skunk.

This is why even the simple act of being mindful of the breath, attending to the inhale and the exhale, is so radically different than how we usually live our lives. We most often take our respiration totally for granted until we suffer from an illness, or asthma, or some other medical condition that interferes with our ability to breathe. Then we begin to feel how truly precious this energy of breath is. Instead of waiting for an unwanted and frequently unexpected limitation to teach us not to take life for granted, what would it be like to be completely aware of it now? What would it be like to connect the energy of breath with the energy of our life and become aware of how precious and delicate life truly is?

As we strengthen our human ability to be aware by returning over and over to the direct sensations of an experience like the breath, we begin to expand to a larger landscape that mindfulness can also hold. We exercise awareness, just like we would exercise any muscle of the body through physical activity, or the mind through intellectual activity, or the heart through emotional connection. As we increase the capacity of our mindfulness, we open the field from the physical sensations of the body to sensations of the mind and heart—the terrain of our thoughts and emotions. And we begin to include both easy and difficult experiences; those things that are pleasant for us and those that are unpleasant for us.

We value and hold tenderly all the infinite joys and sorrows of our life and not overlook any moment—including our last.

For Reflection

How often do you pay no attention to your breath?

How often do you take your ability to breathe for granted—this energy of breath that feeds the energy of your life?

What else might you take for granted in your life?

What do you not give a second thought to in your life's activities?

What or whom would you miss dearly if they were taken away from you or absent from your life?

4

Nobility of Truth

THE MOMENT-TO-MOMENT nature of contemplative awareness, with its observation, inquiry, and reflection through all experiences of joy, pain, or boredom, has changed my attitude toward each of them. As has oft been said by spiritual teachers in many practice traditions, meditation does not so much change our lives as it changes our relationship to our lives.

Many times this is enough change to create a greater sense of well-being. For me, when stories of separation or oppression are retriggered or re-created, I have a new curiosity about the deepest nature of my experience as opposed to denying or repressing it. This curiosity allows the suffering to be held in a larger context, a larger space. Experiences of joy are held with a new sense of value and respect, knowing that they too will change and lead necessarily to other events. Joy emerges, not as something to be attached to but rather as an occasion for deep appreciation not to be taken for granted.

With mindfulness meditation, noting sensation after sensation—whether sitting, eating, walking, or going about my daily life—without needing to become involved in the sensation or to interpret it strengthens my ability to be present and aware in my life. It strengthens my capacity to traverse the experience of suffering and the first noble truth without circumventing or denying it in any way.

Increasingly, I experience a growing number of moments of letting go—surrendering each experience as a new one arises. Being open to what is emerging instead of trying to control the outcome of things can be such an important skill when it comes to the complexity of life.

When we naturally let go, we give the present experience permission to fully fill our awareness. When we do this, a certain peace and ease of mind persist regardless of circumstance or story. As our minds begin to ease up, so do our lives. It's simple to read about and understand this, but, of course, not so easy to live it in real time.

I remember one poignant example when I was rushing to meet a friend for dinner and had to get some cash from the ATM that I always use near my home in San Francisco. I waited impatiently for my turn on a busy sidewalk during the rush at the end of a business day. I was mindful of the time because I knew that getting to the restaurant would mean going through a lot of stop-and-go crosstown city traffic, with the added necessity of finding parking in an area of narrow, small streets, where availability was limited.

As I reached out to insert my ATM card in the machine, I stopped abruptly, stunned by what I saw. My awareness became sharp as a knife. Scratched into different areas of the ATM faceplate were the words "Chinese Garbage," "Chinese Trash," "Chinese Shit."

If my life were a movie, in this moment it would have shifted abruptly into slow motion. Plans for dinner all receded into the distance and my focus telescoped onto strong emotions of anger, hurt, even fear. Looking inward, I asked, *What is happening right now? What is my internal experience?* The rush of blood to my head, the pounding of my heart from increased blood circulation, dizziness, and detachment from my surroundings—all of these were immediately identifiable. I turned toward the emerging feelings as they forced themselves to the surface of my mind.

I felt aversion and the inclination to escape from and push away the present moment.

I did not want what was happening to be happening.

I felt again the impact of past experiences of harm caused by racial discrimination in different periods of my life as the child of Chinese immigrants.

I felt again previously experienced forms of oppression that our society still perpetuates, including homophobia.

Stories and scenes cascaded by association into my consciousness.

I could hear the self-deprecating voice that aversion uses to minimize abusive experiences, floating stories through my thoughts that these are kids simply misbehaving and wanting attention. "That's all it is," the voice said. "Don't get so upset."

In that moment I just waited, not needing to believe those conditioned voices.

I waited to feel and clearly determine what was really happening to and within me.

As I lifted the veils of aversion, anger, even rage, a tremendous sadness revealed itself for myself and for those like me who are targets of cultural abuse.

I felt again losing my innocence when I first encountered racism as a child.

I felt again the grief of feeling different throughout my adolescence and questioning whether my life was worth having.

I felt again the injustice of life being unfair, both as a child and as an adult.

It broke my heart to stay with these feelings, and even though I hadn't been standing at that intersection for more than a minute, it broke my heart further to be aware that I still carried all these injuries with me over all the decades.

A frail, elderly Asian couple brushed against my elbow as they walked by me, leaning on each other for support as my mother and father have done so many times. I wondered about their stories and how their lives have been impacted by discrimination and historical oppression, large events and small, that broke their own hearts and burdened their minds.

I felt my heart embrace their experience and wonder what their responses might be to the disparagement of their Asian identity presented by this hate graffiti, had they stopped to consider it. I saw others passing by who were as akin to me as a younger brother or sister, and I felt their injuries of feeling different in their lives, regardless of the reasons. As the circle of my awareness widened, my heart broke open again and again, and I came to feel the injury of the injurer.

The perpetrator of this hateful graffiti must have been deeply wounded in order to want to create such harm for others.

In the subsequent minutes, while meeting this experience with kind awareness and gentle attention, even when it concerned triggering pain over past injuries, I realized that my attitude toward such events had changed. This was a new experience for me.

My life had changed, not because there was more or less suffering in it but because my relationship to life's sorrows had shifted. This development of spaciousness allowed me to hold the pain in a larger picture and also to learn more deeply what will lead to less suffering in my own life and in the lives of others.

As we nurture and cultivate our capacity to be mindful and become more aware of the full range of our lives, we begin to see how much suffering there is in the world. We encounter the fullness of the first teachings that the Buddha offered after his own awakening—the four noble truths. Even after more than 2,500 years there is relevance in our current lives to these ancient teachings. There is the veracity in the first noble truth.

But what is the nobility of these truths, why the word *noble*?

These truths are the embodiment of the Buddha's teachings. The Buddha states in the Majjhima Nikaya that he teaches only about suffering and the end of suffering. He teaches the conditions that lead to freedom in our lives. That motivation toward freedom distinguishes the nobility of these truths from other truths in our lives. The four noble truths lead to a clear mind, an open heart, and "extinguishes" (using more traditional terminology) both the causes and impacts of suffering. This is the definition of the path to happiness. There is no higher aspiration we can have.

The first noble truth shares the reality that there is difficulty and suffering in the world and there is harm and pain that we will experience in this lifetime. Of course, we may not look for it and we would rather not experience it, but it is there. Whether it is about our individual lives or our collective experience in communities, bad things happen to good people; bad things happen to bad people; bad things happen to people.

My encounter with the racist graffiti on the ATM is an example of the first noble truth arising. It was not something that I could prevent or avoid. The circumstances were also not something that happens only to me or other individuals. Racism, like suffering itself, emerges from deep patterns of individual and collective unconsciousness.

And, of course, with the arising of pain and distress, there will be things that we would want to be different. I could feel in my own craving that I did not want to have the experience that I was having. The movement of my heart to shut the feelings down and the mind rationalizing the ATM incident as "no big deal" are both part of this wanting another kind of experience. In that craving emerges the second noble truth: that suffering is caused by the attachment of desire for life to be other than how it is unfolding. The cause of suffering is not whether we receive the object of our desire and clinging or not; the cause of suffering is the craving itself.

Generally, the conditioning of our world and our behavior is patterned toward sating our cravings. We have a misguided assumption that receiving the object of our desire will ultimately satisfy us, create contentment, allow us to be happy—and, as mentioned before, our larger culture is constantly training us that "more is better." We have become seduced by the ambient marketing arising that more of everything is better. We see this on a daily basis in our lives—just about every product that is sold to us is about guaranteeing our happiness. Our market economy even tries to convince us that "desire" and "craving" are worthwhile states of being. Echoing a pop song, one advertising slogan read, "I want you to want me." I saw another during the Christmas shopping season on the streets of San Francisco in a retail storefront with a banner that announced, "Moderation kills the spirit." Or we are told, "Obey your thirst."

Not only does our society's collective unconsciousness feed our desires, it promotes them to an extreme—even pathologizing moderation and balance!

What these almost universal advertising messages hide from us is a key awareness that could pierce this prevailing confusion. This awareness is that there are consequences to trying to satiate unrestricted craving and unencumbered desire. The primary consequence is that craving and the attachment that comes from craving can never be satiated by any object.

No object can truly satisfy craving because the goal of craving is not to crave. All craving is the craving for no craving. The real goal of craving is unmitigated attainment of permanent satisfaction. In the search for satisfaction, all craving seeks its own destruction. But sating craving never creates lasting satisfaction; it is always fleeting and temporary. Why? Because the energy of craving and attachment have neither wisdom nor insight. Craving does not have the ability to see truth. Craving does not have the ability to know that the cause of suffering is craving itself. Only our mindfulness can cultivate the clarity and insight into the truths that lead to freedom from craving.

In a Mahayana sutra of Chinese origin, the Buddha gave this teaching in a discourse called, as translated by J. C. Cleary, "Instructions for the Rich":

> You monks who want to escape from all the various afflictions must contemplate [what it means to] know satisfaction. The method of knowing satisfaction is the locus of prosperity, of bliss, of peace and security. Even if they are lying on the ground, the people who know satisfaction are happy and at peace. For the people who do not know satisfaction, it does not suit their fancy even if they are in heaven. The people who do not know satisfaction are poor even if they are rich. The people who do know satisfaction are rich even if they are poor.

Being content with what we have leads to happiness—whether that is materially, psychologically, or spiritually. It is an awareness practice. Are we content with the moment as it is or are we craving for something different?

If you have ever been involved with compulsions or addictions to any kind of activity, food, relationship, chemical substance, or any of our surrounding technology devices, or if you have been involved closely with people caught in cycles of wanting and craving, you know that it is the "high" that the person in addiction searches for and seeks to sustain. The plateau of the high is regarded as the moment of satisfaction—and unfortunately for all of us searching for that high, there is the inevitable, subsequent crash. This dynamic plays out for everyone; it is just more discernible within addiction. We might easily feel that a certain kind of job, or certain house or social status, or even a certain person will fulfill our happiness. But each of those experiences and objects have the ten thousand joys and ten thousand sorrows embedded within them. And there will always be the disappointment and crash that, if we remain unconscious, will drive us to seek yet another object to satisfy our continually arising craving for happiness.

The alternative is this: as we realize that no external object will create freedom from craving, we let go of and drop any object of craving in order to be with the bare experience of craving itself. We are invited to notice and become intimate with the sensations arising and passing away, of the attachment and desire without any connection to any object or focus. As we navigate sensations and emotions, we actually traverse through the experience of craving as opposed to fruitlessly trying to circumvent craving through an object that we imagine will provide happiness.

True freedom is not about getting an object to satisfy the craving. True freedom is in exploring the craving itself, and seeing and feeling what is on the other side of that craving. One of the powerful aspects of awareness arises from the fact that the awareness of an experience is not the experience itself. The experience of being aware of craving and all of its sensations, pleasant and unpleasant, is the experience of not being lost in the experience of craving.

As I stood before the ATM, I could have dismissed my painful experience, repressed or ignored it, or tried to push it away. Indeed, I felt the allure to do so because I could feel how it triggered past injuries of race and racism. In dropping the object of my craving, which was for this moment of hurt to be different than it was, I was able to stay with the sensations of craving. In navigating through these sensations, I saw beyond the boundaries of my own experience and even of this event. I could feel my own pain, but I also felt the suffering of our humanity. I could feel how I would not want to add one more drop of suffering to how much the world suffers already.

When I went into the bank and the local Asian Law Caucus to report the incident, I found out that there had been additional anti-Asian hate-speech violations in the area. Even though I had found some freedom from the suffering of my past conditioning, allowing a different relationship to suffering is not the same as giving permission for the injury itself. Mindfulness doesn't mean being passive to harm and oppression. Allowing myself to clearly experience the hate graffiti opened me to turn toward the first noble truth with greater ease in acting to transform its injustice and unconsciousness.

On this path, which ostensibly leads to the end of suffering and greater happiness, it is perhaps ironic that as we become more mindful, we actually see even more suffering than we had previously noticed. In the assimilation phase of my earlier life, I didn't see how I suffered from internalizing the racist and homophobic messages that are ambient in the larger unconscious culture. I ignored them, pushed them outside my consciousness in hopes that "fitting in" or "belonging" was possible by transforming who I was, instead of being who I was.

Even if it is only at a subtle level, we have always known that sometimes we need to go through more difficulty and pain before reaching the place of having less of it in our lives. Turning toward who I authentically was, despite the pain that is experienced from external conditions of racism, homophobia, and oppressive patterns of the larger culture, is a path to greater happiness and freedom—as contradictory as that might feel.

As we begin the path of mindfulness, we begin to realize that there are actually two kinds of difficult experiences in our life. The first is the pain of this life into which we are born. In one of the Buddha's sermons, this is described as the pain of an arrow piercing our body. We did not shoot it at ourselves, we did not create the arrow, we did not create the conditions of the pain, and yet we are nonetheless pierced by it. The pain of this arrow can be undeserved, unfair, even unjust—regardless, the pain is still there.

The second kind of distress that Buddha taught was the suffering that compounds this painful experience. We take that original painful experience and augment it by resisting it, wanting it to go away, denying it. We push the experience away—and in that process we are said to have shot the second arrow at ourselves.

This second arrow is suffering that we potentially have the ability to transform, shift, and even heal—if we are mindful. When difficulty arises, there might be an internal reaction of anger or depression that also arises. What do we do next? Often, we can get angry at the anger—feeding the energy with more of the same, pouring gasoline on the flames. We can get depressed at the depression, continuing an ever-descending spiral into self-doubt, despair, and despondency. Painful events might be unavoidable, but we do not have to make them worse—this is suffering that we can be free of. This is the second arrow that we can prevent ourselves from experiencing.

What was liberating for me at the ATM was being able to see beyond my past injury and conditioning into the sensations of the present moment. Allowing them to rise and pass away enabled the experience to also arise and pass away. Of course, it was painful, but I didn't have to inflict the pain of repeated arrows of anger, rage, or even revenge. The experience did not have to trigger additional trauma or suffering. In the moment of pain, there was also freedom. Therein lies the third noble truth: that there is freedom from suffering in this life.

The more that we meet the first arrow of pain with the second arrow of suffering, the more we just continue the cycle of both. Our usual pattern is to meet suffering with suffering. This will never lead to the end of suffering. Meeting pain with pain is never the solution. The challenge is to remember that when we are in pain, physically, emotionally, or spiritually, we are less likely to be mindful of what is needed to alleviate it. When I am injured, I will more likely lash out in pain. When I am caught in the vortex of my family's complex patterns, or when I lack the patience with my husband because I am really impatient with myself, or when working toward a nonviolent world under frustratingly unjust conditions, it is an aspect of mindfulness to remember that meeting the energy of injury with the energy of injury is never the solution.

The Buddha said in the Dhammapada (Thomas Byrom translation):

In this world
Hate never yet dispelled hate
Only love dispels hate
This is the law
Ancient and inexhaustible.

If there is lingering doubt over whether this path is really relevant for the life you are living, if you still do not have a foundation of confidence or faith upon which you depend—this is not a problem. The invitation of Dharma practice is to depend upon the confidence and the experience of all those practitioners before us. This is a path and a set of teachings that has been followed by untold numbers of people. The Buddha's teachings have lasted over 2,500 years encompassing countless beings, all of whom felt confidence that the Dharma benefited their lives. We have the gift of their faith to support our own.

What has tremendously helped me as well as others with whom I teach and practice is that these teachings do not *only* articulate the ideal spiritual outcomes of suffering's end—they also show us a way to get there. The Buddha did not speak of an "eightfold *destination*"—but an eightfold *path*.

The eightfold path contains the whole path, and it starts with the components of wisdom: of wise understanding and wise intention. The second cluster of components leading toward freedom comprises those of ethical behavior or moral integrity: wise speech, wise action, and wise livelihood. And while these factors are not linear, they collectively support the deepening of meditation and focus: with wise effort, wise mindfulness, and wise concentration. Within this framework are literally hundreds of practices to support the development of our happiness and freedom. They are all worthy ingredients in our lives, but the recipe is something that only we can create for ourselves. None can be designated as the single way to spiritual liberation, because no one lives our life but ourselves. It is our own practice and experience that will exert the effort, apply the ethics, and gain the insight needed for our own liberation.

Much of the work is being mindful and aware. As we are aware of more and more aspects of our life, we are not lost in the busyness and distractions of our lives. Our awareness does not make the injury or pain of life go away, but it does allow us to create a different relationship to it and it does allow us to diminish our creation of additional suffering. This is key in developing the long-term practice of changing the conditions of the suffering itself. And it cannot happen without awareness.

Awareness gives us options on how to live and relate to our life. We cannot change anything that we are not aware of. Awareness allows us to continually better ourselves and live our lives with more fulfillment. It invites us into living our potential in this lifetime.

Awareness offers an increasing faculty to discern what will lead to more happiness and what will lead to more suffering. Discerning those choice points with awareness, wisdom inclines and guides us continually to make choices toward freedom.

None of this is a passive process.

I know that for many people in the worlds of social justice and social transformation being only mindful can feel like surrendering to the oppression or pain of an unconscious dominant culture without a concomitant course of remedying action to relieve the injustice or oppression. Our practice is not about "not doing" or being passive in the face of the enormous pain in the world. It is being mindful, precisely so that we are not paralyzed into unconscious behavior and can determine what is most needed to change the conditions of suffering and injustice.

Sometimes we experience the sheer amount of suffering in the world and in our lives as an overwhelming flood. We fear for the security of our families when already tenuous economic safety nets are further eroded and the disparities in wealth steadily increase and get more extreme. We may wonder how to provide our children resources for their future when the system of public education feels wounded, not sustainable, even undermined. It can feel like values such as safety and ethics are long forgotten in a world filled with escalating conflict, divisiveness, and continuing warfare. Violence toward African Americans continues at a disproportional rate with police actions, distressingly, creating more violence rather than less. Disparity in the forms of discrimination, oppression, sexism, racism, and homophobia has not gone away from this world that we call civilized.

And in the middle of all that suffering is the unconsciousness, the lack of mindful awareness, that allows it to continue. Even amid our own highest aspirations for social transformation, we so easily slip into living unconsciously. How often have we ourselves caused harm, not intentionally but because we were not aware enough of what was going on? As a social worker, in the profession of helping and advocating for others, one of the lessons that I have had to learn over and over again is not to rush too quickly into solving a problem. Even with the best of intentions to be of service, if we serve without being aware of the details of the situation, if we try to be change agents without understanding deeply and broadly what it is we are trying to change, we can actually make things worse.

I remember as a substance abuse counselor trying to support people getting clean and sober but not taking into consideration some of the suffering and circumstances that were causing their need to self-medicate. This is in spite of the fact that I was also in recovery. I was not mindful enough of all the complexities of people in different life circumstances. My focus was a certain goal, and regardless of how beneficial that goal might be, unless I examined the process and the concurrent factors of their lives, I was less than effective. Taking care of people's basic needs—food, clothing, shelter, medical care—was as important as sobriety itself; otherwise relapse was always a high possibility.

Mindfulness allows us the space to create skillful, meaningful, and transformative action. It allows our actions in the world to come from a deep recognition of the causes and conditions of our lives so that change can emerge from the unencumbered goodness of our hearts and minds, rather than arising from the place of our wounds or injuries. It is this goodness that makes our paths noble.

For Reflection

When craving for the moment to be different than it is arises, explore the possibility of letting go of the object of craving and directly feeling the craving itself.

What are the physical sensations of craving on a moment-to-moment basis?

What are the vibrations and energetic experiences of desire on a moment-to-moment basis?

If there are thoughts or emotions that are prominent, can you feel them coursing through you, as opposed to them being a focus or destination of your awareness? Is it possible not to be lost in the content of your thoughts?

In the face of injustice, oppression, or even injury, what supports deepening your awareness around the experience as you try to remedy the conditions of suffering?

5

Awakening Together

AFTER ABOUT fifteen years of Dharma practice, I went to Thailand and was ordained as a Theravada Buddhist monk. I will carry the experience with me for the rest of my life.

It was during that time that I first encountered the deep and direct experience of community and relationship along a collective spiritual path. Entering monastic life, I entered into a kind of community very different from any I had ever been in, with different norms and expectations, and in a foreign culture with which I had only minimal experience. It was intimidating, to say the least.

What was surprising for me was that I actually *did* belong to the community, whether or not I felt that as an internal experience. The simple fact of my presence within the community meant in a truly important way that I belonged to it. The acceptance of my presence didn't depend on my background, origins, upbringing, or status; my heartfelt intention to practice toward happiness and freedom was a sufficient credential for acceptance.

It is not often in my life that I have felt such a simple, fundamental sense of belonging. For me, there is something special about the basic sense of belonging that came with being ordained in the monastic spiritual community. My usual experience has been to need to be a certain way; think in alignment or agree with a certain group's viewpoints; look or dress to a certain convention; or act appropriately for group norms that often are not explicitly articulated, in order to feel that I belong somewhere. Failing to accomplish these things usually reinforces the narrative that I am unworthy of a fundamental sense of belonging—a basic sense of the goodness of who I am, as I am.

And this is not to say that living an ordained life with this sense of belonging was easy. I remember getting dressed in monastic robes as one of the most difficult initial challenges that I encountered in my ordination. On other monastics the robes seemed to drape in a natural visual flow, cascading down elegantly from shoulder to heel. On me it was as if I had wedged my body into some kind of complicated architectural construction made out of fabric. I was both compulsive in my attempts to get it correct and unsuccessful, at least at first, in managing to arrange all the folds as they should be. Not having a steam iron, every night I would paper clip the folds of my robes together so that they would stay in place once I put them on in the morning, and it sometimes took me an hour to dress in the early hours before sunrise. In one of my overly vigorous attempts to keep the robes properly aligned, I tied my waistband so tightly that the friction of the bound cloth gave me an intense blister on my back.

During those first weeks after my ordination, other monks—whether or not I had met them, whether or not they were senior to me, and whether or not they were my teachers—would walk up to me without so much as a greeting and simply adjust my robes. Nonetheless, I didn't feel any particular sense of judgment from them, and many times they didn't even make any comment. Rather than feeling judged about having done something poorly, I actually felt like the other monastics were lending me their support so that I could look like an experienced monastic and be the best monastic that I could be. It felt like an affectionate gesture, like your mom stopping you as a kid before you dashed out the door to straighten up your hair or adjust your collar or pull down your sleeve. It felt intimate. We were supporting each other to live in our monastic roles—communicating that we could mutually depend on one another. By the end of my time in Thailand, I felt it one of the highest compliments when a Thai lay practitioner in a community ceremony commented to my teacher that I "wore my robes well."

That sense of community grew more expansive and deep for me in the relationship between the monastic community and the lay practitioner community in the village. As with many religious orders, monastics in Southeast Asia provide lay communities with spiritual guidance, teachings, and role models. In return, the lay communities completely support the monastic communities in material ways. The Buddha structured the Sangha in such a way that monastic and lay Buddhist communities function interdependently.

Within the Buddhist tradition it is important that the lay community support monastics and temples by supplying the four requisites: shelter, clothing, medicine, and food. The ordained community, in turn, functions as the vessel within which the teachings of the Buddha are preserved for the benefit of all down through the ages. This interconnection and mutual dependence between monastic and lay Buddhist communities has allowed the teachings to survive these thousands of years.

Moreover, the Buddha says in a Pali scripture called Itivuttaka that

> Householders and the homeless [monastics]
> in mutual dependence
> both reach the true Dhamma. . . .

This mutual support is not only expressed in the larger projects of creating and building temples or meditation centers, but in the day-to-day support of the monastics. Every morning, after the predawn chanting, we would engage in the practice of alms rounds. Every morning we monastics would walk out to collect the food that we would eat for that day. Many Theravadan monastics in cultures like Thailand, Myanmar, and Sri Lanka are not permitted to buy food, to cook for themselves, or to even store food overnight. Unless ill or injured, we walked for our food to maintain that sense of interdependence, connection, and relationship that exists between ordained and nonordained communities. This is an example of community practice, people collectively supporting each other on both the primal level of nutritional food and the elevated level of spiritual sustenance.

This tradition is very different from Western notions of "begging"— it is the furthest thing from that. Our ordinary notion of "begging for food" is loaded in a specific way by our culture of capital materialism and competition. We think about what "food" is "ours" because there are a limited number of pieces to the literal and proverbial pie. If we don't get enough for ourselves, we won't survive. This mindset is based on an assumption of scarcity—that there isn't enough to go around for all of us. In the practice of alms rounds, the monastics walk with their eyes looking down onto the ground straight ahead of them and their alms bowl in their hands. They never directly ask anyone for food; asking for food is actually an infraction of one of the hundreds of guidelines that Theravadan monastics are required to follow in order to be defined as a monk or a nun. Instead, through the incredible and unconditional generosity of the people in the community, food is placed into the bowl.

I remember many times at the village temple when the sky was just beginning to turn a rosy pink as dawn lifted the cover of night, I would slip off my sandals, as is the custom, to feel the dust, the grit, the roughness of the unpaved ground and street paths—to feel the foundation of the ancient earth while engaging in this ancient practice and interchange. The walk for alms and food for the day is done without shoes. When people give food, they also take off their shoes, even if they are in the middle of the street. There is a sense of deep connection, free from hierarchy—just people in different roles touching the ground directly and together. The first time I stepped into the coolness of the morning air in my bare feet with my alms bowl, I felt incredibly vulnerable. It was unfamiliar to engage in this ancient act that has been done for more than 2,500 years. And amid that, I found myself wondering, *Would I do it correctly? Would I be able live up to the tradition well enough?*

I walked directly behind a monastic more experienced and senior to me. There was little activity around the village. Store owners were only just beginning to wash the sidewalks in front of their doors, and the smells of the food stalls cooking their first wave of meals began to waft through the air. As we walked, people came out of their homes already prepared to offer the generosity of their food. Generally, it was the older women of the household who had gotten up in the early morning hours to cook the elaborate meals that were delicately tied up in plastic bags to be carefully placed into monastic bowls.

We would hear the word *nimorn*, an equivalent of "Please, may I offer this food to you?" They would raise the food offering to their foreheads as a sign of respectful giving and gently place it into the alms bowl, starting with the senior monastic first when there was more than one. The lay villagers knelt as they made the offering, their faces showing a warmth that matched the emerging glow of the rising sun. All of this was done in silence, as if this ancient act was unfolding on its own. Then, the monastics would chant four verses that bless the food and those who have offered it. After a pause, without another word, we would move on. Sometimes not even a minute would pass before we heard another voice speak, "*Nimorn*"—"Please, may I offer this food to you? Please, we invite you."

The villagers would sometimes make an additional gesture of pouring water into a bowl as the monastics performed their chant. The gesture signified that whatever "merit"—goodness and value—that came from that act of kindness and generosity is shared with all living beings as easily as water flows. In this way the benefits of our spiritual practice are not only for the giver but for all beings unconditionally.

We enacted this ritual over and over again, each and every morning, and each time it touched a deep place in my heart. I returned to the temple with pounds and pounds of food, always more than the actual alms bowl could hold. I had to carry extra bags with me to accommodate all the donations. Monastics are obligated to accept all the gifts because another equally important aspect of this ritual is providing the community the opportunity to be generous. The practice of alms round and almsgiving offers practitioners an invitation to appreciate their faith and spirituality.

These rituals helped me come to a deep appreciation of life in partaking of the food. It helped me see how our physical lives continue through sustenance and how our spiritual and emotional lives continue through generosity and kindness.

After I ate my fill, the opportunity for me to be generous appeared.

Excess food was usually given to the monastery kitchen to be incorporated into regular meals for the larger temple community—but I figured that our temple was very well supported: it had grants from the government, not to mention offerings from generous lay supporters. So I chose to give differently.

I usually gave the remaining portion of my alms food to the migrant laborer families who live in dilapidated shacks along the border of the temple. Their living conditions were truly marginal: shanties with walls barely held together with string and cardboard or maybe, if they were lucky, scraps of aluminum. The first time I walked out to their huts, the residents, who were eating some plain rice in preparation for their day of hard labor, gave me a questioning look. When the families realized that I had an offering for them, they placed their palms together in the mudra called *anjali* and said thank you in broken Thai and Burmese.

The etymology of the word *community* is from the Latin terms *cum* meaning "together" or "among each other" and *munus*, which indicates giving or a gift or exchange. Integrated into one word, *community* represents a form of exchanging or giving among and between each other. It suggests the development of relationship and the act of relating with each other, since in the act of relating there is exchange and sharing. This source resonates with the Buddhist concept of the practice of sangha. Giving to each other—whether in the form of support in getting one's robes right or in the form of offering food—is a visible and visceral way of bringing community off the page as a concept and into life as a relational reality.

We are all interconnected and interrelated just by the fact that we are alive together in this world. We are relating to each other, but also to the larger aspect of life and the earth. The teachings on causes and effects, sometimes called interdependent coarising or dependent origination, speak to this innate aspect of how things are intertwined, both on the scale of our everyday human life and also in the grand expansiveness of the Universe.

This is explained in the Samyutta Nikaya as follows:

> When there is this, that is.
> With the arising of this, that arises.
> When this is not, neither is that.
> With the cessation of this, that ceases.

The fundamental part of this teaching can feel so true or like a nobrainer that it can seem mundane or feel irrelevant or unimportant. Yet in its succinctness, it invites us to explore how deeply interwoven and interdependent our lives are. Reverend Dr. Martin Luther King Jr. also captures the spirit of this ancient knowledge in writing:

> In a real sense, all life is interrelated. All men are caught in an inescapable network of mutuality, tied in a single garment of destiny. Whatever affects one directly, affects all indirectly. I can never be what I ought to be until you are what you ought to be, and you can never be what you ought to be until I am what I ought to be. This is the interrelated structure of reality.

It is this interrelated structure of our reality that we are invited to live each and every day when we walk within the different groups in our lives.

The different and varied communities within which we walk are defined and described by *culture*. I would define culture as the dynamic, ever-changing way in which a group of people lives together, including their conscious and unconscious behaviors, attitudes, norms, values, institutions, and symbols. This collection of characteristics is communicated verbally and nonverbally, transmitted from generation to generation, and constantly created, collected, and transformed in the process.

Culture necessarily influences our spiritual practice, both explicitly and subtly. Our norms, beliefs, and values influence our mythologies, rituals, and imagery. How we worship and have faith, in turn, is one of the common threads from which our culture is woven.

The organizations and institutions that comprise our Dharma communities are themselves cultural expressions. One view is that when our spiritual practice grows sufficiently deep, our awareness and spiritual development will transcend the influence of culture. I have seen this idea expressed specifically in regard to practice of the Buddha's teachings and even in the context of secular mindfulness and meditation practice. Some may disagree, but I believe that if Dharma practice is meant to be comprehensive—leaving nothing in life outside of its scope—then culture is not to be transcended or left behind. In fact, culture is something to be integrated into the very fabric of our spiritual practice, including the diverse facets of our behavior and identities. Cultural influence is there from the moment we are born until we pass away, from the time when we learn to when we teach others, in all the mundane and sublime elements of our lives.

The way in which the teachings of the Buddha and Buddhism have come to the West is no different: our experience of Dharma is influenced by both our own culture and the cultures from which we have received it. Western cultural norms and inclinations have already influenced our collective experience of the teachings. Even though those of us in Insight Meditation circles acknowledge that Sangha is a practice of being in community, we as Western convert groups do not place as much emphasis on this aspect as practitioners from traditionally Buddhist countries. The dominant culture in the United States can be quite focused on the singular, individual person. Our culture values icons of rugged individualism, the socio-literary narrative of raising oneself by one's own bootstraps, and the psychological ideal of healthy individuation in the process of human behavioral development. Such sentiments do not leave much room for cultivating a larger experience of community.

Mainstream Western society is not very collectively motivated. Our families are small nuclear ones, rather than the extended clans or networks common to so many other cultures. We can live in our densely populated urban and suburban environments but not encounter the people who live right next door. We can hear the teachings of how everything and everyone is interconnected, and yet not be connected to or even aware of the people and cultures in our near vicinity. The Dalai Lama has observed, "In the West, you have bigger homes, yet smaller families; you have endless conveniences, yet you never seem to have any time. You can travel anywhere in the world, yet you don't bother to cross the road to meet your neighbors."

For the past several decades, social psychologists have been exploring the impact that differing cultures have on psychology and human behavior. The current consensus is that nearly every social-psychological phenomenon is culturally dependent.

From this has emerged a description of what might be called two broad cultural archetypes: one that emphasizes, implicitly and/or explicitly, the individual experience and one that emphasizes, implicitly and/ or explicitly, the collective or group experience. The former has been described as an "independent" cultural modality, and the latter as an "interdependent" cultural modality. It is very interesting that, for the past fifty-plus years within the circles of Western Buddhist practice, the wisdom teachings of the Buddha have been transmitted from its Asian cultures of origin, "interdependent" cultures, to the largely "independent" cultures of Europe and the United States.

Just as social-psychological phenomena are culturally determined, so too are matters of spirituality, including the Dharma. Many of our Western Dharma communities largely focused on European American values and norms have yet to examine how the Dharma has been changed in its transition and transmission from interdependent cultures to independent cultures. Moreover, our own cultural reinterpretation of the Dharma is largely an unconscious, unexamined phenomenon.

This reinterpretation by dominant cultures in the Western world will necessarily lead to complex impacts, including how portions of the Buddha's teachings are selectively used by communities outside of the Dharma's cultures of origin. Amid the legacies of colonialism and their oppressive sociopolitical histories, cultural appropriation can be a continuation of those histories of dominance. This appropriation can be expressed through a dominant culture exercising its privilege, ability, and, most important, power to pick and choose what cultural forms to absorb or discard, and what is regarded as worthy or unworthy of consideration in defining Buddhist practice for Western communities. The separation of mindfulness practice from the eightfold path and the rest of its spiritual lineage of ethics in order to be efficacious in secular, corporate, for-profit, market-driven worlds is only one example.

We have also yet to seriously consider the impact of the Dharma as it spreads within multicultural communities. Strong interdependent cultural values, behaviors, norms, and social dynamics are inherent to the identity and cohesiveness of many cultures, particularly cultures of color—Asian and otherwise. Shared experiences of marginalization and oppression within the dominant, European American, hetero-based, and able-bodied normative culture actually reinforce cultural values of interdependency among such groups: we strengthen our core identities in order to survive the unconscious impact of the dominant culture's oppressive unconsciousness. Cultural interpretations of the Dharma focused on individuality and personal experience by teachers of European American descent and their communities do not resonate with those of us who share a cultural inclination toward interdependent ways of living and being in the world. We often experience a subtle but impactful sense of exclusion when the dominant culture's interpretation of the Buddha's teachings is offered through a cultural lens that overlooks the value of togetherness in favor of personal, often solitary, practice.

We see the impact of this interpretation of Dharma in the noticeable lack of emphasis on collectively creating more freedom and less suffering. There has been a great deal of emphasis on the development of meditation practice, awareness and loving-kindness practice, even Dharma and scriptural studies, but these are, by and large, regarded as some things to be personally experienced rather than carried out in community.

Our mainstream culture thrives in the marketplace of "self-help," help for the individual self. The message of self-help is reinforced by the language in which spiritual freedom is promoted: we can do it on our own, we should be able to do it on our own, and there might be something wrong or broken with us if we can't do it by ourselves. This is the subtle message conveyed in many Western Dharma teachings.

And yet, intuitively, we know we need the support of others.

Given that the Dharma's own cultures of origin were very much interdependent, I do not believe that rugged individualism or personalization is the inherent spiritual journey that the Buddha invited us to take. Although most contemporary Western converts to Buddhism are aware conceptually of the importance of interdependence, it may be that our dominant independent culture has rendered the teachings on this subject into conceptual abstractions.

The Buddha was always precise in his guidance, and he elevated community as one of the three most important aspects of our spiritual life in the teachings on the Three Refuges. He did not do this just to pay obligatory lip service to the collective aspect of our spiritual journey. He was inviting us to explore, as deeply as meditation itself, what it means to awaken together in community. He was inviting us to explore community itself as a practice of meditation or cultivation.

The more interdependently we feel, practice, and offer these teachings, the broader the reach and impact these teachings will have in our contemporary world.

The Buddha taught not only by his own example but through encouraging us to practice and bring the teachings into our own direct experience. The Buddha did not design a container for spiritual awakening that depends solely on personal effort. Out of the interdependent communities of lay and ordained practitioners, the Buddha wove the fabric of his vision for practicing together. The archetypal practices of daily alms rounds and offerings are an invitation to be in relationship with each other, to support each other out of necessity, to reduce our collective suffering out of compassion, and to awaken each other with joy. Let us bring this spirit of togetherness inclusively into our Dharma communities; let us thereby envision, create, foster, and evolve as practitioners, preserving the possibility of awakening and freedom together.

The Buddha's path is not a spiritual practice that encourages practitioners to go into a cave and escape the world, somehow becoming enlightened by the separation from others. Rather, the Buddha is inviting us into a practice of awakening using the full energies of our ever-evolving collective experience—of community. This is awakening together.

For Reflection

How do loving-kindness and compassion practices manifest as communal experiences?

How do they affect the objectives and outcomes of our collectives, groups, and organizations?

How do members of one sociocultural community develop, maintain, and deepen their awareness of a different sociocultural community?

What harm would we be able to avoid and diminish if we were to pay attention to different forms of being conscious collectively?

How would that impact efforts to diminish and eliminate the causes of collective unconsciousness and suffering of oppression, racism, and disparities based upon gender identities, physical abilities, and economic class?

How would the three pillars of our spiritual path—generosity and giving, ethical behavior and integrity, and meditation and mindfulness—manifest if we considered them to be things that we experience and develop together?

6

Refuge in a Multicultural World

THE EXPERIENCES of my childhood, whether related to race or the unnamed sexuality I felt, helped to shape the multiple cultural worlds into which I was beginning to live. These experiences in the multiplicity of cultural experience, its challenges, and its pain began for me a line of questioning that has extended throughout my life.

Early on in my spiritual path I wondered how I would succeed in a mainstream culture that makes things really difficult, even oppressive, for those who appear to be different. Where is it that I can feel I belong? How could I be who I am, while simultaneously trying to "fit in"? How does being unique and different relate to the universal connections that I feel and we all share in our lives? Do I try to blend in with and assimilate mainstream norms without questioning them? Do I differentiate even further to stand out, be different, or even try to be better than the "them" of the dominant culture?

The values of the dominant culture had a powerful impact on the experiences I had growing up and the life I was growing into. I felt the pain of exclusion and the desire to be included. I became aware that I walk between cultural worlds and wondered where my place, my home, and a sense of safety could be found.

The three jewels of spiritual practice, the Three Refuges, are one of the core Dharma teachings all Buddhist traditions share. The Buddha offered these refuges to create a sense of safety and a spiritual home. The word *refuge* connotes a feeling of safe haven. And of course the aspiration to find refuge reaches beyond formal Buddhist practice.

The yearning for a spiritual sense of home is an expansive and common experience. One teaching I received from my time in Southeast

Asia was that whenever we invoke the Three Refuges at the beginning of a meditation retreat, a practice session, or even our everyday sitting period, we can be sure that the refuges are being invoked by someone else in the world at exactly the same moment. It is because there are always others who are seeking the same sense of spiritual safe haven that we seek. The specific refuges that we envision in the Buddhist tradition share in the larger human aspiration for a sense of belonging and protection. The intentions and energies behind the refuges to facilitate peace and safety in the world are universal to the human spirit and prevalent across all cultures.

In Buddhist practice, these three safeguards of our path to freedom are described as refuge in the Buddha—the capacity for human life to become free from suffering and awaken to its true nature; refuge in the Dharma—assured guidance through teachings, practices, and experiences that have been time-tested by hundreds of generations of previous practitioners; and refuge in the Sangha—a community of like-hearted and like-minded spiritual friends and companions who support each other's growth on the spiritual path. We are able to find refuge in these potentials of our human lives because, ultimately, these teachings make us more at ease with ourselves, our lives, each other, and the world. There is a freedom in that sense of ease.

These refuges are also intimately tied to our cultural experience.

The Buddha's notions of freedom and awakening have always accounted for culture, diversity, and the infinite variations in human experience. Within Western Insight Meditation communities we are sometimes predisposed to idealize aspirations of spiritual practice and to assume that the highest aim is to transcend the vicissitudes of this life, to somehow obviate the sorrows of this lifetime so that we only experience the pleasant, peaceful, or sublime. Thus, I have heard some Dharma teachers avoid talking about diversity and culture, saying something like, "Why dwell on our differences? The point of practice is to see our similarities"—as if differences inevitably lead to suffering.

But it is a fact that our lives are not just made up of our similarities. Like any manifestation of nature—like any snowflake, leaf on a tree, or shape of a cloud—we all have attributes that are unique and characteristics that are common. It is through seeing the deep nature of our differences and how they are a part of our lives that we can also see the deep similarities of our human experience. We all feel different at some point in our lives; in that experience of difference is a similarity common to us all. Just as we cannot have a life without both joys and sorrows, we cannot have a life without both differences and similarities.

The Buddha recognized the importance of culture as a path to freedom. There is a story in the Vinaya, one of the primary scriptural volumes containing the Buddha's teachings for monastics:

> The occasion was this. There were two monastics called Yamelu and Tekula. They were of brahmin stock, and they had fine voices and a fine delivery. They asked the Blessed One: "Lord, now the monastics are of various names, of various races, variously born, having gone forth from various clans. They spoil the word of the Blessed One by using their own language. Let us render the words of the Buddha into classical meter."
>
> The Buddha, the Blessed One, rebuked them: "Misguided men, how can you say 'Let us render the words of the Buddha into classical meter'? This will not rouse faith in the faithless or increase faith in the faithful; rather it will keep the faithless without faith and harm some of the faithful." Having rebuked them, he addressed the monastics thus: "Monastics, the word of the Buddha is not to be rendered into classical meter. Whoever does so commits an offense of wrongdoing. I allow the words of the Buddha to be learned in one's own language."

So, what is the significance of this story?

The two monastics—who were of the dominant culture and class—were concerned that the teachings of the Buddha were being "spoiled" by people different from them assimilating the Dharma to their own cultural-linguistic expression. The two suggest that the Buddha codify the spiritual teachings into a singular, unified cultural expression—in keeping with their own cultural values. But the Buddha replied in no uncertain terms that his teachings should be learned in the languages native to the various disciples, in the idiom of the people, and this point is essential to understanding the deeper level of the Buddha's intention.

The Buddha lived in a historical time before written script. This means that all communication of his teaching was oral. In the absence of the printed word, it was very difficult for languages to survive and thrive outside the geographic area of their cultures of origin. Thus, a specific language was one of the determinants of a specific culture. Language and culture mutually influence each other in significant ways. We can see the message implicit in the Buddha's statement above is that it is misguided to offer teachings in only one cultural form or to somehow impose homogeneity on Dharma practice. It is the Buddha's opinion that teachings should be offered in the context of the practitioner's own culture.

For me, it is a relief to know this, particularly in this modern age when access to technology, the ability to travel, and the sheer scale of humanity have brought a greater convergence of diverse peoples than has ever occurred before in history. As the filter to our experience of Buddha's teachings, cultural identity is an important aspect of the path to freedom. It is as important to recognize this today as it was during the Buddha's time. We must recognize our uniqueness in order to recognize our sameness.

Culture and the Refuge of the Buddha

In taking refuge in the Buddha, we take refuge in the possibility that we, like the Buddha, can be freed from greed, liberated from hatred, and awakened from delusion—this is one of the ways enlightenment is described. We do not take refuge in a deity or power higher than ourselves. We find faith and confidence in the idea that enlightenment is possible because the human being Siddhartha Gautama—as the Buddha was called before his enlightenment—was able to exemplify that potential for humanity in his awakening. We take refuge in a potential that is deeply human.

And embedded in that humanness is an invitation to explore one of the central spiritual questions of being human: "Who am I?" This question doesn't only exist within one particular spiritual tradition but rather is found across cultures and across wisdom traditions because it is central to our human experience.

There is, of course, no generalized answer for everyone, and so each person needs to find their own answer in the context of their own life. Our cultural experiences and specificities—whether in the form of race, ethnicity, gender, gender identity, orientation, age, physical ability, economic and/or educational level, or any other characteristic or experience—will necessarily form part of our exploration of who we are. No part of our humanity falls outside the scope of that question. There is nothing in our lives unworthy of our loving attention and mindfulness. The Buddha awakened by deeply exploring his particular experience of the human condition.

We all share in common the experience of the human condition, but we each experience it in unique ways. None of us lacks the potential to awaken to a greater sense of freedom and clearer mind and heart.

Unfortunately, though, the exploration of culture and identity within some Dharma circles has a tarnished reputation. Some say that using experiences of culture and identity contradicts or is antithetical to the teachings of *emptiness* or *nonself.* Reasoning in this way, some people dismiss cultural experience altogether as a potential object for personal mindfulness practice and discourage collective awareness of these themes within Dharma communities. Some say that not only is exploration of multicultural experience not really Dharma practice, it can be divisive and lead to a greater sense of separation and suffering, rather than less.

This is a reflexive reaction of the culturally unconscious.

Unconscious of how culture shapes the experiences we examine in practice, such views hastily cast aside culture as a basic human experience—ignoring it or denying it in a multitude of ways.

Those who belong to the dominant or mainstream culture are usually most unconscious of their own cultural experiences. The values and behaviors of the dominant culture are taken as norms. These norms of the dominant culture "dominate," so to speak, and as such, are taken for granted and go largely unnoticed by those who own them. This is not only true for the larger society but also for spiritual communities, regardless of denomination; spiritual communities are not separate from or different than other forms of community. So the same dynamics of cultural unconsciousness appear in communities of Dharma practitioners as well.

This cultural unconsciousness that happens within dominant cultures can severely limit how we understand spiritual inquiry into who we really are, because the lack of individual, interpersonal, and collective consciousness distorts how we perceive the nature of this "we."

How do people who are marginalized or who are different from the dominant culture encounter the Dharma when it is filtered solely through a dominant cultural lens?

There is an idea at the heart of the Buddhist teachings that each of us has the same potential for enlightenment the Buddha had. Does this idea really manifest for those of us outside the scope of mainstream culture when, due to cultural ignorance and insensitivity, our stories are overlooked, instructions are not made relevant to us, or the dominant cultural interpretation of the Dharma is assumed to be the only interpretation possible? Having the same potential for enlightenment is different than being the same, having the same lives, or living under the same conditions.

People of color are constantly challenged to find for ourselves how the teachings are relevant to our lives, particularly in terms of how they can be applied to our very real experiences of discrimination and oppression. For example, people with physical limitations are left behind when instructions are given for walking meditation without any alternative options.

A Xicana psychotherapist friend of mine has shared with me the particular challenge that the teachings of nonself present for Latinx* cultures who have a healthy sense of self as interdependent and integrally bonded with the collective whole. The way self is construed in these

---

*Latinx, sometimes Latin@, is the gender-neutral term used for the previous binary identity descriptions of Latina and Latino.

cultures differs from individual-oriented psychology paradigms, and so teachings tailored to European American experiences do not always resonate with the Latinx cultures.

It is precisely our refuge in the Buddha—the idea that all of us are worthy of awakening and can attain it—that justifies and requires that there be culturally specific teaching and practice venues to skillfully meet the differing cultural needs of diverse communities.

We have seen such responses develop within some of our American Dharma communities. It began with women's residential retreats in the late 1970s and early 1980s offered by Ruth Denison, Christina Feldman, Julie Wester, Debra Chamberlin-Taylor, and Anna Douglas, among others. In the mid-1990s, retreats for lesbian, gay, bisexual, transgender, intersex, and queer (LGBTIQ) communities were pioneered by Arinna Weisman and Eric Kolvig. And by the late 1990s and early 2000s, retreats for communities of color finally emerged, first at Vallecitos, and then at Spirit Rock in California and Insight Meditation Society in Barre, Massachusetts, through the efforts of Ralph Steele, Marlene Jones, Gina Sharpe, Linda Velarde, Michele Benzamin-Miki, Jack Kornfield, Margarita Loinaz, George Mumford, Joseph Goldstein, Sharon Salzberg, and myself—among many others. These retreats set the foundation for the development of local sitting groups for each of these cultural groups within broader Dharma communities. In 2007, East Bay Meditation Center was founded in downtown Oakland, California, with the expressed mission of including cultural diversity as one of its organizational priorities based on recognizing that the teachings of the Buddha do not stand apart from cultural experience but are interwoven with it.

Of course, these developments have not occurred without resistance.

Some are of the opinion that there really is no need for culturally specific retreats, such as retreats for communities of color or for the LGBTIQ communities. Even recently, in the aftermath of the culturally charged events of Ferguson, Charleston, Orlando, Baton Rouge, Tulsa, and so many others, when cultural refuge is so urgently needed, there are still meditation centers that not only disallow culturally specific retreats but disallow teachers who believe in the benefit of these retreats to teach any other kinds of retreats at their centers.

Even if there is not an active dismissal of the needs of diverse communities to explore spiritual teachings in a culturally congruent way, there can be a passivity that often arises in the mainstream, that "diversity and culture are not *my* problem; they are someone else's issue." This becomes another example of the inability of a dominant culture to see beyond its own experience. This inability is not passive; it is an active manifestation of oppression.

It isn't my intention to simply draft a list of grievances—after all, what better and more meaningful place is there than our Dharma communities to engage with the practice of conscious awareness and attention? It is precisely by practicing mindfulness with respect to our own unconsciousness that we begin to wake up!

None of us can deny the forces of our own cultural experience. It is part of our human existence. When we are not mindful and aware of the ways in which our cultural experience influences our perception and can limit our understanding of things, we prevent ourselves from penetrating to a deeper experience of interconnection and relatedness. Interrelatedness is critically important to the experience of what is beyond ego. We move into and through our cultural experience, just as we move into and through the ten thousand joys and ten thousand sorrows of this lifetime.

We cannot go around them.

We find what lies beyond the layers of our experience by probing deeply into them, not by ignoring them. We cannot simply say that culture doesn't exist, isn't important, or isn't part of our spiritual path. All of our lives are part of our spiritual path.

The Buddha's awakening and the refuge of the Buddha are very much about culture.

Culture and the Refuge of Dharma

Dharma is the word used to encompass the teachings of the Buddha and the lineages of teaching that arose from them.

The Dharma, too, is very much about culture.

Throughout the course of the historical movement of the Dharma from a relatively circumscribed region in northeastern India to central and southeastern Asia, over the Silk Road into China, Mongolia, Tibet, and eventually to Japan, the words of the Buddha have been amplified over and over again through different linguistic and cultural expressions. If anything, history seems to show us that the Dharma has survived multiple adaptations to the languages and cultural contexts of those who receive it. Since the Dharma is always necessarily expressed via a language and a culture, Dharma necessarily comes to reflect the different cultural experiences of different cultural communities.

After the Buddha passed from this world, differences in interpretation of his teachings appeared. Interpretations of the teachings may have been generally agreed upon in the immediate wake of his death (albeit not without some controversy, as is documented in the scriptures), but within seventy years of the Buddha's passing a major disruption of the unified interpretation of his teachings occurred. At the Buddhist council held at Vaishali, ten points of controversy were raised, wherein one group of monastics accused another of sullying the purity of the Dharma and committing various offenses. Such offenses included things like storing salt in a horn, eating after midday, eating once and going on alms round again, carrying out official acts with an incomplete assembly, following a practice because it was done by one's teacher, consuming strong drink before it had been fermented, using rugs that were not the proper size, and using gold and silver.

Many of these points of controversy seem irrelevant to us today, but the cultural context in which the conflict arose is not. At the time the Dharma was spreading to areas of western India where there was a much more diverse mix of peoples with different needs, lifestyles, and values. When the Dharma came into contact with other cultural perspectives, multiple ways of interpreting it arose between those who remained in the Buddha's native region and those who migrated outward into the larger world.

This is quite relevant for us, and we should take note of it.

Cultural complexity and intersectionality are major factors in the struggle between those of any religion who identify themselves as valuing "pure," "traditional," and (ostensibly) "original" teachings and those interested in adapting the teachings to make the Dharma relevant in the new worlds it encounters. This classic, archetypal tension has not just to do with the content of scriptural interpretation but also with the dynamics of societies as they converge and meet. In the contemporary Dharma world, debates and controversies continue to explore whether there is an expansive nature to the Buddha's teachings that allows them to be interpreted, reinterpreted, and further interpreted without losing core principles.

In the past two and a half millennia the Dharma has moved through numerous cultures, and there has always been tension between the Dharma as expressed in its source culture and the new culture into which it has been received. One clear historical example is how the Buddha's teachings filtered into Chinese civilization and culture. Some legends say the first Chinese contact with the Dharma happened during King Ashoka's time (250 BCE) and Buddhist icons and statuary were installed on the Silk Road around 120 BCE. Official emissaries arrived in the Chinese court in 67 CE, but it took until 500 CE for the Buddha's teachings to really begin to rival the indigenous traditions of Confucianism and Taoism. It could have taken 650 to 750 years or more for Buddhism to permeate Chinese culture and become an established, honored tradition. Today we perceive Buddhism to be absolutely integral to Chinese culture and experience. So why did it take so long?

There were, of course, enormous variances in cultural norms and values when the Dharma first came into contact with Chinese societies. Tremendous cultural resistance arose. I don't want to reduce or oversimplify a complex cultural interaction and evolution, but for our purposes, we will consider just a few of the most salient indications of the dissonance between the culture of the Dharma that entered China and the way of life that already existed there. These included: (1) the Buddhist focus on personal enlightenment, as exemplified by the arhat ideal, undermined Confucian values of family lineage and ancestor worship; (2) monastics were not viewed as filial or respectful of elders (a highly prized Confucian ideal) because they went forth into homelessness and home-leaving (as ordination was called), renouncing their families of origin; (3) monastics were perceived as nonproductive members of society because they lived off of alms and donations; and (4) last and probably most emblematic of the cultural dissonance, Buddhist monastics could not bow to the emperor or any higher authority.

What happened to ameliorate these conflicts and allow the Dharma to become so ubiquitously infused into Chinese culture? Over the course of hundreds of years of cross-cultural contact, new Buddhist traditions gradually evolved: (1) "merit" or the goodness of one's spiritual efforts could be transferred to one's family and ancestors; (2) novice monastics were trained to be "filial" to senior monastics in keeping with the traditional Chinese family structure; (3) monasteries developed commerce, and trade and even took on government administration, thereby becoming "productive" institutions within Chinese society; and (4) the emperor came to be considered an incarnation of the living Buddha, making it appropriate for the monastic community to bow to the emperor.

From the perspective of culture, the evolution of the different Buddhist schools (Theravada, Mahayana, and Vajrayana) was not strictly a matter of scriptural development and interpretation but also a matter of the Dharma being transformed by the cultures with which it came into contact. In a real sense, culture has been extremely influential in producing the different lineages of the Dharma. Their development is sometimes couched in the language of multiple "turnings of the Wheel of Dharma," the origin of each lineage constituting a different "turning." But we can also say that distinct Dharma lineages blossomed into the fullness of their teachings as the Dharma encountered and was integrated into particular geographic, social, and cultural worlds.

When European colonizers arrived to dominate many regions of Asia, they initially believed that each culture had its own distinct religion. To the foreigner observing superficially, the spiritual traditions of regions such as Sri Lanka, Burma, Thailand, Vietnam, China, and Japan appeared very different. It took European colonizing examiners years to realize that they were not encountering different spiritual traditions in each of these countries but were seeing a single spiritual tradition that had become uniquely adapted to a multiplicity of cultural contexts. This is one piece of evidence for the great malleability of the Dharma.

When I revealed to my Chinese-born parents that I would be ordained and take up practice as a Buddhist monk in Thailand, even after accepting the radical life change I was about to undertake, they were still slightly bewildered because the various practices, the process of ordination, even the way that monastic robes and temples looked were all very different from what they were accustomed to in China. Yet when I talked about the core teachings, there was an immediate recognition.

The Dharma tends to profoundly influence and transform the cultures into which it is received, and it has an incredible resiliency, even when adapting to local cultures and forms. Moreover, there was probably never a monolithic "Dharma" free from the influence of multiple cultural contexts. The teachings of the Buddha are transformative of individuals and of communities, and are transformed by them as well. The Dharma changes every culture it meets, and in turn, the Dharma is changed, transformed, and uniquely lived within each culture—and yet remains the Dharma.

All of us can ourselves learn something from how the Dharma has been lived differently. We can embody it even more fully for the multitude of cultures it touches within our lifetime and for those who will experience this human condition in the future. Let us attend to how the Dharma will change our cultures, our relationship to those cultures, and our relationship to the Dharma itself, and let us attend to how our cultures transform the Dharma into variegated expressions of our creative humanity.

It took six to seven centuries for the Dharma to permeate the Chinese culture until ultimately becoming an inseparable part of it. What will the process be like in the West?

The Dharma was first brought to North America by Asian communities as they migrated in waves beginning in the mid-1800s. In the early and mid-twentieth century, European American spiritual seekers began to visit Buddhist cultures, bringing their interpretation of the Dharma back to the Western cultures from whence they came. Even now, we are still at a relatively early point in the encounter between these Western cultures and the Dharma. We must discover for ourselves how to distinguish what we might think of as "indispensable core teachings" from what represents the cultural interpretation that has always taken place to make the Dharma accessible to the specific communities into which it has now migrated. We must learn what the differences are between a natural integration and synthesis of the Dharma into a new culture and the cultural appropriation that occurs when a dominant culture unconscious of its power, privilege, and resources takes only what it wants, while disregarding cultural context or a communal respect for cultural origins. Working through these issues is to be expected. It is a vibrant and creative time for all of us to encounter the Dharma as it just begins to flourish in the multiplicity of our cultures. As has been the case down through its history, the Dharma continues to be intimately tied up with culture.

The lineage of the Buddha's teachings, the refuge of the Dharma, is very much about culture.

Culture and the Refuge of Sangha

Sangha is the word originally used to refer to the community of ordained monastics but has come to carry new meanings beyond this traditional definition. In many places *sangha* has come to encompass the larger spiritual community of practitioners and friends supporting each other as they work toward freedom. It has come to mean broadly the assembly of communities who will provide a healthy foundation on which the Buddha's teachings can be sustained far into our future. It is important to explicitly state that *sangha*, community, is very much about culture as well.

Social networks (technological and their noncomputer, in-person forebears) and their cultural dynamics—including their achievements and celebrations, conflict and resistance, integration and synthesis, evolution and transformation—all influence how the Dharma develops and how it is lived in the present and shaped for future generations. Communal culture is one of the doors through which the Buddha's teachings are being transmitted into the diverse communities of the West. This is one of the primary reasons that culturally specific or identity-focused support—such as retreats for people of color (PoC); lesbian, gay, bisexual, transgender, intersex, queer (LGBTIQ) communities; women; or young people—is so important.

At a recent Buddhist teachers' conference there was an exercise in which attendees were invited to write down a question they considered important to discuss at the gathering. Anonymously, participants informally voted on the questions so created. One of the questions read something like, "When can we end the proliferation of special-interest retreats like LGBTIQ and PoC and return to the unity of One Sangha?"

The allusion to the "One Sangha" is an incomplete reference to the unity of our common existences in the realm of Absolute Truth. But as we know, within the teachings on truths, there are two truths, both equal in their importance: the relative and the absolute. Spiritual freedom is not about privileging one truth over the other—not about imposing the absolute over the relative, or preferring the relative over the absolute. To do either negates so much of being human in the simultaneity of our different cultural experiences and common universal experience and performs what John Welwood has classically described as a spiritual bypass.

In a recent interview, Welwood describes this phenomenon in these words:

> *Spiritual bypassing* is a term I coined to describe a process I saw happening in the Buddhist community I was in, and also in myself. Although most of us were sincerely trying to work on ourselves, I noticed a widespread tendency to use spiritual ideas and practices to sidestep or avoid facing unresolved emotional issues, psychological wounds, and unfinished developmental tasks.
>
> When we are spiritually bypassing, we often use the goal of awakening or liberation to rationalize what I call *premature transcendence*: trying to rise above the raw and messy side of our humanness before we have fully faced and made peace with it. And then we tend to use absolute truth to disparage or dismiss relative human needs, feelings, psychological problems, relational difficulties, and developmental deficits.

A spiritual bypass implies a shortcut—and the tendency of the mind to incline toward the pleasantness of obviating the complexity and messiness of human differences by prescribing unconditional harmony and homogeneity upon the collective experience. This artificial imposition of one-sided truth only creates more suffering.

We know that we need to go through the first noble truth in order to see the other side of suffering—to gain freedom from it. If we circumvent, repress, deny, or bypass the first noble truth, we will only create more suffering in the future. This is true of any experience in our lives: we need to turn toward it in order to fully comprehend, fully feel, and fully live that experience. The same is true for our cultural experiences. We need to go through the uniqueness of each of our lives in order to live the connection and interrelatedness that is beyond the differences.

Shunryu Suzuki writes in *Zen Mind, Beginner's Mind:*

> Strictly speaking, there are no separate individual existences. There are just many names for one existence. Sometimes people put a stress on oneness, but this is not our understanding. We do not emphasize any point in particular, even oneness. Oneness is valuable, but variety is also wonderful. Ignoring variety, people emphasize the one absolute existence, but this is one-sided understanding. In this understanding there is a gap between variety and oneness. But oneness and variety are the same thing, so oneness should be appreciated in each existence.

John Welwood comments later in the same interview mentioned above that

> We need a larger perspective that can recognize and include two different tracks of human development—which we might call growing up and waking up, healing and awakening, or becoming a genuine human person and going beyond the person altogether. We are not just humans learning to become buddhas, but also buddhas waking up in human form, learning to become fully human. And these two tracks of development can mutually enrich each other.

We need both: the absolute aspiration of universality, and the relative path of our humanity. Regardless of how we understand the question of One Sangha, as long as we have diverse communities newly coming to the Dharma, and as long as we intend to welcome and encourage their participation in practice and the community, identity-based retreats will beneficially support their spiritual efforts. So, the basic answer to the question, "When can we end the proliferation of special-interest retreats like LGBTIQ and PoC and return to the unity of One Sangha?" is "Not any time soon."

So long as culture remains a primary influence on human experience, there will be a need for these retreats as a skillful means for diverse practitioners to access the Dharma. The single unity of the Sangha has always been diverse in nature.

Diverse folks making the tender entry into spiritual practice necessarily have varied needs. To successfully transmit and receive the Dharma into diverse cultures, we must support the differing processes of each person, so that all can share a feeling of safety and being acknowledged within the teachings. This is a universal quality of our human experience, even within communities of the mainstream, dominant culture. The large sanghas formed within the European American mainstream in the United States are a recent development. Since the mid-1800s many Buddhist temples and spiritual centers had already existed within North American Asian American communities. There were already Chinese, Japanese, Tibetan, Thai, Burmese, Cambodian, and Vietnamese Buddhist communities, among others.

Over time, particularly during the twentieth century, many Westerners from the dominant European American cultures traveled to Asia and returned with profound experiences with the Dharma as a spiritual path to freedom. Some of these individuals would become prominent Western meditation teachers, and many of those are still with us and actively teaching.

It is interesting to reflect on why European Americans returning from Asia did not practice and teach in the Asian Buddhist temples and communities already established here. Why did European American practitioners feel the need to form their own communities, to practice in retreats that served mostly "their own kind," in spite of the existence of Asian and Asian American Buddhist practice venues and communities?

I do not want to overgeneralize, but I suspect that it was at least partially because European Americans did not see themselves reflected in Asian American spiritual centers and communities.

The way the teachings were expressed in Asian American centers likely did not reflect the worlds of life within the dominant mainstream cultures. Perhaps the cultural forms in Asian American Buddhist centers, whether devotional, linguistic, visual, or psychological, did not reflect how these European Americans saw or felt about themselves. Those pioneering European American Dharma teachers wanted to offer social conditions in which the Dharma could be made as relevant as possible to the cultural experience most familiar to them. So European American practitioners created communities focused upon European American experiences. Culture allows the teachings to become relevant to specific communities—even for the dominant culture. Culture is what begins to connect the dots to show people that "Yes, this practice is for me too— not just for others." The reasons that European Americans chose to form their own sanghas can be the *exact same* reasons that PoC, LGBTIQ, and other culturally distinct communities also feel the need to create experiences of the Dharma that are specifically relevant to their experience.

Indeed, while it might seem counterintuitive, what we all share in common regardless of our backgrounds is the tendency to view ourselves as culturally different. We all respond in common ways to cross-cultural circumstances, even if the details of our specific stories differ. Recognizing this gives us insight into our interconnectedness and the universality of human needs. Everyone, not just PoC or LGBTIQ communities, feels more at home in a community when the culture and identity of the community are shared—just as folks from European American cultures found.

We are all human. We all want to feel safe, to feel we belong, especially in the vulnerabilities at the beginning of our spiritual paths. In the service of this, it is helpful to see ourselves reflected in the teachings, reflected in the teachers who share them, and reflected in the spiritual community surrounding us.

Spiritual explorations require intimacy and tenderness, and it is very hard to relax into what is an open, vulnerable state when our defenses already have to be in place to protect from the injuries and traumas caused by unconsciousness and patterns embedded in the dominant culture. To deny nondominant cultures the same sense of intimacy and safety that those of the dominant culture enjoy, at the very least, simply continues a pattern of cultural unconsciousness and insensitivity. At worst, it aggravates a pattern of oppression that denies those outside the dominant culture the ability to be fully who they feel themselves to be.

It is clear that American mainstream culture has not yet transcended or healed the tremendous harm wrought by racism, homophobia, and other forms of oppression and discrimination. As members of this society, we cannot separate ourselves from the innumerable events surrounding Oscar Grant, Trayvon Martin, Tamir Rice, Sandra Bland, Eric Garner, and Orlando, Florida; Flint, Michigan; and Charleston, South Carolina, as well as the continued hate violence toward transgender communities, the active hostility to voter rights protection and immigration reform, or the vitriolic xenophobia expressed in our 2016 electoral political discourse. Our spiritual practice is not detached from these experiences.

On the contrary, we call on spiritual practice specifically to create the skillful means that will enable us to extinguish such harms. Creating identity-specific practice events for communities of color or LGBTIQ communities is one such skillful means. It allows practitioners to gather, secluded from the incessant barrage of racism, heterosexism, and other types of oppression, and experience some relief so that they can better explore the deeper calling and benefits of spiritual practice. I use the word *incessant* here because even when overt physical violence and aggression are absent, microaggressions can occur that comprise the proverbial "death from a thousand paper cuts" that many outside the dominant culture experience on a daily basis.

Of course, simply creating culturally specific practice venues, like PoC, LGBTIQ, women's, and young people retreats, isn't the ultimate goal of practice. It is only a skillful means of engendering a sense of safety for communities who feel they don't belong or relate to mainstream cultural settings so that they too can access the Dharma. Even though a mainstream sangha may have the intention of being totally inclusive, unless dedicated and inspired attention is paid to culture and diversity within the group, the outcome will likely fall short of the intent.

This yet-to-be-achieved deep inclusivity is in part due to our collective cultural unconsciousness, which includes legacies of racism, homophobia, and other sorts of discrimination. Collective practice of awareness can elevate our communities so that we fulfill the aspiration to a "Beloved Community" developed by Josiah Royce, a philosopher of the early twentieth century, and expanded upon and timelessly described in the speeches of Reverend Dr. Martin Luther King Jr.

Beloved Communities are envisioned as those that embody the values of love and justice in every aspect of their being, even when circumstances are difficult or oppressive. A Beloved Community assumes that all our lives are interrelated and the social nature of our humanity is not secondary to any other aspect of life. As Dr. King reminds us over and over again, "We are tied together in the single garment of destiny, caught in an inescapable network of mutuality."

Eventually the Dharma invites the deepest intention from all communities—communities of color, European Americans, queer folks, hetero-normative folks, young people, people of different physical abilities—to be able to practice anywhere, with anyone, under any circumstance, and to be able to practice together, in "unity," as a gathering of Whole Communities.* It will take a concerted effort from all of us to raise the level of our personal and collective awareness to fulfill the intention to truly live together in a way that embodies nonharm, nonoppression, and nonexclusion.

And it takes time—and a lot more of it than anyone would like.

In 2010, there was an opportunity at Spirit Rock Meditation Center for a multicultural gathering to practice over the Martin Luther King Jr.

---

*My gratitude to the Center for Whole Communities in Waitsfield, Vermont, for introducing me to the terminology of "whole communities." One of CWC's founders, Peter Forbes, describes Whole Communities as being "the sum of healthy relationships between people, and between people and place. A community is made complete or whole when people are fully visible to each other, reaching their potentials within lasting relationships to real places made of rivers and soils and human creativity that can thrive forever."

holiday weekend. Out of ninety participants, half were from communities of color and half were from European American communities. The gathering wove together difference and commonality, connection and diversity, and was over twenty years in the making. It took that much time to cultivate in the practitioners, the teachers, the board members, the management, the staff, and the organization itself the degree of multicultural awareness that would enable such an event to happen. The bad news is that it couldn't have happened sooner (or else it would have!) because the conditions of cultural skill and sensitivity were not sufficiently present to enable truly diverse communities to be authentically together in spiritual practice without causing harm. The good news is that it did happen. And we did it again in 2012, understanding deeply how rare and precious it is anywhere in this world to be able to gather such diverse communities together with deep spiritual intention, and that it is our profound responsibility to continue such efforts.

When we create practice opportunities so that both culturally specific populations and the larger community can gather in cultural mindfulness and awareness of our shared humanity, we are invited to move from the question "Who am I?" to a broader exploration of "Who are we?" What kind of path is possible leading to collective liberation?

The Buddha said that he would not teach that which is not possible or that which we cannot do. We can do this.

We all share the need to feel safe and at ease in our spiritual journeys so that we may deeply explore our places of healing, our places of injury, our joys, and our sorrows. We are vulnerable and tender when we undertake such explorations. And just as we are so much more than who we think we are as individuals, we are also so much more than who we think we are as communities. As we enlarge our spiritual capacity to be with all of our experience, we also gain the capacity to be with the experience of greater numbers of beings and greater numbers of communities. The Dharma invites us into the unconditional, into the expansiveness that community and Sangha represent, into the vast connectedness we share as a Universal Family.

This is why the Sangha is very much about culture.

This is why the Three Refuges are all inextricably woven into our experience of culture.

For Reflection

What allows, invites, makes room for enough safety in your life?

What does refuge mean to you? How do you feel it and embody it?

How can refuge support you in your aspirations and actions?

What could you do, who could you envision yourself to be, if you fully felt the benefits of refuge?

How is your sense of refuge determined by your cultural experience, your culture of origin, or the cultures of your familial lineage?

7

Beautiful and Beloved Communities

O NE PLACE I teach is at the East Bay Meditation Center (EBMC). EBMC sits in the middle of downtown Oakland, California, and we are immersed in the bustle of multiple communities coming together to work, to shop, to play—and even to protest.

Protest can be a collective form of mindfulness practice.

Protest can be a vehicle for advocacy—exerting political and social pressure on controversial issues—and a chance for people who do not have a voice in mainstream culture to make themselves heard. One of the principal purposes of protest is to reveal what is usually hidden, not seen, heard, or acknowledged by the larger society. In this way, protest can be viewed as a collective mindfulness practice that articulates and reveals experiences that are invisible to the mainstream dominant culture. Protest is also a method of speaking truth to power, especially when the sources of power have little or no accountability.

During the height of the Occupy movement of a few years ago, Oakland, California, and Occupy Oakland became one of the focal points for community discussion and action for social justice and transformation. When a general strike was organized as part of the Occupy Oakland movement, I was moved to see actions designed by the EBMC meditation community adding to the emerging collective voices. One EBMC practitioner, Max Airborne, writes on Buddhist Peace Fellowship's website about the inspiration from the "vast array of artistic, cultural, philosophical, educational, and practical contributions coming from so many people and communities . . . seeing so many folks who are really showing up, and masses of people who are acting like it's possible to create the world we want to live in, acting like liberation is within reach."

A small group of EBMC practitioners had the idea of doing sitting and walking meditations in front of a branch of a major banking institution that Occupy activists had identified as contributing to the disparity between the 1 percent and the rest of our society. As they prepared for their action, they thought to expand the action to include something that would transform the idea of what a bank represents. To counter the values of making money from other people's money and the belief that disparity of opportunity is simply an inevitable byproduct of our capitalistic economy, these EBMC protestors decided that rather than making money at the bank (as the 1 percent does), they would give it away. They would extend the practice of unconditional generosity to anyone who walked past the bank. They gathered as many one-dollar bills as they could and offered them freely to pedestrians as they walked by.

There were a wide range of responses to this symbolic act of protest— from not wanting any contact with the protesters whatsoever to expressions of need for the money to appreciating the idea and planning to pass the gift forward to others. At the same time, in order to prepare for the perceived possible "danger" or "risk" posed by Oakland Strike protesters, the bank kept its doors locked, despite being open for business, and only allowed customers to enter one at a time. The slightly befuddled security and bank employees watched the nonviolent protest in the form of unconditional generosity from behind the lobby windows—although one bank teller even came out to offer to change larger bills for one-dollar bills so that protestors could continue to give.

The openness of the gestures of generosity stood in sharp contrast to the locked doors of the bank itself.

Things got even more interesting when another group of protestors arrived, not associated with EBMC. This second group was operating with a very different attitude and tactical strategy. They were yelling loud, angry chants and blocked the entrance to the bank. When one of the EBMC practitioners, in a gesture of generosity, offered some of them a dollar bill, the impact was palpable. The angry, rage-driven energy shifted to surprise, questioning, amusement, and maybe excitement. Some of the latecomers joined the EBMC folks in their practice of generosity by making their own monetary offerings to others.

Some might question the effectiveness of this effort.

Max Airborne, who was one of the organizers behind this collective practice and who shared the story with me, had an answer to this concern. They write:

> All actions that address injustice and greed are needed in these times, both internal and external, large and small. We weren't shutting down the bank, instead we were doing our part to shut down human greed by digging a new pathway in our minds, and the minds of all those we encountered. So to ... [those] who asked if our action had been "successful," I say "Absolutely, without a doubt."

This type of action may not seem to approach the scale of other massive social-change efforts, but perhaps that isn't the point. The profound objectives of social justice endeavors can sometimes be so expansive that they become intimidating or overwhelming to would-be activists. We can be paralyzed by the sheer size of the issues. Perhaps the point of this smaller protest action was to approach issues not only on a massive scale but in each moment and each intention in our lives. Even in our small actions, we can accomplish them with our highest values and vision. We make a difference, no matter how seemingly limited our acts may be, because we affect each other's lives.

Even handing a dollar bill to someone we don't know has some impact, because we do not live our lives in isolation, even when we think we are alone.

The Occupy movement was complex: it involved diverse interests, goals, visions, needs, and communities, and not every group in the movement agreed with one another or always saw eye to eye. The intense feeling of pressure exerted by omnipresent surveillance and containment imposed by the police and city political leaders added another layer to this complexity, and everyone involved in the movement had to be constantly vigilant and on guard against that pressure. As the energy of the Occupy movement grew, the topic of *diversity of tactics* came to prominence within group discussions. This term refers to possible justifications for the use of force and violence as a viable means to counteract oppression and injustice in the interests of social change—and here *diversity* indicates an openness to using any means possible because the ends might justify them.

Many members of our EBMC community—already activists from communities of color, differing gender identifications, differing sexual orientations, differing physical abilities—were involved in the Occupy movement. Coming from a practice community that sees itself as a center for spiritual support to social activists, we were familiar with this inclination of the mind to use any means possible to justify outcomes. But our spiritual practice asks that we pause and reflect on whether such acts really lead to personal and collective freedom. For us, the practice of social justice is not different than or separate from our spiritual practice.

So how do we meet even struggles for justice and equity with a heart that is both tenderly open and deeply wise? What is truly beneficial in the face of oppression and inequity? As mentioned above, in the Dhammapada the Buddha teaches "Hate never yet dispelled hate."

This is such a simple teaching, but it is repeated because it is so profound and so complicated to practically implement and actually live.

In other words, the creation of justice and the diminishment of injustice must and indeed can only happen through just means. We cannot create justice through unjust means. Justice created through unjust means is not justice, nor is it freedom. Justice can be supported only by our conscious awareness and by the deliberate kindness that allows us to transform and heal the suffering of the world in a way that doesn't create more suffering. The means of violence and injustice only perpetuate cycles of individual and collective human suffering.

A reactive heart and mind may want to meet the forces of injustice with force, but our spiritual practice challenges us to determine whether the force we marhsal emerges from the power of love and wisdom or from a strong aversion to obliterate pain.

In this way, we can live and breathe into the oft-quoted words of Reverend Dr. Martin Luther King Jr., which have such congruence with the message of the Dhammapada:

Returning violence for violence multiplies violence,
adding deeper darkness to a night already devoid of stars.
Darkness cannot drive out darkness;
only light can do that.
Hate cannot drive out hate;
only love can do that.

In another example of how spiritual wisdom crosses cultures, Nelson Mandela writes in *Long Walk to Freedom*, "For to be free is not merely to cast off one's chains, but to live in a way that respects and enhances the freedom of others."

Once at a teaching event by His Holiness the Dalai Lama, an audience member asked about the complexity of the issue of the conflict between Tibet and China. "Why didn't you fight back against the Chinese?" the person asked. His Holiness paused—a nonverbal way of expressing softness and tenderness—before replying, "Well, war is obsolete, you know." He paused again briefly, and then added, "Of course, the mind can rationalize fighting back. But the heart, the heart would never understand. Then you would be divided in yourself, the heart and the mind, and the war would be inside you."

We hear this teaching from so many of our iconic spiritual and social justice role models—Mahatma Gandhi, Martin Luther King Jr., Audre Lorde, Thich Nhat Hanh, and many more too. As we so often hear from such leaders, we must endeavor to *be* the change that we hope to see for our society. We must create peace in the world from a peacefulness that resides in ourselves. We cannot create world peace from a place of violence in our own hearts. The idea that peace in our inner worlds supports the creation of peace in our outer worlds is woven into the mindfulness teachings themselves.

Sayadaw U Pandita, one of the Burmese meditation masters who was the teacher of many of our Western teachers, said:

Practicing [the foundations of mindfulness] means building peaceful little worlds within each of those who practice. Without peace in our little worlds, crying out for peace in the Big

World with clenched fists and raised arms is something to think about.

During the height of the Occupy movement (and to this day), experiential workshops were offered at EBMC on Kingian Nonviolence Conflict Reconciliation led by highly skilled facilitators and trainers, like Kazu Haga from the East Point Peace Academy and Communities United for Restorative Youth Justice. The workshops invited our communities to remember and internalize the wisdom and power of our justice elders, like King and Gandhi, and continually to train in this way. The act of remembering is itself a form of mindfulness practice that we apply personally and collectively as well. During the most intense and tense periods of street activity, members of our spiritual community provided places for meditation and stillness, even in the middle of the many actions and activities that were part of the protests.

There is a famous story about a meeting between a warlord general and a Buddhist monk. The warlord was conquering the countryside and violently taking over the lives and property of all its inhabitants. When he came upon the temple of a renowned meditation master, he intended to ransack it and destroy all of its resident monastics. As the warlord entered the meditation hall, he beheld the temple's meditation master, sitting perfectly still in its center, calm, composed, and with complete poise as if nothing were happening around him. Charging up to the sitting monk, the warlord roared, "Do you realize that I am the kind of person who can run my sword through you without batting an eye?" And without missing a beat or even the length of a breath, the meditation master replied, "And do you realize that I am the kind of person who can sit here while you run your sword through me, without batting an eye?"

The response stopped the general in his tracks.

The master's nonviolent action was much more powerful than any force that the general could muster. The general not only stopped in his tracks, he stopped his rampage across the countryside. The warlord became a monk under the tutelage of the master and developed a life of peace. And, of course, when the violence within the general was extinguished, the violence in the countryside also ceased, and the people thrived in the peace that resulted from his transformation.

There is an intentional relationship between personal spiritual practice and how we live together in community in the world. What we do when we meditate and are mindful is directly connected to what we do in our lives when we are off the cushion. The peace and stillness that we are inclining toward, strengthening, and cultivating in ourselves are no different than the peace and stillness we wish to see in the larger world. The shifting of our inner lives toward the clarity of discernment and wisdom and the gentleness of heart and spirit can be forces to transform the larger world around us.

You may think you are meditating with the purpose of attaining peace in your own mind or tenderness in your own heart. You may think that meditation practice is about creating a deep awareness and mindfulness in your own life so that you can choose what leads to happiness for you rather than what leads to suffering. You may even feel the benefits when wisdom and insight arise and your mind and heart grow calm. But there is something else that happens at the same time.

By emphasizing the refuge of Sangha, the Buddha was connecting personal practice of mindfulness to a collective form of awareness. I believe he was interested in transforming our collective experience into a higher order of consciousness not bound by individual experience but inclusive of the diverse experiences of all of us. As practice expands from the personal to the collective, from the internal to the external, from the particular to the universal, it comes to embody the value of inclusion of all things, of all people, of all differences. All of our experiences are invited and belong; none of us is marginalized or excluded. In this way, we are being invited to create beautiful and Beloved Communities.

From the perspective of Dharma, *beautiful* doesn't refer to an aesthetic quality but rather to the qualities of mind and heart that lead to happiness and freedom—the end of suffering. Sayadaw U Pandita speaks of "the state of mind called beautiful," the mind of awakening. Beautiful is the capacity to be tenderly aware in the landscape of mindfulness and allow the transformative wisdom that arises from that landscape to be seen and acted upon, thereby changing us all. Beauty is nurtured and sustained by the awareness and the love we bring from a spacious mind and tender heart.

Because it is not an aesthetic characteristic, beauty is not necessarily pleasant to experience or easy to create. Like the rest of our spiritual practice, it requires effort, concentration, integrity, discernment, intention, and mindfulness. In actuality, beauty requires the panoply of teachings that create freedom of the mind and heart. It is the complexity of life that challenges each of us every day to accept the ten thousand joys *and* the ten thousand sorrows to be nothing less than beautiful.

I like to place this notion of *beautiful* in parallel with the concept of the Beloved Community. We walk the path toward Beloved Community through acts of nonviolence and nonharm—that is, through acts of love and kindness. We act this way with respect to ourselves and all those around us, whether we are similar or different from each other, whether we are in friendship or in conflict. The terms *beautiful* and *beloved* refer to the spacious qualities that allow us to hold and navigate the inordinate complexity of our human experience—that we can love and create a better world even in the midst of the challenges complexity brings. Bridging the expanse between cultural differences and origins, geographic distance, and chronologic time, the intention of Beloved Community is congruent with the Buddha's beautiful practice of taking refuge in Sangha, creating a community within which all of us awaken together.

Beautiful, Beloved Communities do not appear just because we want them to, or because we deserve them, or because we feel entitled to them, or because we think they are the way things should be. They are built from the ground up, with the inner materials of our own spiritual intentions and practice, laying the foundation brick by brick, plank by plank, nail by nail, beam by beam.

Make no mistake: this takes effort and diligence.

This kind of community building is difficult and time-consuming but so necessary for our collective journey.

We must meet the moments of our individual and collective lives just as they have come to be, and we must have compassion and insight so that we will know how to proceed in order to create the most benefit and cause the least amount of harm possible.

This is growth.

This is evolution.

This is development.

This is living into our highest potential of supporting each other into greater freedom.

For Reflection

Invite yourself to use a meditation practice period as a period of contemplation.

Ground your sitting period with a simple practice of awareness of the body or breath. Invite your mindfulness to become present with the sensations arising in the present.

Within this landscape of stillness and expansive mindfulness, open yourself to the questions that appear below.

Don't try to "completely think through" or "definitively answer" or "totally figure out" these questions. Don't formulate responses, interpretations, or solutions. Just reflect on them in quiet.

Allow yourself to see what emerges from these seeds of inquiry. Whatever emerges is useful.

Encourage yourself not to judge anything that arises, even if what arises are judgments.

Reflect on the following:

- What aspects of a community to which you belong have been inspiring, been elevating, and provided deep learning for you?

- What aspects of that community have been challenging, difficult, perhaps even harmful for you?

- How is it for you to experience both the joy and the sorrow within one community?

- What have you learned from even the difficulties or conflicts?

- If there has been a conflict that the community navigated "successfully," what qualities, what causes and conditions, supported that?

- What would you be most moved to share with a younger community in development about your own community's experience?

8

The Precious Experience of Belonging

I REMEMBER the very first loving-kindness and *metta* retreat I went to as a participant.

It was a ten-day residential retreat, and I was anxious, intimidated, even fearful: ten full days of wishing kindness to the world seemed impossible, if not ridiculous, given my ingrained skepticism! My predominant experience with spiritual and religious traditions that purported to teach unconditional regard was that they were typically unable, unwilling, or unskilled at directing love toward those aspects of life important to *me*, someone outside the dominant hetero-normative American culture.

The retreat was in a beautiful, newly constructed meditation hall with a towering ceiling that soared spaciously above our carefully appointed cushions and chairs. Amid our intention of renunciation, I was somehow assigned the luxury of a single room. And all my meals were beautifully prepared by a kitchen staff that looked after everyone's nutritional needs.

The basic guidance took on a grandeur simply by virtue of having been spoken in such a sublime architectural space. I felt small—smaller than the aspirations of the building, smaller than the simplicity of the instructions.

But more than small, I felt totally inadequate.

All I could focus on was that I was the only person of color out of about a hundred people—and how awkward, lonely, and even unsafe I felt. Of course my experience was partially due to my own psychological conditioning at the time (itself societally influenced), but it was also due to the external conditions of how the teachings, teachers, community, and organization had manifested.

Given my anxieties stemming from past injuries, current discomfort, and projections of future harm, I was feeling anything but lovingly kind.

Not feeling what I thought I should be feeling—that is, compassionate and full of *metta*—led me into further self-judgment, which in turn made my tension and sense of isolation and exclusion even worse. I tried to stay with the physical experience of the stressors—the vibration of fearful energies, the heat of a history of anger, even rage, that had no beginning and no end, the brokenness and despair of sadness and frustration.

There was nothing in the Dharma talks that felt connected to my circumstance or story.

What I was experiencing was a profound sense of not belonging in this space, no matter how sacred it seemed.

The gap felt insurmountable. I couldn't connect the dots of what was being spoken in this glorious meditation hall with the inglorious life I felt I was living. When I couldn't connect to the room because there was nothing inviting my differences into this spiritual practice, I began to feel I had to leave this part of my life—my experiences as a person of color, as a gay, queer man—outside the door.

These were aspects of myself I felt were unwelcome, unseen, and unappreciated in the retreat space.

I experienced the nonacknowledgment as a subtle push to go back into the closet and repress the difficulty or deny suffering that was arising.

I felt that by being implicitly encouraged to leave portions of my identity outside of the hall, I was also being told to leave tender aspects of myself outside of my spiritual aspirations. The message I felt was that those aspects were not worthy of awareness and kindness, and by extrapolation, I myself was not worthy of this practice.

The guidance from the teachers, which ranged from "sit with the feelings that arise" to "more practice is required," were not sufficient to meet me where I was. I struggled in isolation, and the isolation compounded the struggle.

Silent retreats have the ability to create an open space from which tenderness and vulnerability can emerge and be deeply experienced. Part of the teachers' role is not only to share the traditional content of the Buddha's teachings and their own experience with the teachings but to connect meaningfully and authentically with how the practice is landing with respect to the tender vulnerabilities of practitioners. It can feel extraordinarily painful for the practitioner when there is a disconnect, a denial, even a dissonance in that relational process.

These days as a Dharma teacher I hold such experiences as tremendous bittersweet memories. Although the experiences were quite distressing, they also taught me how to do my very best not to replicate those conditions in my own teaching. And if I unconsciously do so, to invite and learn from the immediate feedback of the practitioners involved.

Part of my experience in learning my craft as a Dharma teacher is to learn from the example of my own teachers about what they did well and also what they did not do so well. We all learn by positive and negative examples from our role models. In my current teaching, I endeavor to meet practitioners however they self-identify, not denying any aspect of their backgrounds or cultural experiences. Especially in one's entry into the Dharma, invoking the complex teaching of not identifying with one's self can be experienced as a spiritual bypass of a practitioner's reality in the world's external conditions. Telling practitioners to simply "sit with" their feelings and thoughts may not be a sufficient reflection or respect for their realities and life issues. Naming how I have been caught in the complex feelings of identity and intersections of multiple identities can invite connection and relationship with the practitioner's own experience. From a teacher, this kind of self-disclosure can build the relational connection so that the Dharma can be shared.

It is sometimes said that Dharma practice is a process of purification. The image of purification isn't meant to connote unblemished perfection versus sullied imperfection but a process of moving through and healing from the ten thousand sorrows of our life so that they no longer wield compulsive power over who we are. Only half-facetiously have I said to myself that these silent residential retreats can be more intense than any psychotherapeutic process that I could imagine (and I myself am trained as a psychotherapist!). At least when it comes to therapy, I only have to attend and be present with my suffering for one hour per week, two at most if it was really a psychological emergency and I could afford the luxury of an additional hour of therapy. During a silent retreat with the absence of myriad distractions, we are functionally alone with ourselves 24/7.

Not being able to distract oneself from all the unresolved dilemmas, the demoralizing conflicts, the unfulfilled or unrequited desires, the no-win situations, the frustrated searches for meaning—all of this is part of the purification process. Indeed, our whole lives arise on the meditation cushion.

That can be intense, especially because we are often not in control of what arises on the cushion to be purified.

As I sat with my feelings of not belonging in the meditation hall, recollections cascaded into my consciousness of all the times I had felt excluded, not seen, dismissed, not appreciated for who I was, and even actively discriminated against or injured. It triggered memories of those still-delicate times in my childhood that were so difficult because I was not like other kids in so many ways. It brought to the surface exactly what I had tried so hard to forget.

Looking back, I know that even if the teachings could hold all of my experience, there was nothing about how the retreat was designed that could have supported me in that moment. I intellectually knew that the practice was supposed to be about purification through obstacles, but what I felt was a reduction into insufficiency.

When we broke into small spiritual practice groups at the retreat, I only heard discussions about heterosexual relationships and families, or issues from communities who were predominantly white, or about upper-middle-class economic values. I wondered what relevance this practice and this community had for my life, and I puzzled over what I was doing there.

It was ironic that I was questioning my place in Buddhist practice. My parents were from Buddhist cultural backgrounds, and the Buddha statue in front of the hall had features that looked like mine. I wondered how to invite *that* Buddha to move with life into my consciousness.

Looking back, this experience and others like it showed me how the collective unconsciousness of the external world can determine how we experience things as individuals. I came to realize just how much I had internalized external messages of racism and homophobia and projected them onto myself. I saw that I had internalized the message that I was not worthy to be in the space, a part of this practice, in this community, in this lifetime.

That was for me a moment of waking up.

And waking up gives us the power to choose to move toward what is calling us to be free.

Like everyone, I wanted to hear the teachings and cultivate the wisdom that would allow me to be happier in life and to reduce suffering. What was most important to me was how the practices of mindfulness and meditation were relevant to what I was actually going through every day. And of course I would imagine this to be true for most practitioners, regardless of the circumstances of their background, families of origin, or difficulties that they have experienced.

So it was challenging and painful to never hear mentioned such central examples of suffering in our modern world as racism, heterosexism, discrimination, or wealth disparity. The silence on these topics relevant for anyone who experiences marginalization in their personal or communal lives felt like a turning away from suffering instead of meeting it. It felt like the opposite of what Dharma teachings invite us to do.

And this seemed at the time like a form of spiritual hypocrisy.

It still seems that way today too, when a multitude of racialized events are happening in rapid succession in our larger culture but unacknowledged by our communities in the Dharma or our conversations in Dharma practice.

Those of us who feel ourselves to be connected to such racialized events, whether we wish to be or not, quickly come to feel that this lack of acknowledgment means ignoring, overlooking, and even denying what are important life experiences for us. And this denial leaves us feeling unattended, unloved, unseen, and even harmed. The act of paying attention to them, on the other hand, has a sense of kindness embedded in it. Meeting the complex and difficult moment for what it is, with total acceptance, without needing it to be different, without needing to feel differently about it, truly is an act of kindness. And its opposite, actively not paying attention to the moment, is a kind of act of harm.

It is likely not the intention of a community of homogeneous practitioners and teachers to make anyone feel this way, but the lack of cultural awareness and sensitivity can feel oppressive to those who are different when they try to enter that community. When people feel unseen and not validated, especially in a space purported to be sacred, this can evoke memories of all the other times in their lives when cultural harm has also occurred.

Although my own experience has to do with specific aspects of my story—including my cultural upbringing, historical injuries, and personality type—the larger truth beyond the scope of my own story is that we all can feel, and probably have felt, different, excluded, or that we do not belong. It is never an easy or pleasant experience for anyone, regardless of the reasons or the stories involved. The details of the particular suffering each of us has to contend with in our lives may differ, but the feeling of isolation that comes from that suffering is the same.

Some may not feel marginalized due to injuries around race and orientation, but may feel marginalized due to disparities in treatment based on gender, the range or limitations of their physical abilities, their economic or educational status, type of employment or lack thereof, or the history of trauma or abuse they carry. For some, feelings of isolation may come from deeply conditioned self-judgments laid down in childhood and consistently reinforced, or life-changing events like illness, divorce, loss, and death.

Regardless of the specific reasons, it is painful to feel "separate from," to feel that we do not belong. Despite all of our differences, cultural or otherwise, the need for this precious experience of belonging is something we all have in common. We are social beings, connected beings, and beings who feel supported when conditions of community and Sangha are safe enough. If we are able to move through the feelings of isolation into connectedness, not only will it foster a sense of healing but it can provide a template for learning how to live more fully, openly, and authentically together.

My dear friend and colleague Shahara Godfrey, who now teaches at the East Bay Meditation Center, once wrote, "When few around you look like you, and when the cultural expressions used to teach the Dharma are not your own, it can make it really challenging to practice." Those early retreats in my own experience were incredibly challenging. I still am shy to admit it, but that particular *metta* retreat was so difficult for me that I exited the retreat before it was over.

I am not proud of that. I wish it had been different.

I had written a note to the teachers, needing to meet with one of them to discuss how unsafe I felt and how it was so painful to be the "only one" in the meditation hall and feel so isolated. The response that came back to me—even though the words were kind—felt invalidating. They pointed to my need to continue to "sit and practice with my internal experience" and suggested this topic would be good to discuss at the end of the retreat.

Because I already did not feel connected or seen in that retreat, this bit of instruction did not resonate with me. It didn't feel helpful but rather evasive and avoidant, like another form of denial and repression of an arising experience. It felt like the same old patterns of advice marginalized folks receive in the everyday world—that the pain of exclusion and marginalization is somehow "our" problem and issue to deal with. How can retreat practice support me when the same patterns of unconsciousness of the external world is replicated within the retreat container? The suggestion to "practice with it" made sense in principle, but I was flummoxed as to how applying it might be possible.

In time, I did return to *metta* retreat practice, and I returned to practice with those same specific teachers. During an interview at a subsequent retreat with the same teacher who had told me to continue to practice, an apology was offered for this previous guidance that had initiated my departure two years before.

At the time, some circumstances had changed; some of the pain and suffering had been transformed. I had found other teachers with whom and methods with which to sustain my practice through and beyond feelings of exclusion and the blatant demographic disparity in the room. And by returning to the same retreat of my initial painful experience, I was beginning to exercise my own capacity to sit with any community, under any circumstance, with any teacher. There was freedom emerging from the practice.

Even during the Buddha's time, the conditions for hearing the teachings were critical to successfully absorbing them and realizing potential transformation. The Buddha was said to have had the ultimate and impeccable skillful means as a teacher: he could simply hold up a lotus blossom without saying a word and someone in the audience would be enlightened by the grace of that nonverbal gesture. But it is also true that not everyone in the crowd was brought to enlightenment—the conditions were not right for those people. Given the imperfection of our humanity and the fact that we lack the Buddha's perfection in skillful means when teaching, how can we still create the conditions that will best allow the teachings to be heard, learned, and integrated by the most diverse audience possible? Pursuit of this inquiry, both on a personal and communal level, can broaden the reach of the Dharma in our times.

An example of skillful cultural means within the context of mainstream Western Buddhist practice is the experience of silence. The container of meditative silence has become a highly respected format, treasured and revered. It is called "noble silence." Unquestionably, the nobility of silence is not only beautiful but allows us to explore our lives beyond the chatter both external and internal.

However, if we honor the sense of a larger sangha, the practice of silence should not occur without a broader awareness that for some communities, and in some cultural contexts, silence can become repressive, especially when one is new to this form of spiritual practice. It does not take much for people who have been continually discriminated against or who have been injured repeatedly to feel that the silence itself is oppressive. This sentiment was expressed in the LGBTIQ communities during the height of the AIDS crisis through the slogan SILENCE = DEATH. The lack of explicit words, actions, involvement, and collective awareness on behalf of the government and the public at large to address the human devastation of AIDS was killing us in queer communities. The intent of silence can have radically different impacts on different cultural groups.

In my *metta* retreat, when I was redirected back to the container of silence, I would have found it supportive if I had experienced simply being seen and witnessed by the teachers—that might have been enough to allow me to tolerate the inner pain I was experiencing. Just being acknowledged, itself a form of loving awareness, can provide a healing and precious experience of belonging that can transform an experience.

In the same way that silence is experienced differently for marginalized communities, mainstream European American communities also experience some things differently due to cultural associations. In Western iterations of Theravadan practice, few practitioners, much less teachers, practice devotionally. Bowing is not taught as a practice of mindfulness in many Western centers, even though it is a highly prized form of practice in Asia. Not unlike the queer communities' association of silence with repression, for individualistic Westerners bowing can feel like submission or capitulation. The lived cultural experience is dissonant from the original intent of the practice. For some, such as those of monotheistic cultural identification, it might be spiritually contraindicated to bow to any statue or object that could be interpreted as an idol. This would be in conflict with teachings of the Old Testament and the Koran. For others, particularly those who are secular-minded, bowing may be associated with religious ritual and cultish conformity.

As diverse communities practice together, it is important to be sensitive to such cultural norms and values. The more the differences can coexist, the more inclusive the space will feel. Practices that are most congruent for each of us may not just be about personal preference or choice; they may have cultural influences important to the practitioner involved. The more we can create a sense of safety and a sense of congruence for our different communities, the more folks will feel they truly belong in the moment.

Part of awakening as a community is acknowledging how people's differing needs may affect how safety is generated differently for various groups. For everyone, it is difficult to release our defenses when we have been injured, particularly if we feel we are still at risk of re-experiencing being wounded. It is difficult to settle into contemplative stillness or silence when we are still guarded against potential risk or harm that we know has happened in the past. It is hard to develop trust in the environment when there has been injury, because we are often the only ones who were able to take care of ourselves. Creating that container in which safety and trust can emerge is fundamental to deepening one's spiritual exploration.

And of course, we know both intuitively and experientially that there is no space that is 100 percent safe for anyone in this world. After all, therein lies the reality of the first noble truth—there is suffering and a subsequent lack of safety from suffering. In the development of collective practice together, the invitation and aspiration become how we can create a safe-enough space for diverse communities to practice together.

We walk in a world that more frequently than not tries to define who we are, who we should be, what we should be doing, how we should be looking, what we should be thinking, even what we should be feeling— whereas returning to the depth of our own experience can be called a kind of spiritual homecoming. As we move into exploring our identities, we create an acceptance of who we are *completely* and a sense of being able to be at ease no matter how difficult the conditions of our lives might be.

Maya Angelou writes:

> The ache for Home lives in all of us,
> the safe place where we can go as we are,
> and not be questioned.

When we constantly have defense mechanisms in place to protect ourselves from suffering, it is difficult to trust and relax into the space that has been created, even one with the highest spiritual intentions. It's so important to find that practice of sangha, that experience of community, because when we're only dealing with the defended reality, when we're only dealing with survival, we can't let the rest of life in.

Finding refuge and safety in a supportive community is so critical to deepening spiritual practice. And yet, just because a community says it is welcoming and inviting of everyone's experience does not mean everyone will feel welcomed or invited. Many meditation centers claim they do not discriminate and would welcome any and everyone into their space. And therein lies a potential problem: it is "their" space into which people are being invited.

I have heard many Dharma students and friends who identified either as people of color or as gay, lesbian, bisexual, or transgender say that they attempted to go to a particular sitting group or meditation center but never returned after the first visit. I had that experience in my early years of practice. It is something I call the "ricochet effect" or the "bounce-away factor." People who are sensitive to issues of whether they fit in or belong may come for a single visit and then bounce off and never come back.

Often, although not always, there is no explicit injury experienced, no act of discrimination perpetrated—and yet there is also no inclination by the practitioner to return, because there was nothing about the environment or atmosphere that created enough of a sense of cultural safety. Creating a space that is safe enough to feel as if one belongs requires more than just the intention to do so and a few words from the community. It requires a set of actions, behaviors, and attitudes to support those intentions. It means creating a space that people will feel not just invited into but also connected to and can fully participate in.

Attempting to create conditions of safety and belonging without cultural awareness may even produce experiences of injury and harm. The unconscious conditioning and patterns of the larger culture, which are still imbued with disparity, unconscious privilege, and oppression, appear in our sacred spaces or meditation halls more easily than we might think.

One practitioner of color reported:

> Helpful as I found Buddhism, I had experienced some painful misunderstandings when white Dharma teachers, meditation instructors, and yogis seemed to be threatened or baffled by my bringing up experiences with racism. Or they seemed not to think that it was important for African Americans to be exposed to Buddhism and welcomed by that spiritual path.

One visiting Dharma teacher asked me, "Why would they be interested? Don't they have their own churches?"

This sense of safety and ability to completely be who one is, without leaving any portion "outside" the door, is why culturally specific practice spaces and retreats are so important for communities to develop and deepen their practice. Over the past twenty years, this need has been recognized by a few centers and groups, but not necessarily by the larger Insight Meditation community. Culturally specific practice events and retreats, like those for people of color or LGBTIQ communities, provide the safe space that mainstream retreats are currently unable to offer. Culturally specific venues allow safe spaces to become sacred spaces through the exploration of Dharma and meditation practice. They invite the universality of the teachings to be felt through the particulars of one's own cultural experience—to see and directly experience how relevant these teachings are to each life. The sense of connection and interrelatedness can flourish based on insight into the universality of the teachings. Even the highest teachings have difficulty reaching us when we feel like we must defend ourselves from injury.

Eventually, as I became progressively more familiar with the teachings and felt the direct change they were having on my life, I could grow and stretch my practice. Over time, I have come to be able to practice anywhere, with any community, with any teacher, under any condition, even when there is cultural unconsciousness in the room. While I still notice the demographics of the room as a part of my awareness practice, they are no longer an obstacle to my being present or deepening my practice. It is liberating to not be buffeted by the external conditions of the world. There is freedom in that progressive experience.

Some may fear that specifying culture as an aspect of Dharma practice encourages separation and division. That fear is completely unfounded. Our awareness practice invites us to go through the experience of our lives in order to be aware of what is true. It does not ask us to circumvent an aspect of our lives because of what we think enlightenment or awakening ought to be. In order for us to see what is beyond the experience of our cultural identities, the teachings themselves guide us, with awareness, through the experience of identity, to see how substantial or insubstantial they really are for each of us.

We never reach a place of clarity or discernment by going around a situation. Mindfulness is the invitation to go through our lives—rather than performing a spiritual bypass—in order to see, feel, and understand that we are so much more than who we think we are.

Culturally specific retreats whether they are for communities of color, queer communities, women, or young people are not the endgame of the spiritual journey. They are doorways into the Buddha's teaching on freedom.

And just as culturally specific retreats for marginalized communities are not the endgame or the ultimate goal of the spiritual journey, so also the much more numerous culturally specific retreats for the dominant culture (which are generally still almost all upper-middle-class, European American, binary-gender, and hetero-normative) are not the endgame. Although it may yet dawn upon mainstream consciousness, the retreats that the dominant culture have been creating to meet their own cultural needs and sense of safety (for example, not going to the existing Asian temples or practice communities that have been long extant) should not be clung to or viewed as the end of the path of creating community. Mainstream retreats, while they might seem to be the norm, are not formed with the goal of beautiful and Beloved Community. They are not the standard to which other communities must adjust. The deeper practice of a community living together in diversity occurs when we have practice venues that attract an equal or greater demographic of diverse populations to the retreat. When those numbers are consistent, then we will have an indication that we are going in the direction of a truly inclusive community.

The Buddha points to the importance of this in the following passage from Uposatha Sutta:

> And furthermore, just as whatever great rivers there are—
> such as the Ganges, the Yamuna, the Aciravati, the Sarabhu,
> the Mahi—on reaching the ocean, give up their former names
> and are classed simply as "ocean"; in the same way, when

members of the four castes—noble warriors, priests, merchants, and workers—go forth from home to the homeless life in the Doctrine and Discipline declared by the Tathagata Buddha, they give up their former names and clans and are classed simply as "contemplatives, sons and daughters of the Sakyan Buddha.". . . This is the amazing and astounding fact about this Doctrine and Discipline that, as they see it again and again, has the monastics greatly pleased with the Doctrine and Discipline.

I find it particularly significant that this must be seen and appreciated "again and again."

There is a sense of belonging that goes beyond what we experience in the places with which we feel most comfortable or familiar. As we grow more authentically connected to ourselves and to the life we are living, we become aware of how we are an indispensable contribution to its totality. As recounted by Jack Kornfield, Buddhadasa Bhikkhu, a prominent Thai monastic teacher and social justice activist from the twentieth century, had particular advice for Westerners with their psychological propensity to low self-esteem, self-hatred, judgment, and the inner cultural wounds that often come up in meditation practice:

First, their whole spiritual practice should be enveloped by the principles of *metta*. Then they should be taken out into nature, into beautiful forests or mountains. They must stay there long enough to realize that they too are a part of nature. They must rest there until they too can feel harmony with all life and their proper place in the midst of all things.

Patterns of self-hatred and self-blame, while not exclusive to marginalized groups like communities of color and LGBTIQ communities, can grow deeply internalized by the aversion, discrimination, and even violence of the external dominant culture. We learn to internalize our unworthiness, and this affects us for the rest of our lives unless the awareness grows that all those messages are not who we really are. We begin to create internal limitations for who we think we are and who we think we can be. We effectively restrict ourselves with glass ceilings that we ourselves put in place as barriers to reaching our potential in this lifetime. With mindfulness practice we can begin to examine and then gradually dissolve the conditioning of a lifetime. What has been conditioned can be reconditioned—and transformed.

One queer practitioner writes of his early practice and experience on a LGBTIQ meditation retreat:

> In the company of heterosexuals, I am always to some extent on guard. I am old enough that when I came of age being queer was still listed as a mental disorder. Boys in my high school used to boast of going and "rolling queers." With a very few precious exceptions, sex was something desperate and dangerous, done with someone you didn't know. Nowhere I looked—nowhere—were there any positive messages or role models. I have dealt with debilitated self-esteem and depression all of my life.
>
> So, in the Queer meditation retreat last weekend, I experienced a momentary thawing of my frozen heart that I am quite sure would not have happened in a general retreat. It was so beautiful to me to be in the company of other gay/bi men, each having humbly come to practice. This huge lump of unprocessed pain began to move.
>
> I have work to do, and I will seek out queer Buddhist environments to do it in.

This "momentary thawing" is the initial movement, the small step, the beginning of a journey leading to greater freedom. One Buddhist aphorism frames awakening and enlightenment not as a destination to be reached but as small moments, experienced many times. Our journey is composed of these incremental moments of insight and compassion, over and over again, woven together many times into this precious fabric.

We are invited into the experience of being part of and belonging to all of life. If anxiety, memories, depression, tension, pain, or even oppression arises, explore whether there is also somewhere in your experience a place that might be a spiritual sanctuary of refuge or home to which you completely belong no matter what happens. Maya Angelou's "safe place where we can go as we are, and not be questioned" is where all of us belong, where all of us can go. That place is the seat of your practice and awakening—and that place is in the middle of all of life, excluding no one.

As gentle and tender awareness allows us to return to our natural state of being over and over again, we tap into a grand and spacious sense that no one can oppress, that no one can take away. We begin to feel that we belong to the family of life, the family that excludes no one—the Universal Family. Our practice strengthens this sense of belonging so that it becomes unshakable, regardless of where each of us are on the path and regardless of any external conditions of the world. Our ability to hold our collective experience in the family of life is generated through our capacity to hold with kind awareness every single aspect of our experience. This is the ability to hold all of who we are, not in spite of who we are but because of who we are.

The spiritual homecoming to the precious experience of belonging is something we gradually internalize as we practice it over and over again. And as we do, we start to take that sense of home, of safety, of belonging into whatever we are doing, wherever we go, whomever we are with.

That is a measure of freedom.

For Reflection

What is the experience of belonging for you? How does it feel in the body? What sense doors are engaged? How does it feel in the heart? What emotional states emerge from this reflection? How does it feel in the mind? Is the mind relaxed, agitated, dull, busy, or calm?

What qualities allow you to relax into being present and feeling that you can be authentically who you are without any pretense or mask?

Even though there might not be any space in the world that is 100 percent safe, what allows you to feel safe enough that you can soften the defenses that can hide or protect or even pretend the nature of your reality?

Having reflected on your own experience with belonging, how might others feel about the experience? What might others who are different from you need to feel that precious sense of belonging in the world, in their life?

9

A Place to Call Home

Not finding a spiritual community within which to root myself, for many years I practiced meditation on my own, and I read books and tried to learn meditation from recorded talks. I periodically attended meditation and Dharma sessions at different places, but always bounced out of them because I never fully felt that I belonged in those settings. Nevertheless, I kept trying again and again—manifesting what I have come to appreciate as a kind of deep determination to engage with the Buddha's teachings even when they were expressed in ways to which I could not relate.

Eventually I encountered an LGBTIQ Insight Meditation retreat in Northern California. It was a modest-size retreat held at a small Catholic center, north of San Francisco, led by the only "out" Insight Meditation Dharma teachers at the time: Arinna Weisman and Eric Kolvig. They were pioneers in creating safe spaces for queer communities, and I am so grateful to them.

In that retreat, for the first time I heard how Buddhist teachings were relevant to the sufferings of one of my tribes, the community of queer folks. Though not every aspect of my identity (such as my person-of-color identity) felt supported in this LGBTIQ retreat, I felt safe enough that I could stay in the room and absorb what was being shared. That retreat was a doorway, the proverbial Dharma gate, into how the teachings of the Buddha could be experienced within my own life using the intimate and vulnerable method of silent retreat practice, amid people who were like me in important ways.

I fell in love. Repeatedly.

I had numerous fantasies about the gay men in the meditation hall and how I would live the rest of my life with one of them. This was the first time I was able to allow myself to feel the presence of gay men in a spiritual practice space, and allow myself to be attracted to them. Who knew there were other gay spiritual men to be attracted to? Who knew a safe-enough space could be created even to explore *that* portion of my identity and experience? It was revelatory.

I didn't know that it was possible to relate to guys on both levels of sexual attraction and spiritual exploration; those parts of me had each been placed into some kind of different categorical box in my life, without any contact between them. I might have conceptually known, but I had not had the chance to experience that sexual attraction and relationship were intimate portions of the spiritual path.

There was safety and a sense of belonging even in this visceral movement of bodily sensations within me, and in this space. In all the other meditation spaces I had been to, I felt I had to avoid, deny, or push away any of those vibrations in the body, palpitations of the heart, and romantic fancies of the mind. Without those defenses, I felt more freedom and spaciousness to be who I was in that moment.

I felt the emergence of a spiritual practice called "being a gay man."

But much more than the people and personalities around me, what I *really* fell in love with was the Dharma. The safety of a community creating a stillness and sense of peace together was thrilling to me. On a personal level, the rampant thoughts of feeling judged, or excluded, or not understood were, surprisingly, absent. I began to see the power of those thoughts and how the absence of them not only allowed the mind to relax, but permitted the body to release itself into the sitting posture. I was able to physically sit in the sitting posture on the cushion without agitation or discomfort vastly longer than I did usually.

And even more important, my heart began to relax.

In that relaxation I softened and opened to my own experience and life—and I could feel the benefits of not judging my experience. I could see that this nonjudgment was an act of kindness, one both enacted by and experienced by me.

The conditions in that retreat were not perfect—the community of practitioners was still not very culturally diverse—but it was good enough, safe enough. And it let me realize that insight and realization do not need perfect conditions.

The sense of safety and connection was enough for me to stay in the seat of my practice and strengthen my concentration. Living a human life inherently entails uncertainty, discomfort, and risk—no moment or place is ever utterly and unfailingly safe.

So what does it mean to feel safe enough to stay present? What constitutes enough safety that I could strengthen the capacity of my practice to be with difficult experiences in a different way? Having some sense of connection and spiritual homecoming with regard to one major aspect of my identity seemed to be enough for me in that moment—enough to prompt my interest in deepening my engagement in the Buddha's teachings.

In the Dharma talks during the LGBTIQ retreat I heard the direct connection between ending suffering by changing our relationship to experiences of pain and difficulty and how that process was relevant to our experiences of the social and cultural pain and difficulty of oppression and homophobia. More than hearing it, I viscerally felt the safety of being in a community that shared similar life stories and experiences.

I fell in love yet again as I heard in the Dharma talks and meetings with teachers' life experiences that addressed specific issues in my life as a queer person—the joys and the sorrows of our politics, the issues of a desire for intimate relationships, the losses from the AIDS epidemic at the time, and how to counter the feelings of self-hatred and judgment.

I fell in love with my faith.

I fell in love with my faith in spirituality and humanity.

And I fell in love with my own humanity—without needing any piece of myself to be any different than I was. I fell in love with learning to pay attention to, to care about, and to love myself. This was a deeper sense of ease than I had had in any other practice space—and this in turn allowed me to do my work in relating to my feelings, my thoughts, and all of my experience differently. It allowed me to more easily let go of the thoughts of difference or questions about whether or not I belonged in this group. From that state of ease, my practice blossomed and transformed.

When I was first beginning to consciously walk on a spiritual path, I visited many retreat centers, tried many practices, and experienced many teachers from multiple traditions and lineages. My own search included different traditions from Sufi to Zen, from Native American sweat lodges to Hindu ashrams, from different lineages of the Buddhist teachings to different traditions of yoga. And I went from Episcopalian churches to Unitarian ones. Somehow I was searching for a home that was always outside of me. Only when I tasted the possibility of an *external* sense of resting could I explore what an inner sense of peace and stillness could look and feel like.

This was my journey: to come home to a home within myself and carry that with me. It might not seem like such a big deal that I could actually be more aware, once I could stop thinking so much about surviving, fitting in, and belonging—but it was. It wasn't the cognitive, understanding aspect of the process that was transformative; it was the direct experience of being able to let go and relax my heart, which began to recalibrate the suspicions, worries, and fears that were conditioned into me. This is how the heart can heal.

Accessing a true experience of belonging, I could begin to allow life to unfold however it might—even and perhaps especially in spaces where I didn't feel an external kind of belonging. Sometimes this meant I might find a sense of relief, sometimes a joy, and sometimes it meant I discovered injury left unexplored because it hadn't felt safe enough in the past to turn my attention to it. I could allow all of that to cascade into my consciousness without feeling the need to defend myself. I felt a sense of relaxing into a life that was being lived however it arose. Underneath all of the defensive protection that worry, fear, and anger brought was the beginning of a stillness, a calming of anxiety, a more stable, peaceful state of mind.

In that calm, my mind could begin to be aware of itself.

Until the conditions of the sacred space crossed a certain threshold in terms of safety, just to survive external suffering was a struggle; it was all I could manage.

Yet mindfulness practice is not simply about living a life of mere survival.

Mindfulness invites us into the opportunity to live to our fullest potential; it invites us to explore the true nature of who we really are.

And so, who am I? What is my "true nature"?—to use another common form of this question. And what does it mean to realize it?

Insight into our "true nature" emerges from the gentle yet persistent exploration of the questions "Who am I?" and "Who are we?" within the specificities of our particular life. The path toward freedom does not go *around* the experience of identity or transcend it but goes through the experience of identity—however identity manifests for us.

At some point in their lives everyone asks some version of these great spiritual questions, sometimes even as young children. Of all the identity descriptors I had for myself as a queer gay man, as a person of color, as an Asian American, as a social worker, as an activist, as a therapist, as a meditator, as a son, as a brother, none seemed to completely describe me fully, none alone or together seemed to capture all of who I am.

So if no descriptor is adequate or complete, what then? What lies beyond the question and experience of identity? What happens when the question subtly transforms to become "Who am I *really*?" As my practice of awareness became more and more refined, the question became more and more nuanced.

These early LGBTIQ retreats taught me what to pay attention to in practice.

I learned to pay attention to identity—not to ignore, bypass, overlook, dismiss, repress, or transcend it. And in going through the door of identity, the world of our lives opened up to my awareness in much more expansive ways.

This has influenced my own Dharma practice: how I live the Dharma, how I create organizations and communities around the Dharma, and how I teach and lead from the Dharma.

Later in my journey when I was teaching culturally specific retreats for different communities, one practitioner of color wrote the following about a retreat for people of color that he attended:

> Just a few weeks before, I had discovered that I would not be able to attend a different retreat that I had been trying to register for, where I would have been one of six African-American attendees in a crowd of over 700 participants. My acceptance at this PoC retreat was fortuitous because, at the time, I was in

a wounded place in my spiritual practice and had been wrestling with issues of basic trust, feelings of vulnerability, and hyper-defensiveness. My sense was that these issues arose, in part, from what I had perceived to be a lack of empathic attunement on the part of some of my teachers towards my struggles with the myriad forms of discrimination that I'd suffered, and the reactive stratagems I employed in my life to feel safe.

Until the PoC retreat, I had never stopped to consider the psychic toll in terms of the paranoia and stress-induced bodily constrictions and the sheer exhaustion that my ever-ready defensive posture was exacting on me. My unease in certain meditation practice settings seemed always to be close at hand. Dr. W. E. B. Du Bois coined the term *double-consciousness* to describe aspects of this peculiar affliction, "this sense of always looking at one's self through the eyes of others, of measuring one's soul by the tape of a world that looks on in amused contempt and pity." A subtle shame often accompanies my "double-consciousness" when I attend many a New Thought Movement or Buddhist Dharma talks where my minority (Other) status often appears in stark relief against a predominately white body of practitioners. For some people it is hard to feel fully accepted where so few of one's peers really relate to a black man's experience or worldview.

And so it was with this considerable chip on my shoulder that I came to the PoC retreat seeking ease and comfort for a burdened body and soul. In the span of seven days, I had walked hallowed grounds, communing with nature and making offerings to the enlightened ones and at every manner of impromptu shrine erected by a grateful group of yogis. By night, I reveled in the joyful noise of sacred chants and drank liberally from the inexhaustible fountain of wisdom that is the Buddhadharma taught exquisitely by culturally congruent teachers of color. Many an afternoon I contorted my body into a sweaty yogic bliss-state that laid the foundation for meditations so deep, peaceful, and still that even breathing seemed optional. And all of this took place amid a radiant community of color who had gathered in this majestic place for the celebration and liberation of spirit and our lights shown as bright as the birth of a new Sun. For one of the few times in my life I felt as if I actually belonged right here and right now!

That sense of belonging "right here and right now" allows the landscape of awareness to expand with a growing sense of stillness and spaciousness beyond how we want life to be to how life actually is.

I still contemplate and reflect on questions of identity.

They are questions that do not feel like they need the succinct and clear answers that our logical and intellectual brains would like us to have. The paradox of my experience is that it took finding a supportive place in which to express my identity in order to explore and feel what lay beyond that sense of identity itself. I needed to find a spiritual home with enough safety, enough refuge, and enough sense of sanctuary in order to leave that sense of spiritual home and explore what, in my experience, had no boundaries, conditions, or even definitions.

When my life itself, the worthiness of *this* precious life, becomes my true home—not a geographic place or a particular community—I have achieved a measure of freedom.

This sense of home and refuge, for me, came from searching for and finding others who could support me, validate me, mirror my experience. It was not something that I could have done by myself. I'd needed a community that I could call home in order to embody and internalize deeply for myself that I am worthy of belonging in this world, regardless of external conditions.

This is one of the fruits of waking up together, in community.

10

The Beauty of Transformation

As an adolescent I grew up amid the energy of change and experimentation in the United States of the late 1960s. The generational ferment in our social, political, sexual, cultural, and spiritual lives was well under way by then. It was a time to do things differently, to look differently, to try to think and act differently. My generation hoped that the change and idealism of the times would positively transform our society, stretching far into our future.

Being different became a mantra, a life aspiration, and also a kind of style. Visual and aesthetic cues connected those of us who were raised differently, thought differently, and acted differently. We came together in a common recognition of each other.

The iconography of difference and change included patched blue jeans, unisex beaded necklaces, peace signs, any tie-dyed piece of clothing—and all kinds of protest buttons. One symbolic expression of change across all genders, but more clearly a declaration for men, was long hair. What shoulder-length (or longer) hair almost immediately came to represent was an alliance with the growing counterculture of the times, and its associated slogans: "Power to the People!" "Make Love, Not War!" "Black Is Beautiful!" "Give Peace a Chance!" and "Never Trust Anyone Over Thirty!" (This last slogan is particularly poignant, as most of us who came of age in that era are now entering our sixth, seventh, and eighth decades.)

Like so many, I too grew my hair long as a teenager—despite the verbal and nonverbal objections of my assimilated-by-necessity but still traditionally Chinese parents. In fact, until I was fifty years old, I had hair that I could pull into a long ponytail, flip with annoyance, and use to add a dramatic gesture to a point I was making.

As I've said, after I had been meditating and practicing the Buddha's teachings for more than a decade, I decided to get ordained as a Buddhist monastic in Thailand. Although I had developed great faith in the Dharma and saw clearly how spiritual practice benefited my life, I was cautious about joining any organized religion or community; my experience with religious dogma and judgment, especially as a gay man, restrained my enthusiasm.

As I deepened my involvement with Buddhism, I really felt the need to explore what was relevant about this ancient tradition and practice. The monastic form has survived for over 2,500 years, albeit with many changes as it migrated from culture to culture, continent to continent, and across the millennia. I was curious about what this practice from the Buddha's time had to offer. I had reached a point in my spiritual practice where I was ready to face the unknown and undergo a ritual ceremony that was as foreign to me as anything that I had ever experienced: ordination. I was prepared to become a Buddhist monastic.

The year prior to my ordination my then-partner (and now-husband), Stephen, accompanied me to Thailand to visit different temples and monasteries at which I could potentially receive ordination—perhaps about a dozen of them.

When we got home to the United States, and as my embarkation on my solo spiritual journey progressively became more real, I decided to let Stephen, choose the monastery I would commit myself to, ordain at, and live in. The ordination was an intimate part of my spiritual exploration; it was something that I had to do for myself. But I was also intimate with my life partner. Ordination may be part of my spiritual journey, but it did not diminish the reality that interpersonal and intimate relationships are also major parts of my spiritual practice.

It was important to have my partner intimately involved in the journey that lay ahead of me, which was in many ways as intimate as our relationship itself. After all, he would be impacted by my ordination as much as I would be, if only in terms of my absence; and he would be in spiritual retreat as much as I would be. After considering all our options,

Stephen chose a temple a little less than forty miles south of Chiang Mai, Thailand, in the village of Chom Tong.

When I arrived at the village temple, Wat Chom Tong, as a preliminary to ordination I intensively practiced meditation daily for three weeks, sometimes for fifteen hours a day, and then for nearly twenty-four hours a day as the date of ordination drew closer, all under the guidance of the temple's abbot, Ajahn Tong. This undertaking was meant to show my sincerity, dedication, and respect for the tradition. As the date of the ordination approached, I had much to prepare, gathering supplies and paying respects to my sponsors. An eighty-nine-year-old elder Hakka-Chinese-Thai woman who had heard about a Chinese American who wished to ordain wanted to become one of my sponsors by offering me a set of monastic robes, clothing, and supplies. She cut a lock of my hair as a precursor of the hair shaving ceremony to occur the day after my visit to her.

Shaving one's head is a key element of Buddhist monastic practice. In Thailand the practice extends to shaving the eyebrows as well. I understand it as an invitation to let go of all the ways we express ourselves through our appearance in the world. How we look, dress, and adorn ourselves is, for the most part, some expression of vanity, attachment to individual self-image. When one shaves one's head and eyebrows and dons the same saffron robes that all other monks wear, one loses the outward signs of one's individual identity. One has no embellishment, no creative statement to identify who one is apart from a monk. This had an impact on how I held my internal experience of identity as well.

My head was shaved at nine o'clock in the morning in front of the meditation hall where other lay practitioners could watch and participate in the ceremony. They could probably see my growing nervousness and inability to stay still. In Thailand, even in mid-November, we were not far enough away from the tropics to escape the pervasive humidity and heat. By midmorning, all our light cotton clothes were drenched in sweat.

My meditation teachers at the temple took the first snips of my long hair, but I wanted Stephen to cut my ponytail off. The scissors must have bruised his thumbs: it took a while for the shears to sever the thick bundle of hair. Then one of the senior monks from the monastery lathered my head with shampoo, took out an old-fashioned Gillette safety razor from my father's time—the kind that one has to unscrew from the bottom of the handle in order to place a double-edged blade on top—and proceeded to strip clean the right side of my scalp. I felt a chill that I had never experienced before as the blade passed back and forth, smoothly removing the black of all my hair.

As the razor revealed skin that hadn't seen the light of day for more than thirty-seven years, memories of the vanity that I had in my hair cascaded into my consciousness. I remembered the different hairstyles I had tried and the many arguments I'd had with my parents when they wanted my hair to be short. The stories of this head of hair flooded my mind along with the emotions each story brought. Since half my scalp was already exposed, all I could do was sit there as all the sensations arose. There was nowhere to go and nothing to be done. There was certainly no turning back, even if I'd wanted to.

I came to a memory from when I was a thirteen-year-old deciding to grow my hair long. I stood in front of the upstairs bathroom mirror and absolutely hated how I looked. I hated that I didn't look like the other kids at school. I hated the almond shape of my eyes, the color of my skin, and the round shape of my face. I always thought I had a rotund, overweight face.

In that moment in Thailand, at the more jaded age of fifty, I felt it all again: the hatred of my adolescence, hating myself and who I was at the tender age of thirteen. Even back then I was enough of an aesthetician, possibly presaging my experience as an "out" gay man, to realize that if I grew my hair long I could maybe lengthen the look of my face, and also take attention away from the features of my face that I was so critical of. And so the decision was made, forgotten, and buried over the long years, deep in the shame, internalized racism, self-judgment, and self-deprecation that followed me over the succeeding decades.

As I sat with the memory as it unfolded and felt it deeply on a nonverbal level, I was able to be fully present with it in a way that I never had before. It had been such a repressed experience I hadn't even known I'd had the memory of it.

As the razorblade uncovered more and more of my naked scalp, it also brought about a profound healing. And I began to sob.

Everyone probably thought I was sobbing from joy emerging from the ordination. But I was sobbing because what was being shorn away was a deep attachment to my own suffering—an attachment I had to looking a certain way and to wanting to look like someone I was not. I was realizing that I no longer needed the unconscious and unrelenting thoughts that being a person of color in a white world was somehow ugly, unattractive, or inferior.

Each moment that my heart broke open, more was revealed—and I saw the truth that I am a beautiful, worthy person wherever I am in the world.

The path of spiritual practice is often called purification of the heart. We don't have a choice about what we purify—rather, what needs purifying shows up in our lives. The question is whether we can be mindful enough to be present to it.

Sometimes the suffering and pain we internalize go very deep, deep into the core of who we think we are—whether it is a thirteen-year-old boy's feeling of hating how he looks, other judgments we make about ourselves, or the multitude of judgments the world can make about us. The practice of mindfulness invites us to see that we are so much more than who we think we are and our full and beautiful lives are so much more than just our suffering. Can we be present for all of that too?

When we simply meet an experience for what it is, with gentle and tender mindfulness—not needing to change it or force it to be different—and move through it, we gain the healing that comes from passing to the other side of the suffering. When we have kindness and awareness, we are able to move through our suffering instead of around it, which is how the unconscious mind would like to direct us. Taungpulu Sayadaw, a twentieth-century Burmese meditation master, said, "If you know suffering, it will break. If you do not know, it will go around and around."

If we see our suffering clearly, it will change and transform. When we do not see suffering clearly, it continues to feed itself.

This was what I experienced with my own negative self-image and internalized criticism—it changed. And now, when those thoughts arise (as they still do), my experience of them is not the same. I don't believe such thoughts and feelings as much anymore. They don't carry as much weight as they used to. I don't have to take them so seriously and can move on to what is more important in my life more easily.

This is letting go: we move through suffering and get to the other side without getting dragged down or stuck in the story or the personalization of the story. We usually try to repress, dismiss, or otherwise throw away our unpleasant experiences. When we do that, we actually throw a piece of ourselves away. But when we meet our experiences, even if they are experiences of pain and suffering, with gentleness and the simple kindness of awareness, they don't stick.

Ajahn Chah, a Thai meditation master who taught many Western teachers, said, "If you let go a little, you will have a little peace; if you let go a lot, you will have a lot of peace; if you let go completely, you will have complete peace." He goes on to write:

> Even though we can't yet let go, we are aware of these states continuously. Being continuously aware of ourselves and our attachments, we will come to see that such grasping is not the path. We know, but can't let go: that's fifty percent. Though we can't let go, we do understand that letting go of these things will bring peace.

So my hair was cut after thirty-seven years. I had to smile when I heard my mom lament that I had cut off all of that beautiful hair. After decades of trying to convince me to wear my hair short, it was now *she* who did not want me to cut it off. The reality that all things are subject to change is another core Buddhist teaching. Everything is impermanent—even the opinions from our mothers.

After I disrobed and returned to the States, I kept my hair short in a buzzcut. This surprised my family and friends. Over and over again I heard variations of "It was so beautiful. It was so 'you.' Will you grow your hair long again?" Without hesitation, my answer always was, and continues to be, "I don't know if I will. But I do know that if I do grow my hair long again, it won't ever be for the same reasons that I grew it long before." I have let go of those reasons—and there is freedom in that letting go.

Our reasons for practicing mindfulness meditation can be profound. The value of our practice lies not only in its potential for personal healing but in its potential to heal us collectively as communities. The value lies in our investigation of who we would be to ourselves and to each other without our personal, interpersonal, and internalized group messages of self-hatred. What would it be like to be with and support one another through the process of healing?

These teachings invite us to a greater freedom and deep change. Something as seemingly insignificant as cutting my hair brought an inner transformation that led me to a deeper understanding of who I was and who I could be in this life.

The beauty of ordination and the beauty of the Dharma invited me to let go of the experiences of identity to which I was so deeply attached. Letting go, I was transformed. As we transform ourselves, we can support others in their transformation. Together we can all come to see the joys and sorrows, differences and commonalities, the injuries and healing so that we can all be more open, awake, and connected with each other.

Of course, even when we taste freedom, we will still experience suffering. The dance between suffering and freedom from suffering is intrinsic to the richness of our lives.

11

Aware Within and Without

A WHILE BACK I participated in a nonresidential weeklong meditation
retreat.

The retreat was in a tradition that differed from what I was familiar
with, but several friends assured me that it would support my own mindfulness practice in the Insight Meditation tradition. I find it beneficial
to seek out teachings from different perspectives and through the lenses
of different lineages. This has helped me see the Dharma from different
points of view, culturally and otherwise, and to feel how wonderfully
variegated these universal teachings can be. I found this to be the case at
the retreat, in both expected and unexpected ways.

The retreat teachers had rented a space from a local Dharma community. The teachings from this tradition had a deep Dharma lineage,
were extremely nuanced, and were brilliantly detailed in terms of guiding folks to cultivate the ability to rest the heart and mind in unbounded
spaciousness. We could describe the practice as resting in awareness in
its broadest, most expansive scope. I also learned at this retreat how we,
with our inevitable human frailties, can be aware and simultaneously
unaware of how we apply our practice to the actual life experiences that
arise in front of us.

This retreat took place at an intimate meditation center along the border of business and residential neighborhoods in a small Northern California town. The gathering of around forty-five to fifty participants had
a large impact on the sleepy streets of this community—primarily in the
form of parking. Even with carpooling, it was still hard to fit thirty-five
to forty cars in the local area. And not unexpectedly, when one retreat
participant found a spot with parking spaces, other participants quickly

went to park their cars there as well. Eventually, during the week of the retreat, the residents of the neighborhood complained that they could not park on their own streets due to the number of cars from the retreat. Because the retreat ran for eight to ten hours each day, during which time retreat participants' cars remained parked on the streets, the retreat severely and negatively impacted the neighborhood.

Once feedback from the local residents made its way back to the retreat, participants tried to find different places to park, but while retreat participants did find alternatives, they also collectively followed each other to the same neighborhood that had seemingly empty curbsides. They then proceeded to park their cars and fill the streets of that neighborhood just as they had done in the first neighborhood. A few of us found parking farther afield and did so individually so as to try to minimize the effect of additional cars in the neighborhood, but most continued to park together in a group. The group as a whole was unaware of the collective impact they were still having.

Ironically, although the inside of the meditation hall was peaceful, calm, and spacious by the end of the retreat, the external community was progressively more agitated, angry, and upset. The Dharma teacher grew exasperated with the constant intrusion during teachings by neighborhood residents, who kept walking into the hall to voice their complaints, and refused to have anything to do with them. The community in the neighborhood around the meditation center eventually complained to the town's zoning officials.

Soon after the ending of the retreat, the Dharma community that had originally rented the space to the retreat teachers lost their own lease on the space. It was unfortunate that the practices being cultivated and strengthened inside the meditation center did not translate into the practice of collective awareness so needed simultaneously outside the meditation hall.

Mindfulness practice is never only about our own personal experience. While we continue to be aware of our thoughts, emotions, and intentions, we do not just stop at the boundaries of our own bodies, minds, or hearts. Sometimes when I've become distracted while meditating in a silent retreat, I've found that it was actually the sound of the breath of the person next to me that reminded me to return to the sensations of present moment and brought me back to awareness of my own breath. If we allow awareness to be present for both our inner and outer experiences, those experiences can mutually support each other.

We develop an intimacy with each other in the silence and in the field of mindfulness. When we are open and available, we care. In silent retreat practice, we not only notice and become intimately familiar with the breath of the people next to us but come to recognize them by their walk, the way that they eat, or their feet from the ankle down. We become aware of the details of our actual collective experience and the relationships around us. When we turn our ability outward to pay attention with care and nonjudgment toward others, kindness, compassion, and all the energies of the heart become present and available to us.

Just as mindfulness of the body and breath is only the beginning of awareness practice in our lives, noticing the surface aspects of another's experience is the initial point around which we begin to see our impact in relationship with them and our mutual impact on each other in deeper and deeper ways. We begin to include in our awareness how we practice together and to observe and note our impact as a collective community on individuals and other groups. Our mindfulness is continually invited to go beyond the simplicity of what we think we know or understand to include the great diversity and mystery unfolding for all of us.

As we deepen our practice together with each other in community, if we are mindful, we get to know people beyond our assumptions of who we think they are. We usually only experience this kind of intimacy—in which, for example, we come to recognize someone by the rhythm of their breath—with our partners or our families. The invitation of this community practice is to extend such intimacy beyond our closest circles and, in so doing, to get to know others without assumptions, judgments, stereotypes, or influence of external messaging. When we do this, we can discover who we really are as a larger community and as a larger interaction of communities.

The Buddha taught very clearly that mindfulness is a relational practice that does not stop with being aware of just our own experience. In the Satipatthana Sutta, the formal teaching in which the Buddha gave detailed guidance on mindfulness practice and how to expand the practice into all the experiences of our lives, the Buddha says (as translated by Bhikkhu Analayo), "The Noble Ones abide contemplating internally, they abide contemplating externally, they abide contemplating both externally and internally."

This teaching is not mentioned just once in the sutta but is a refrain throughout it, repeated thirteen times with each and every cumulative instruction on mindfulness. Buddha is inviting us to be aware of more than just ourselves; he is inviting us to be aware of our communities, our culture, and our world, and finally to be aware of the relationship between all of ourselves in the totality of our experience together.

The portion of the Satipatthana Sutta with which Western practitioners are usually most familiar is the part on internal mindfulness, which is most often the primary focus of silent practice in both retreat and in daily life.

The first part of mindfulness is attending to one's inner experience, as impacted by the external world. We might illustrate that like this:

But there is more to the Satipatthana Sutta than that. The Buddha teaches a second part of mindfulness, in which we direct our mindfulness externally. Thus mindfulness moves in the direction of external input and takes external events or people as object of attention. This would include being aware of our impact on other individuals, groups, or communities. We could illustrate that like this:

In the third part of this practice, we turn our mindfulness practice, moment-to-moment, toward both internal and external experience. Diagrammed, this would represent awareness going in both directions, including both experiences of internal and external:

This practice, as a whole, lets us explore what creates successful, meaningful relationships as an experience of mutuality—avoiding the ego-oriented extreme of focusing only on our own internal experience and the codependent extreme of attending solely to the needs of someone or something else. The balance between the extremes that creates healthy relationships is the multidirectional aspect of awareness that notices both internal and external impacts—our external impact on others, their impact upon us, and the relational dynamics that arise from our mutual interactions.

Functionally, this is combining our insight with our empathy. The Tibetan Buddhist tradition has a practice of "exchanging self for other" that goes right to the heart of this. It requires almost no more instruction than those four words. How would you feel if you were sitting in the other person's life? What would you learn and how would you live your own life differently having learned from exchanging yourself with another? It is the classic question that all parents ask of their children when they have made a mistake or done something to cause harm or injury while playing around. Parents will say, "Put yourself in the other person's shoes. How would you feel if this happened to you?" We can call this common sense. It is also the sense of what is common to all of us as human beings: we all appreciate that empathic resonance that connects us. If we focus solely on inner awareness, we can become preoccupied with our own experience at the expense of our awareness of the experience of others and how our own actions impact them.

I travel frequently as a Dharma teacher, teaching retreats that take me away from my home and family. Sometimes, it's inevitable that I return home from a retreat in one part of the country only to do a quick turnaround within a day or two to leave for another retreat in another part of the country. On one such occasion, there was only one day I was home between retreats.

When this happened, Stephen seemed distressed. I looked at my husband and asked, "What's wrong?" Even before the words left my lips, I sensed what was going on. I could already feel what was wrong before I asked. In that moment, I sensed deeply that it is always hard to be the one continually left behind when one's partner travels for retreats. Regardless of the specific reasons for the travel, even when it is for good work in the world and worthwhile activities, it is always hard to be the one left behind. The more frequently it happens, the stronger the feelings arise, whether they are sadness, loneliness, frustration, irritation, or resignation. While I could understand how my travel schedule had impacted my husband because we had discussed it many times previously, in that moment my awareness was attuned to it and I *felt* it. I didn't only understand it in my head, I held it in my heart and body. That awareness allowed me to realize what would be skillful given the feelings that were arising, and I dropped what I was doing to spend some dedicated time with a partner who unconditionally supports me in what I do in the world. It was both the inner and outer awareness that allowed me to observe the situation arising with him, feel it internally myself, and recalibrate by actions to shift the impact. It might have taken all of one second.

All three levels of mindfulness were operating at once. The experience I just described above could be diagrammed like this:

This is the dance between being fully present to our inner world and what is happening in the outer world. This is a relational experience created by being mindful internally and externally, from within to without. We use this relational experience to begin to feel, understand, and live the teachings that we are all interconnected and interrelated.

It is when we go out into the world and enter all the groups and communities with whom we interact that awareness is most needed and relevant. Without awareness, when we get together we may focus only on our inner experience or only on the collective group experience. We quickly bond with those who are familiar or similar to us and often don't even notice this happening.

Being mindful within and without is a simple invitation but difficult to manifest and live fully. How often are we not aware of our impact on others? As we live in world that is diverse, multicultural, and different than us, how often are we as both individuals and communities not aware of how we impact others even as we're right in the middle of practicing mindfulness, as in the case of the parking difficulty between the meditation community and the local residential community?

It's often the case that when we're part of a group or community with which we are comfortable, our awareness of what's going on outside the boundaries of our community diminishes. Our gaze narrows and we look only inward, to the comfort of people who are familiar or similar to us, rather than looking to the larger picture of both inward and outward, where experiences and communities diverge.

Unless we are careful to balance this aspect of mindfulness between individual experience (either as an individual person or as an individual community) and collective experience as people and multiple communities, we may tend to assume that our reality is the reality of others. This is relevant to how we live our lives, whether in terms of a mundane issue like parking or of the very serious needs that different communities have with respect to health care, education, politics, equity and disparity, housing, childcare, job opportunities, as well as myriad gross and subtle ways that the dominant culture dominates and oppresses marginalized communities.

With practice, every action and behavior can be an invitation to be mindful and aware of how we impact the world and how we live our lives together.

The internal focus of mindfulness can be represented visually as a series of learning events: individual awareness of personal intentions and actions transforms unconscious actions into conscious personal responses in our lives, which leads us to be progressively mindful of how our actions impact our experience, which increases our awareness to allow us to find increased opportunities for new learning, which feeds back into our personal practice of mindfulness, further recalibrating our awareness and allowing for even more skillful intentions. A diagram of that might look like this:

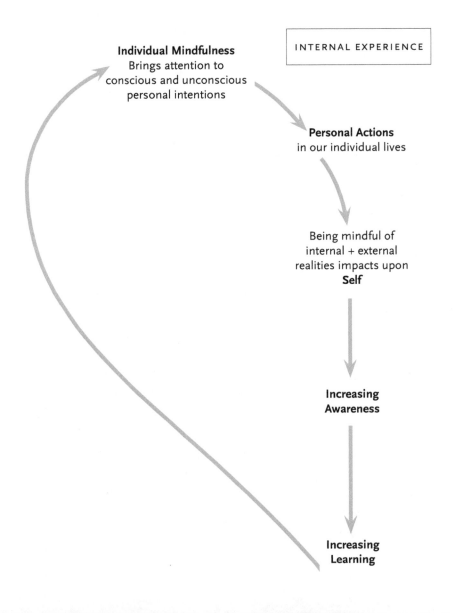

Individual Mindfulness
Brings attention to
conscious and unconscious
personal intentions

INTERNAL EXPERIENCE

Personal Actions
in our individual lives

Being mindful of
internal + external
realities impacts upon
Self

**Increasing
Awareness**

**Increasing
Learning**

Likewise, the outer practice and external focus of mindfulness can also be envisioned as a series of learning events: communal awareness of collective intentions transforms unconscious reactions into conscious collective actions within our communities, which leads us to develop mindfulness of how our actions impact all of our experiences, which allows our awareness and new learning to increase, which feeds back into our collective practice of mindfulness and increasing the effectiveness and benefit of our communal intentions. Like this:

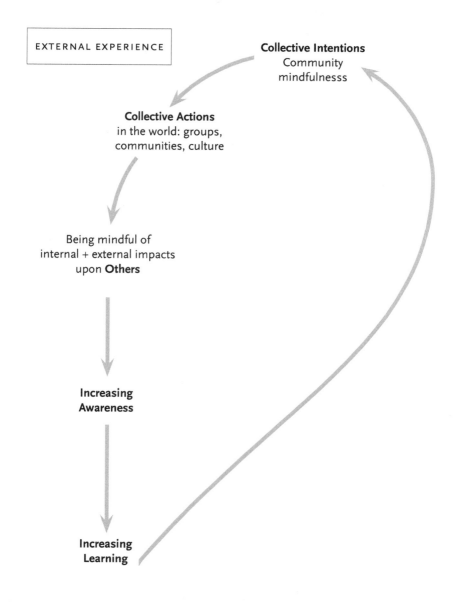

EXTERNAL EXPERIENCE

Collective Intentions
Community
mindfulnesss

Collective Actions
in the world: groups,
communities, culture

Being mindful of
internal + external impacts
upon **Others**

**Increasing
Awareness**

**Increasing
Learning**

The practice of community mindfulness is the same as individual mindfulness but with its focus expanded from the individual to the refuge and practice of sangha and community. These interwoven practices that cycle over and over again, from left to right and right to left in the diagram, internally and externally, deepen the experiential manifestation of a shared sense of mindfulness—and as that happens, we meet the entirety of our individual lives and all of our collective lives as they are with kindness and understanding. This is the experience of collective love and being able to collectively love each other. When we are meeting each other's communities and loved ones with tender understanding—as opposed to judging assumptions or detached indifference—we are loving each other already within the vision of the beautiful and Beloved Community.

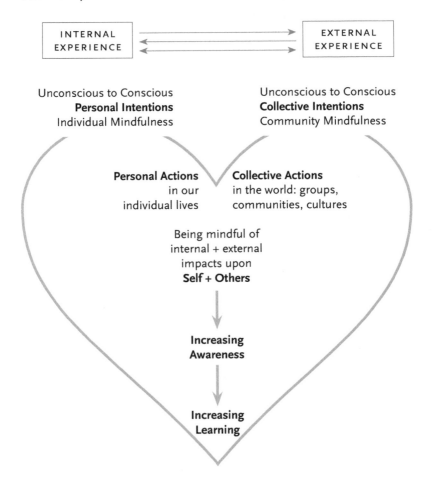

In my earlier professional work—as a park ranger, a marketing designer, a social worker—I consistently remained silent during team meetings and staff meetings unless my opinion was explicitly solicited. I remember feeling frustrated because everyone else around me seemed to be aggressively trying to make their own points, often quite effectively. I had a personal sense of always being on the periphery of the conversations in the room.

Over time, I came to recognize that I had acquired values from my Asian culture of origin of being humble, not being too assertive, not standing out too much, and not diving in unless invited, and these were not the same as the dominant cultural values enacted in those meetings. As with most cross-cultural situations, it is the people outside the dominant norms who must—out of adaptive necessity—learn about a culture different from theirs in order to function and survive. Moreover, people in a dominant culture are often not aware of norms and values other than their own and may also be unaware of how their own values are culturally specific rather than universal. Consequently, they rarely evince an interest in different ways of being in the world.

Based on my newfound awareness, I learned to be more proactive in naming the cultural patterns of communication in the room—elevating the awareness of the group and also being more definitive and assured in my own expression, thereby offering myself the choice to act within my own cultural paradigm or differently from it. To have choices is to have more freedom to do what is most beneficial in the moment without being locked into a pattern I determined for myself or externally imposed. That choice and freedom can only come from being aware and mindful.

In the larger scale of relationships, how can we be aware of how we impact each other and learn how to live with each other with greater ease and harmony? When our attention is focused solely on the groups of people in which we are most comfortable, this can easily lead to a collective self-focus. We can become preoccupied with ourselves as a group at the expense of noticing how our collective actions and behaviors are impacting other groups around us. In the larger world, the potential effect is magnified when there is a collective unconscious underlying cultural norms or actions. When we are not aware of the impact, we are more likely to cause harm. When we are not aware of the effects of racism, sexism, or homophobia, we are much more likely to discriminate and exclude, even if our intention is otherwise.

I was at a recent meeting of Dharma teachers when one of the European American teachers made a jest with cultural overtones that showed a lack of sensitivity to race and culture at the opening circle. I am sure that the speaker was focused more on using wit to make their presence known in the circle, rather than on the impact their statements would have on the two teachers of color in the room. I was one of the two teachers of color among the twenty-two other white teachers. No one held the teacher accountable. I could feel the unspoken pressure to ignore what had happened and to assume that the lack of offensive intentions was sufficient to allow the incident to pass by unnoticed.

This form of multicultural awareness practice always presents a dilemma: do we elevate the consciousness of a dominant cultural group that does not notice such an event, or do we continue the patterns of unconscious behavior and unconscious harm and thus participate in collective ignorance, despite our own awareness of it?

It is a crazy-making situation when teachers who espouse awareness are seemingly unaware. I often wonder whether I might be the one who was crazy and not the situation: was I delusional to feel how I was feeling? I could feel my own internalization of external messaging. This is the impact of external upon internal. What I realized is that I could not with integrity become somehow unaware of that which I was already aware—I could not be unaware of my experience. That was my internal experience beginning to influence the external event.

I did not feel safe enough (even among Dharma teachers!) to comment to the larger group about the experience. I was still too uncertain of my own voice among many more experienced teachers at the time. Eventually I spoke about my experience in a smaller group, and my comments subsequently made their indirect way back to the original speaker. The ensuing discussions included the feelings of white teachers who really did not want to move through life "walking on eggshells." However, what is the delicacy and intimacy of mindfulness other than to treat life, all life—not just life that is similar to one's own—as so very precious and worthy of respect and caring that it deserves as much care as egg-shells? Being mindful means moving with delicacy around everyone's experience. That is the loving nature of awareness.

The full learning potential of this situation was truncated by the fact that the impact was never addressed in the larger group. The implied message to the larger group was that it was okay for a teacher to exhibit this level of public unconsciousness without needing to be challenged or to change patterns or behaviors. In this case, this is the privilege that a predominantly white group has—to determine and frame the experience for everyone, usually at the expense of people of color who are most impacted.

The group didn't pay attention to some of its members' experience. This is the definition of marginalization. And there was no opportunity for the group itself to learn how not to re-create similar acts of uncon-sciousness in the future. It was a missed chance to learn and increase our collective awareness of each other or the communities we are part of.

When we are in a group of people, when we are in community, mind-fulness invites us to be aware of our impact on others. Even though we might intend to treat people well and fairly, the reality of our collec-tive unconscious does not always match our intentions. For instance, unconscious group dynamics in the twenty-first century still usually allow men in the room to speak longer, more often, and with greater perceived credibility than women or other genders. People of the domi-nant mainstream culture still tend to overpower people of other cultures and take up space, time, resources, and energy. This is the unconscious conditioning of how we currently are with each other.

In the United States, most white folks can generally get more airtime, more opportunity, and more privilege than folks of color. We rarely con-sider people with different or restricted ranges of physical ability in how we move through the world; they have to adapt to the way the world is for the larger whole. For example, how many Dharma teachers give "walk-ing" meditation instructions that are truly accessible to those who have difficulty walking or moving in the world?

For such people, the experience of conscious or unconscious disparity and discrimination can be truly disabling—even or especially when they don't experience their physical abilities to be an impairment. The more we become aware of each other, as individuals and as groups, the more we begin to sense, feel, and live the reality that we are all interconnected despite any differences between us.

Our needs are not solely an individual matter, even though we might feel them personally. It is the practice of sangha to naturally take care of others with grace and ease—to share our joys and sorrows together in communion with the full range of our collective experience. Likewise, while the needs of each community might seem different and specific to that particular community, the Dharma is about being aware of the needs of all communities, not just our own.

The issues of different physical abilities or limitations are not just about accommodating the individual needs of people who experience those limitations. It is an issue for all of us, particularly since all of us will surely feel injury, infirmity, and incapacity at some point in our lives.

Sexism and violence toward women do not just involve the experience of women, particularly when the perpetrators are not women. It involves all of us.

Homophobia is not just a problem for gays, lesbians, bisexuals, and transgender or nongendered folks. Racism doesn't just affect or involve communities of color.

All of these issues require awareness and involvement from all of us. This is how we are interrelated. As Dr. King wrote, "It requires a shift in consciousness from all of us."

Our Dharma practice invites us to stand in community, solidarity, and connection with all of our collective joys and pain, in order that we may heal and awaken together to a greater sense of freedom. Dharma has such great potential to impact our multiple communities. Each time we practice awareness, we are transforming our own worlds and transforming the world we share. Are we aware of that? Are we willing to be aware of that? Are we willing to extend the breadth of our awareness practice internally, externally—and both internally and externally?

The practice is not just about our own personal awakening, enlightenment, or freedom. The path is not just about personal salvation. It is about our collective journey and transformation toward a shared experience of wisdom and tenderness.

There is a deep relationship between what we do in our meditation practice, whether in retreat, in a weekly sitting group, or in a chair at home, and how we live our lives in the world. The creation of peace in the world, which so desperately needs it, is no different than the creation of peace within ourselves.

Our practice is not some postponement of our freedom into some unknown future. We are creating freedom in this moment for ourselves and the world and worlds yet to be—those of our children, of our successors, and of all future generations.

That is the magnitude of our practice—that it is the collective embodiment and the possibility for transformation of our spiritual path into a collective awareness and movement to awakening.

This is the great journey toward our internal individual and external collective freedom.

12

Heart and Mind, Together

W E NECESSARILY BEGIN with our own minds and hearts.
We start by coming from a place of personal peacefulness in order to create and sustain peace in the world, and we do our inner work so our work in our communities will have the deepest possible impact. We develop the capacity to be aware and to pay attention to ourselves in order to know more deeply how to pay attention to and be mindful of others and the whole of life around us. This expanding template of awareness is constantly inviting us to deepen the spiritual practice of cultivating internal and external awareness of our inner and outer worlds.

As useful as the word *mindfulness* is, it does not completely capture the full scope of the endeavor. If the meaning of *mindfulness* is to bring our whole presence to bear on the experience arising in front of us, there is an element of heart that also calls to our attention.

The psychologies of Buddhist and Asian traditions use a term that encompasses the Western notions of both mind and heart—thoughts and emotions. In Sanskrit, this word is *citta*. While in Western culture and psychology the mind and heart may be seen to function separately, the Buddhist framework integrates mental and emotional experiences, linking all formations of thoughts, ideas, and concepts with the field of emotions, feelings, and vulnerabilities.

Let me take the example of my father. During his life and for most of his career, he was a professor who taught electrical engineering. Even amid his heavily intellectual and scholarly world, his cultural conditioning with respect to the relationship between heart and mind never wavered. Usually, when Western people say, "I think . . . ," they will gesture to their head, but even if there is no physical gesture, the general assumption is that thoughts emanate from the brain. But whenever my dad said, "I think . . . ," he would gesture toward his chest, his heart. Perhaps a way of languaging *mindfulness* more closely to its cultural intentions is to use a description of "mind-heartfulness."

This isn't to suggest that one or the other cultural perspective is right or wrong, or even that one is better than the other. Eastern and Western perspectives are mutually complementary and can create a larger picture to hold our different cultural interpretations, but it is worthwhile to note that we may introduce cultural valence even in the way we express the term *mindfulness* in English. Many of the core concepts of Western psychology are grounded in the Age of European Enlightenment. Descartes's famous *cogito ergo sum*, or "I think, therefore I am," is emblematic of the Western philosophical elevation of the cognitive function of the mind to a position of primacy in defining who we are as humans. The mind and the self have become culturally equivalent in the dominant Western perspective. But what of different cultures that have differing relationships to heart, mind, and self? What of options wherein the experience of heart and mind are balanced?

Within the cultures of origin of the Dharma, awareness practice is experienced with the totality of mind and heart together, whether one arrives at the teaching through the two doors of mind separate from heart or through the single door of mind-and-heart. Paying attention encompasses both the experience of knowing what is happening and meeting it with the acceptance of kindness.

In this way, the energy of the heart is integrally woven into the mindfulness of paying attention. Whether we are parenting or have parented young children or not, we have all been children. My three young grandchildren have taught me the reality of children: if we do not pay attention to our children moment-to-moment, they don't actually feel loved. We can verbally tell them that we love them all we want, but if we are not paying attention to them, they won't feel it. We are really no different as adults.

When we are not paying attention to someone, we are not turning the fullness of our mind-hearts toward them. In response to this nonattention, a person might feel disrespected, ignored, not cared for, or unimportant.

Paying attention—mindfulness—is a direct act and experience of love.

As we apply this attention inwardly and pay attention to our own experiences, we give ourselves this act of profound love. It may not feel like the love that we fantasize about—but by simply paying attention to our experience, we are loving ourselves by accepting ourselves in each moment of awareness. This love accepts all of who we are in this moment and allows us to be with all the facets of ourselves right now.

The more we've experienced this unconditionality, the more we are able to be present to being mind-heartful. And through practicing it with regard to ourselves, we learn to offer the same attention, the same acceptance, the same energies, and the same presence of our hearts and minds to others.

In a smaller retreat of about thirty practitioners that I co-led with a white woman colleague, we intentionally created a demographically mixed retreat with people from many different cultural backgrounds, including from the dominant mainstream cultures. As a teacher of color, I felt a responsibility for co-creating and supporting that "safe-enough" space for folks who had experienced marginalization in their lives, including through race, gender identity, orientation, and ability. Part of developing that safe-enough container is naming the need for safety and inclusion—in the introductions, in the welcome, in the Dharma talks, and in the group meetings.

At that retreat, I received the blunt input from a white, middle-aged, male practitioner concerning how I was holding the container of the retreat. The lengthy note contained many outlined points to which he objected: my using exclusively passages from authors of color (presumably including the Buddha); my selecting quotes based upon race and also identifying their cultural background when quoting them as racist and divisive upon my part; my mentioning the experience and concept of people of color and that I was a person of color being exclusionary and polarizing. He also wanted me to know that even though people of color have their unique suffering, so do white people, and he suggested I deal with my political issues elsewhere but not in a retreat setting.

Reading this feedback, I could feel how injured this person was when he entered the retreat, and how by paying attention to an aspect of life experience (namely diverse racial and cultural experience) that he didn't generally relate to (but was nonetheless part of the life experience of others in the room), his wound got amplified. This man needed to express this pain.

As one of the teachers, and the teacher to whom he directed his words, it was my role and responsibility to assist in holding that pain—and to care for both him and his pain—during the course of the retreat. My task was a mindfulness practice in teaching: I could notice his pain, I could notice my own pain, and I had the ability to not be lost in either. It was my responsibility to attempt to do what would best serve this practitioner's heart and mind together—which I could not have done had I not experienced my own screenplays of suffering first. But having gone through my own version of racial pain, I could then open my heart and mind together for his benefit.

I do feel my own pain here and I do feel this man's pain too, but I also feel the pain of the larger social unconsciousness that his words represented for me. It is the same social unconsciousness of the mainstream culture that feels injured, threatened, and excluded when awareness—the kindness of paying attention—is given to the sometimes acute and urgent needs of people on the margins. It is the same social unconsciousness that resists the reality and necessity of "Black Lives Matter" with the defensive counter-statement of "All Lives Matter." Of course, all lives matter, but until the landscape of our sociocultural, even spiritual, world levels and shows some equity, it is absolutely necessary to offer our collective attention and mindfulness toward that which has been paid little or no awareness. Alicia Garza, one of the founders of the Black Lives Matter movement, states, "When we address the disparities facing black people, we get a lot closer to a true democracy where all lives matter."

We are too often pulled away from what calls for our deepest and most precious attention so that we miss the chance to create less suffering in a world that already suffers so greatly. We too often do a spiritual bypass and pretend that the pain of difference doesn't exist because we somehow should always be connected to the spirit of the Universal Family. When we allow ourselves to believe thoughts of how life should be, we may end up bypassing again—and denying what is really happening in the moment.

When we use our awareness practice in our lives, we are invited to pay attention—but *not just* to pay attention. We must also bring intention and purpose to bear. We can be mindful of anything that happens in life: we can be mindful when we are willfully hurting someone's feelings as much as when we are offering them our love. For mindfulness to be Dharma practice, it must be done with the intention of being mindful primarily of what will lead to less suffering and more freedom in all our lives. This is the crucial choice point awareness offers us: diminish suffering or amplify it. Once we are aware, we must apply this to everything that arises. The purpose of becoming aware of our breath, bodily sensations, or even our thoughts, emotions, worries, and fantasies is not to fixate incessantly upon them but to strengthen our capacity to be aware in all aspects of our lives, especially when we really need it to reduce suffering in this world.

The aspect of attention and love directed toward our collective experience is as vitally significant as the aspect directed to our own experience. Both realities—external and internal—must be attended to with love.

In a world that often seems to be eating itself alive with violence and hatred of difference, we desperately need the ability *as communities* to pay attention, to demonstrate respect and caring, and to be able to learn about other communities. Can we pay attention to communities who are marginalized, stressed, receive ongoing harm on a sometimes incessant basis? Can we pay attention to communities that do not have a voice or visibility within the dominant culture? Can we learn as a culture to pay attention to something other than just ourselves? How can we do that?

We can start where we are, in our Dharma communities, and pay attention with love to how imbalanced the cultural demographics are in so many Dharma communities in the United States. We can begin to explore the conditions and reasons why almost all of these communities are composed of white, middle- to upper-middle-class, highly educated congregants. Within my own Insight Meditation community, this involves turning attention to the reality that, to date, in over thirty years of training Dharma teachers for residential retreat practice, only ten or eleven out of more than three hundred have been teachers of color.

For members of dominant cultures, this means paying attention to what we usually do not pay attention to—and practicing collectively invites us to do this. There is an urgency requiring us to examine and learn how unconscious and unacknowledged power and privilege serve to keep mainstream social patterns of white dominance in place.

The best that most mainstream Dharma centers have been able to do is to be passively accepting of "diversity" and share publicly the message that they welcome everyone. These efforts are no longer sufficient—and have never been adequate conditions to include diverse communities to participate in the Dharma. Mainstream communities need to pay closer attention to not only what would welcome diverse participation but what would allow multicultural communities to thrive and grow in the Dharma. This is a very different strategy because it may mean changing the very infrastructure of the organization. If the infrastructure of the organization is not a level playing field, if the system is supported by racism and white dominance, then the system will need to change in order to become truly inclusive. And the fact is, inclusivity as a practice is much more difficult to retrofit into an organization or community already shaped by a mainstream culture that is already white dominated.

In 1999 at a talk that an experienced Western white teacher gave one evening, I asked why they thought Dharma communities were so homogenously monochromatic (that is, "white"). Their answer was that when a group of young, passionate practitioners returned from spiritual practice in Asia in the early 1970s, they began to teach meditation to their "friends." Soon friends of their friends were showing up, and that is how the community of this lineage got started. This, they felt, was a wonderful, organic, and natural way to bring the teachings into North America—through the direct experience of people relating to others, who were generally friends of one another. Although it is true that many of our current meditation centers began in this way, this methodology of friends-of-friends building community will not ultimately create a Dharma community that reflects the needs of all of the groups within our society.

When we pay attention to only our friends, and friends of our friends, we are almost certain not to reach many people with different life experiences and backgrounds. It takes intentional, conscious, and proactive effort to do the latter—and, again, this is especially true when the dominant cultural norms have already been patterned into an organization. This teacher's response to my question, if examined deeply, indicates a deep level of collective inattention from a mainstream community to the larger set of diverse peoples beyond their own experience. It took until the winter of 2011 for the conversation on diversity and racism to emerge enough into mainstream consciousness for an article in *Buddhadharma* magazine to show up titled "Why Is American Buddhism So White?"

And of course, we are not speaking about the totality of the North American Buddhist experience when we ask that question. The title of the article refers to how white-dominant culture has come to develop and control many of the communities, resources, press, and even definitions of Dharma practice in the West—with very little interaction or involvement with their own tradition's Asian cultures of origin or with diverse cultural groups who are potential practitioners. While there are lineages, including those represented by Soka Gakkai International, Nichiren Buddhism, Jodo Shinshu Buddhism, and the Buddhist Churches of America among others, who have attended to this in their community development, there are many Dharma communities in North America in which awareness of this issue is completely absent. Despite the lack of mainstream consciousness around the issues of developing inclusive communities, many Dharma practitioners of color and leaders of color hold this issue at the forefront of their minds and hearts. Over the past twenty years, we have managed to patch together a pipeline of experience, practice, and consciousness that leads toward diverse participation in the Dharma. Communities of color and our allies in leadership have created, often outside formal institutional designations, introductory and beginner classes, daylong events, weekend retreats, and residential retreats for people of color.

Making the Invisible Visible, a report we published for the International Buddhist Teachers Conference in 2000, articulated the needs and issues related to creating truly multicultural communities through the personal stories of practitioners of color, and these stories are as relevant today, more than a decade and a half later. Communities of color have advocated for consistent and ongoing organizational diversity and multicultural training and have been involved in the diversity councils and committees of our mainstream communities for over twenty years. We have initiated funding to support PoC practice and retreats, and we have become board members at mainstream Dharma institutions. We have influenced and directed community Dharma leadership and senior Dharma study programs. We have created Dharma centers, like New York Insight Meditation Center (New York City), East Bay Meditation Center (Oakland, California), and Flowering Lotus Meditation Center (Magnolia, Mississippi), based on the priorities of diversity and inclusion within the Dharma. We have designed and taught retreats and Dharma events in which there has been a radical shift in demographics in the practice space. We were part of efforts to re-vision the conditions of the multi-month silent residential retreats to develop a much higher percentage attendance of practitioners of color. For these extended retreats, these efforts included addressing aspects of funding, training of staff, multicultural skills training of Dharma teachers, and outreach and continuing support for communities of color.

All of those conditions have created formidable positive circumstances for training teachers of color. Before 1999, it is estimated that there were less than a hundred unduplicated practitioners of color on the mailing lists of Insight Meditation centers. In 2015, the estimated number of unduplicated practitioners of color on the mailing lists of just five centers—Spirit Rock Meditation Center, Insight Meditation Society, New York Insight Meditation Center, East Bay Meditation Center, and Insight Meditation Community of Washington, D.C.—is estimated to have grown to seven thousand—a 6,900 percent increase. That growth over fifteen years produced a pipeline of practitioners of color, some of whom are now qualified to enter training and development as Dharma teachers of color in the Insight Meditation tradition. These efforts are having a significant impact beyond the friends-of-friends networks, and in the future, we hope to see the impact of these numbers motivating the development of diverse teachers in the Dharma.

In addition to the explicit aspects of racism, there are other subtle forms of racism that maintain the supremacy of dominant culture and white culture as the status quo. Part of the nuance occurs in language, in particular what is referred to as "coded" language. One example of this coded language is the use of Dharma practice to reframe cultural experience. The experience of "anger" is languaged to communicate insufficient progress in meditation or spiritual practice (for example, in the phrase "It seems like you're feeling a lot of anger in response to racism. You should 'practice' with that anger so that you are not quite so reactive and more appropriate in your speech"). The use of the word *appropriate* in relationship to actions and behaviors connotes "skillful" or "good"— but according to what cultural standards is *appropriate* being measured? Who is creating the definitions and interpretations of the Dharma? Can "anger" ever be "appropriate" given the inequities of our world? What if a culture-of-appropriateness is a primary method through which white dominance imposes the projection of inappropriate behavior and/or actions onto folks outside the white mainstream?

I refrain from using the term "senior Dharma teacher" these days— another term I increasingly regard as a kind of coded language. I know of no current Dharma teacher of color who will ever reach the status of "senior Dharma teacher." Therefore for me, it is coded language for exclusion, dominance, and control by the white culture. It feels useful to stop using that terminology until that colored glass ceiling is shattered. And in order to shatter that ceiling, the unlevel playing field of infrastructure needs deep transformation.

The challenge for us now that is truly relevant to diverse communities is to train and empower teachers of color. It is not about getting a diverse group to conform to the norms of the kinds of trainings that have occurred in the past. One experienced white teacher has expressed support for retreats for people of color at their center and the aspiration to offer the "exact same retreat experience that white people have to people of color." This is a flawed understanding of the needs of diverse communities.

We are not simply giving people of color the "exact same experience" as "everyone else" (which is only further coded language for "white communities like us"). We are not training diverse teachers to assimilate to the dominant culture. Rather, we are training teachers to cultivate the Dharma in their own communities in ways that are culturally congruent and respectful—in their own cultural idiom. In so doing, we must pay attention to the need to provide continuing leadership and teaching to the burgeoning number (more than seven thousand) of practitioners of color currently affiliated with Insight Meditation practice. The fluidity of leadership, the ongoing development of leaders, and the succession of leadership for the benefit of future generations are emblematic markers of a community's health.

These are only some of the issues that face our Dharma communities and calling for our robust and enthusiastic attention. We must turn collectively toward these issues with the love of attention and generosity—because engaging these issues out of some sense of obligation or guilt will not sustain what is needed to actually culturally transform our Dharma organizations. The transformation needed in our spiritual communities is the same transformation needed in the world.

Our world cries out for this transformation. With the complexities of the Pulse nightclub shootings in Orlando, the ongoing state-sanctioned killings and incarcerations of people of color (disproportionately African American and/or transgendered), the unrest of a new generation of university students unwilling to be passive in the face of continuing racial disparities, and the vitriol directed at Muslim, immigrant, and refugee communities, we are being urgently asked to pay attention to those who are different from us in order to dissolve the suffering that springs from indifference to them. If we cannot accomplish this in our spiritual communities with the support of all of our teachings, skills, practices, and faith, how will we ever accomplish it in the larger world?

As global conditions seem increasingly incomprehensible, we can humbly recall these words of Anaïs Nin: "We do not see the world as it is; we see the world as we are." Therefore, the greater the number of *we ares* that we see, the more likely a compassionate response to an often unfathomable life becomes possible. If we only understand life through our own particular lives, we will never feel the breadth of life in general and will always be deluded in our pursuit of true awakening. It is only by practicing in a multiplicity of communities—including ones that might seem in existential opposition—that we will have the opportunity to sense that which connects us all as a Universal Family. From this place, we can extend collective effort with our minds and hearts in fellowship together. Cultivating our hearts and minds, we must pay the broadest attention possible to love fully together all aspects of our diverse lives. This inner sense of community between mind and heart is indispensable in creating the outer sense of community and wholeness that benefits all of our experiences. We turn our hearts and minds together toward the lives around us.

Who are we beyond who we think we are? Our mind-heartfulness is an invitation to journey into the answers that lie beyond the question. When we come to a common sense of the heart and mind together—in common with every spiritual tradition, not to mention every human being—instead of eating each other alive with violence, succumbing to greed, hatred, and delusion, we might start to feed each other with care, in order to awaken our hearts and minds together.

13

Transformation of the Heart

M ANY TIMES I found myself frustrated by not having the inner skills and tools to be the person that I wished to be while doing the work I felt was so important in the world.

When I was a newly trained social worker, I was interested in social justice and change in a world that had so much pain caused by structural and political inequity. One of the men of color with whom I worked as a provider had a history of multiple mental disorders and trauma over fifteen years with concurrent addictions to speed, crack cocaine, and sex. He had relapsed and failed out of five substance abuse programs in the span of eighteen months. I worked in a medical clinic providing social service case management in collaboration with a substance abuse treatment facility—my hours at the treatment facility were limited by facility contract to three hours per week. Against the advice and wishes of my own clinic's and the treatment center's management, I decided to see this man four times a week for intensive behavioral-change psychotherapy. Even though I had the time in my schedule to provide it, there was no funding to support the therapy. I could bill for anything connected to social services—after-care, housing, job development, twelve-step meetings—but I could not bill for mental health treatment.

At every staff meeting I attended, there would be implicit or explicit pressure to make my services "billable." I was treated with suspicion by the treatment facility staff and management because they felt I was trying to show that I was a "better" social worker. After four weeks of successfully managing to stay in the treatment facility, the man was prematurely discharged without housing—and without notice to him or any of his providers, including me. I was told that he became "inappropriately" angry with the staff and the staff had felt physically threatened. When I questioned why he was discharged without housing, I was informed that if I had been doing my job I would have had housing options for him already in place. I received no support from my own clinic management and was told to move on to fill my caseload—with billable cases, of course.

At the next staff meeting I blew up. It was I who became wildly and inappropriately angry with my peers and management, accusing them of racism, of only caring about getting money from insurance companies, and of only wanting to create a client conveyor belt of intake and discharge so that numbers would appear to be higher than would be possible with truly effective clinical work. I was beside myself. One of the physicians was privately able to calm me down and create space for all my intense feelings.

I wrote this passage to that doctor in a note, expressing my aspirations for how I wanted to be in my life:

> I would like to reach a place during one of our meetings where I can express the emotions that are going on within my body and mind, without retreating into rage, fear, resentment, or silence. I would like to not just experience the pain when someone does not hear what I am saying or questions it *ad infinitum* but to cry about it as well. I want to cry when my confidentiality is broken by an inappropriate disclosure, rather than to match energy or prove the person is "wrong." By expressing my feelings without blame, I can be fully in the world regardless of whether some people treat me as invisible or not. I can be as much in the world as anyone else because I will have developed the confidence and certainty of having a place in the world, no matter who I am. This vulnerability is my intention, which I need to articulate to someone. I ask that you witness it.

In working to provide care and advocacy for different marginalized communities, I was always stymied by how difficult it was in my role to offer compassionate care to people—because the systems in place were impersonal, bureaucratic, and many times discriminatory. The service organizations reflected the same unconscious privileged values of the dominant culture. I worked in homeless shelters, public hospitals, health clinics, substance abuse facilities, and different community service organizations, and in most of these workplaces, changing the structures and systems in order to take care of people with compassion and respect seemed to be an impossible task.

With ever-decreasing funding, ever-expanding numbers of clients, and increasing demands and responsibilities added by my clinic's management, conditions were harsh. I felt my clients' anger and pain at being continuously shuttled from agency to agency for services that never seemed to materialize. I felt the anger of communities at not being adequately served in a culture that dismisses and overlooks the needs of people without means, without homes, without resources or benefits. I sometimes even felt anger and rage at myself about feeling incompetent and unable to make a difference.

Much of the time I felt that I was simply part of an oppressive system, even if I was trying to change it, and using that oppressive system to earn the paycheck that sustained my own life and needs. I was angry that I had become disillusioned about my own ideals. I became angry and judgmental of my peers who, like me, were just trying to do their work as best they could. Because I couldn't meet my own expectations and standards, I had no empathic energy left for my colleagues who were in similar no-win situations.

Staff meetings became overrun with intense conflicts and disagreements, often spurred by our mutual, but unspoken, feelings of inadequacy. We accused each other of the same disparities and discrimination that we accused the larger society of imposing on our clients and communities. As social service providers in a difficult and harsh world, we were becoming difficult and harsh ourselves. We became unwitting mirrors as our hearts hardened along with the hardness of the world around us.

I began to ask myself how to live and work in a world that suffers so greatly, without myself causing the same kind of pain. That felt like a profound spiritual exploration to me. In the world's harshness, in the midst of the first noble truth that the world is characterized by suffering, I reflected on whether the mind and heart can still remain open and free.

Reverend Dr. Martin Luther King Jr. wrote, "As you press for justice, be sure to move with dignity and discipline, using only the instruments of love."

But what are "the instruments of love"? This wasn't clear to me, until I encountered the Buddha's teachings, and the step-by-step path that they laid out. The Dharma provided succinct instructions, guidance, and invitations to different forms of practice. Its path is incremental, cumulative, and ultimately transformative—but we do not and need not change all at once. I have so appreciated that in the Buddhist tradition we are not expected to simply magically turn into the spiritual ideal of loving-kindness or compassion. What we are given instead are innumerable opportunities to practice being those ideals by trying them out, experimenting with them, and seeing what works in the reality of our own lives.

One form this practice takes is the *brahma viharas*. *Brahma* means "highest," "sublime," or "divine," and *vihara* is the word for "dwelling," "abode," or "sacred residence." *Brahma vihara* is sometimes translated as the "Divine Abodes." The brahma viharas show us the highest places in which our hearts can reside—namely in the sublime energies of loving-kindness, compassion, appreciative joy, and equanimity.

Loving-kindness, or *metta* in Pali, is the primal, intrinsic energy of the heart that also shares the experience of the present moment with mindfulness. Meeting the moments of our lives as they arise with full and accepting loving attention—not needing the moment to be anything more or less than it is—is an act of kindness. This is why in the practice of mindfulness we are told that even if a judgmental mind should arise in meditation with overwhelming thoughts of right and wrong, good and bad, worthy or unworthy, we should invite ourselves not to judge the judgment. It isn't only that we judge others or ourselves, we can also beat up on ourselves for beating up on ourselves. In this way we pour fuel on a fire that's already raging. When we refrain from judging the judgment, the fires begin to cool on their own. This may seem counterintuitive, but the moment we do not judge ourselves we apply the full force of our heart, of *metta*, and begin to dissolve the judgment itself. This is the transformative quality of kindness within mind-heartfulness practice.

As we bring loving-kindness to bear on the full spectrum of experiences in our lives, that kindness meets all of our ten thousand joys and ten thousand sorrows. It is said that when our loving attention meets the sorrow and suffering of our lives, our hearts begin to quiver. This is the visceral expression of the experience of compassion—*karuna* in Pali. That I could cultivate and strengthen my ability to be compassionate by turning kindness toward difficulty was a revelation to me. Understanding how compassion and suffering are interdependent with each other was equally illuminating. The experience of compassion is intimately linked with the experience of suffering. The irony of our hearts is that we cannot have one without the other. They are two sides of the same coin: life that is bittersweet and poignant.

Thich Nhat Hanh expresses it this way: "Since I was a young man, I've tried to understand the nature of compassion. But what little compassion I've learned has not come from intellectual investigation, but from my actual experience of suffering."

Directing *metta* toward the joys and happiness in our lives increases our happiness, but not, perhaps, in a way that our individually focused Western minds may expect.

This Great Joy is called *mudita* in Pali and sometimes translated as "appreciative joy" or "sympathetic joy." The teachings invite us to expand the scope of the joy and happiness we experience so that we experience a joy that is greater than our own personal pleasant experiences. We are happy with our happiness, but we are also happy with the happiness and successes of others. We can feel this most easily with our loved ones: when our children or partners succeed in or achieve something they have reached for, we feel happy too.

As we heed the invitation of the practice to extend our embrace of happy experiences even beyond our close network of friends and loved ones into circles of beings we barely know or don't know at all, we begin to experience a greater joy. This is a joy that is shared unconditionally with others. It is a joy that does not take any moment in this life for granted.

Whether sublime, profane, or mundane, mindfulness brings caring attention to the moments we ordinarily overlook or ignore—so appreciative joy is also "the joy of being alive," a joy that recognizes the precious value of each and every moment, whether lived in sorrow or in happiness or anywhere in-between.

As we connect the experiences of compassion and joy supported by loving-kindness, as we vacillate between the joys and sorrows, as we directly experience the changing nature of both, we reach a place where our minds and hearts find a sense of balance. The Dharma calls this state "equanimity," or *uppekha* in Pali. Equanimity is not an elimination of highs and lows in our lives. It does not get rid of pain or pleasure. Equanimity supports us in developing a different, more patient relationship with both difficulties and successes.

Finding balance is not unlike learning how to ride a bicycle: in the beginning we constantly fall down. It may not seem that falling into anger, depression, or even the seduction of ecstasy and pleasure feels very balanced—but those things are part of how we learn to ride the bike of equanimity, by falling down. As we practice, our ride becomes easier, and we balance more steadily. However, the reality of balance is that we are always still falling down, in one direction or the other. The difference that equanimity makes is that we catch ourselves more and more quickly and adjust. This is how we balance on a bicycle, too. We continue to fall from side to side—even Tour de France racing cyclists do that—but we catch ourselves faster and faster by making micro-adjustments, until there is a seamless motion and flow to our lived experience.

Mindfulness and the Divine Abodes lead our heart toward awakening.

Ultimately, the awakened heart pays gentle, nonjudgmental attention to all of our experiences. This power of kind regard, compassionate attention, shared celebration and joy has the capacity to tenderly hold the entirety of our lives and is deeply transformative. But it is not an easy practice. Still, even when it is difficult, we are invited to be kind to our own practice of kindness itself.

Here's the invitation: Allow yourself to let go of perfectionism and judging whether you are perfect enough or not. Allow yourself to gently attend to yourself wherever you are, even if you feel that you are falling short of some perceived goal or vision of how you would like to act or behave in the world. Allow the practice itself to be flawed.

Hold the practices themselves with tenderness.

Below is a prayer of aspiration I developed in my own practice to remind myself how broad and deep the practices of the heart actually are:

> May I be as loving in this moment as possible.
> If I cannot be loving in this moment,
>> may I be kind;
> If I cannot be kind,
>> may I be nonjudgmental;
> If I cannot be nonjudgmental,
>> may I not cause harm;
> And if I cannot not cause harm,
>> may I cause the least amount of harm possible

In this way, even in my failure, my heart is still inclining itself toward kindness. Even in the midst of difficulty, the gradient of my experience is still aimed toward love and compassion. This is the best I can do: to be still engaged in and inclined toward the practice of kindness even when I have failed, however miserably, to be kind.

In communities like East Bay Meditation Center we endeavor to be as inclusive as possible of the needs and aspirations of as many forms of diversity as we can. And yet we all are restricted by the limitations of our awareness; we are far from fully cooked, fully awake. I am no exception. Regardless of my intention to learn and be more inclusive of other people's experiences, there are times when I fail due to my own narrow assumptions or lack of experience. This is a hard mindfulness practice to learn as a teacher when teaching, but it is one of the most powerful.

With the help of my community, one of the first limitations I became aware of as a new Dharma teacher was that of my own life native to my body and mind as a cisgendered man, a man whose self-identity is congruent with the gender of their biological sex at birth. I learned that these conditions can limit my effectiveness as a Dharma teacher. In one retreat after giving what I thought was a decent, well-prepared Dharma talk, a woman about my age asked to speak with me. In the most gracious manner, she described to me her experience of not being seen in the Dharma talk because all the stories, quotations, and teachings—even from the Buddha—came from the understandings of men. I was taken aback—not at her input but at how invisible my own gender conditioning as a man was to me.

I wasn't aware I had defaulted to the mode of expression with which I was most familiar. It was as if my own autopilot had steered the talk in the direction of the cis-male experience, without consideration for other gendered or nongendered life experience. Even more poignantly, I had fallen into the same pattern I was trying to bring to the attention of white teachers by pointing out that they tended to use only the wisdom of white folks in their Dharma talks.

That practitioner's kindness, in the midst of not feeling valued at the Dharma talk, allowed me to fully experience my mistake without becoming defensive and judging myself into guilt. It allowed me to open more fully to how I could learn from my error and ignorance. This is the learning curve that kindness reveals.

We don't learn most from what we already know; we learn most from our mistakes. Can we be open and gentle to the experience of mistake-making such that we can fully absorb the potential learning it brings? The compassion of the practitioner allowed me to take ownership of my error and apologize to all the retreat participants without any awkwardness or shame. It motivated me to try harder upon my next opportunity to offer a Dharma talk—not just in terms of gender identity but with all the issues of identity in our collective experience, to the best of my abilities.

Did the practitioner's pain magically disappear? No. Did my self-judgment dissipate completely? No. Did it make a difference? I believe it did.

We were able to hold each other with respect in a relational field that also encircled the harm caused. We did not turn away from the incident.

She did not turn away from her own experience, and I did not turn away from mine. And that is an experience of mutual kindness within the experience of difference and even harm.

Each of us has to determine through our own lived experience whether these teachings make any sense for us or whether they will benefit us. My own experience with these practices has deepened my faith in the process of walking this path together.

In *The Sacred Path of the Warrior*, the influential Tibetan Buddhist teacher Chögyam Trungpa Rinpoche expresses the power of the path of the awakened heart this way:

> When you awaken your heart, you find, to your surprise, that your heart is empty. You find that you are looking into outer space. What are you, who are you, where is your heart?
>
> If you really look, you won't find anything tangible and solid. Of course, you might find something very solid if you have a grudge against someone or you have fallen possessively in love. But that is not awakened heart.
>
> If you search for awakened heart, if you put your hand through your rib cage and feel for it, there is nothing there except for tenderness. You feel sore and soft, and if you open your eyes to the rest of the world, you feel tremendous sadness.
>
> This kind of sadness doesn't come from being mistreated. You don't feel sad because someone has insulted you or because you feel impoverished. Rather, this experience of sadness is unconditioned. It occurs because your heart is completely exposed. There is no skin or tissue covering it; it is pure raw meat. Even if a tiny mosquito lands on it, you feel so touched. Your experience is raw and tender and so personal.
>
> For the warrior, this experience of sad and tender heart is what gives birth to fearlessness. Conventionally, being fearless means that you are not afraid or that, if someone hits you, you will hit him back. However, we are not talking about that street-fighter level of fearlessness. Real fearlessness is the product of tenderness. You are willing to open up, without

resistance or shyness, and face the world. . . . It is this tender
heart of a warrior that has the power to heal the world.

Another example of the power of our hearts to transform the world is
in the story of Michelle Bachelet, the first woman to be democratically
elected to a Latin American nation's presidency. When she was twenty-
three years old, after the U.S.-backed 1973 military coup in Chile that top-
pled Salvador Allende, Bachelet's father was arrested because he was an
air force general who'd opposed the coup. He was subsequently tortured
and died in prison. Bachelet and her mother were then taken to one of
the secret military prisons where she was also tortured and told that her
mother was to be executed. In 1975, she was exiled to live in Australia
and eventually East Germany. She gained authorization to return to her
home country in 1979. At the beginning of 2006, Michelle Bachelet won
the presidency of Chile with 53 percent of the vote over her conservative
opponent. In her victory speech, she said to cheering crowds:

> You know I have not had an easy life, but then who has? Vio-
> lence destroyed what I loved. Because I was the victim of hate,
> I have consecrated my life to converting that hate into under-
> standing, into tolerance, and—why not say it?—love.

There are awakened beings on this planet. Do not think awakening
is not possible.

The freedom we seek from this life of suffering does not occur by
inflicting more suffering, no matter how much pain we are in.

The restorative work of love must be done with love.

This is the transformation of our heart that leads to the transformative
liberation that we seek for our communities and for our world.

It is the path of living together, growing together, and awakening
together.

14

Moving Toward Freedom

J UST AS WHEN working to develop multicultural communities, complexities of needs emerge even in my own process of writing a book about the subject.

A while ago I had decided on the provisional title of "Walking Toward Freedom" for one of this book's chapters. It was only when I was almost finished writing it that I realized how that title could impact folks who have different ranges of mobility and capacities to walk. The language I had chosen to use could create a barrier to people in certain situations; it would be, essentially, a microaggression. Accordingly, I was motivated to rewrite not just the title but the chapter itself.

In doing so, I would like to take one of the most basic, fundamental practices in the Buddhist tradition—the guidance usually given for walking meditation—to a deeper level of meaning and reflection. To most folks walking may be just a mundane activity that can be revelatory when awareness is turned toward it as an opportunity for insight and discovery. We hardly give our ability to walk a second thought. Our mental relationship to our physical ability to ambulate may just be "Yeah, of course I can do that." We may have a kind of benign, banal disinterest with our capacity to walk in the world. Most of us can even be completely unaware of walking, even while doing it.

This may say something about the amount of one's own personal mindfulness at any given moment, but it also reveals something else. When we take our ability to walk in the world for granted and don't give it a thought, we also do not give a thought to those who have a different experience, including no ability at all, to actually take a step and walk. The inability to walk might be the result of injury or disability or some restriction in range of motion. But it might also be the case that this is the life that a person has been given—and that, for the person involved, there is nothing broken or inadequate about that life.

Recall the image in chapter 3 of the sea turtle coming up for air every one hundred years and poking his head through a ring floating in the immense ocean as a metaphor for how rare and precious this human life is. The Buddha didn't say people with more physical ability or range of motion are more precious than people who have less abilities or range. He didn't say that people who can walk are more precious than those who cannot. Likewise, he didn't say that hetero-normative people are more precious than queer folks. He didn't say that one gender expression is more precious than another gender expression. He didn't say that people of a certain race or culture are more precious than other races or cultures. He didn't even say less angry people are more precious than people who are angrier. He simply said all beings born human are so very precious—because we all have the capacity to awaken in the vehicle of this human life.

Unfortunately, all the translations of traditional scriptures exclude differently abled communities simply by using the word *walk*, such as in the classic descriptions of the four postures of meditation: sitting, standing, lying down—and walking. In reality, all of us have had times in our lives when we have not been able to walk, or even sit, in one posture with ease and comfort, and some medical conditions preclude sitting for any length of time at all. The question is whether our awareness and cultivation of freedom of mind and heart depend on our physical abilities. Mindfulness has no limits, even though our bodies might. Awareness, insight, and compassion are not restricted by physical ability. These human attributes of this precious life are without boundaries, as indicated by the expansive qualities of the four foundations of mindfulness in the Satipatthana Sutta.

Beyond the physical characteristics of "walking" with one's feet, the larger metaphor points to turning our loving attention to how we "move" through our lives. Do we move through our lives with mindfulness and clarity or mindlessness and distraction? Mindfulness of movement is the invitation to bring our practice and attention to the journey we make through any action or activity. Moreover, we do not make our way through our life's journey or navigate our spiritual path alone.

I was doing a three-week retreat with one of my close spiritual friends. In this retreat center, practitioners are given no detailed schedule. You fall into a rhythm of practice that emerges from your own conditions: formal times of meditation, movement, eating practice, rest and sleeping periods depending upon the conditions of your body and mind at the time. Without checking in with each other, my friend and I came and went, in and out of the meditation hall and the dining hall, at times that we determined by ourselves for our own retreat process. One day we ended up in the same hall doing movement/walking meditation. By two weeks into the retreat, I suppose we were both quite still and tranquil in our mind-states.

Something happened in that room. The experience was profound in the sense that there were times during that movement period in which the external world fell away. There were just sensations revealing themselves, in an expansive sky-like awareness. It was as if the sensations of the body were immersed in an infinity pool—one of those gorgeous swimming pools that have the visual illusion of having no edges or boundaries to them. The brilliance of my sensory experience was like a gigantic, fizzing, carbonated drink bubbling and extending in all directions.

What was extraordinary was that while any meditation period is usually experienced as insular and private in its contemplation, my connection to my friend was tangible in the ineffable field of awareness. We had not planned to have any experience together in the retreat, but in that movement/walking session I felt a connection to a human being in ways that I could not have predicted. I was not experiencing this person in the room simply as a friend doing a concurrent period of movement; I was experiencing a simultaneously interwoven connection that felt embodied, psychological, and spiritual. I felt this living being not only as someone I knew, but as all forms of beings—as my sibling, my mother, my father, my child, acquaintances in my life with whom I had no strong bond, my adversary, my teacher, my ancestor, my descendant, all beings across all generations. In the movement meditation I traveled to a place beyond my understanding of space and time.

After the retreat was over my friend and I checked in with each other and found that we had experienced remarkably similar sensations, even though there was no intentional verbal or nonverbal communication between us during the retreat. Perhaps one interpretation is that the experience we had was *folie á deux*, which is the clinical term for two people becoming mentally imbalanced at the same time due to the same causes. Or maybe it was a reflection of the deep interrelatedness and feeling of unity still possible in the midst of the busy-ness and frenzy of our modern-day, impersonally technological world.

Even though our Western cultures often emphasize the individualistic aspiration to achieve awakening or enlightenment or awareness "on our own" or through our individual efforts, we are never actually alone in the world. Sometimes it takes getting as internally still as possible to viscerally feel that quality of interconnected existence.

We are never practicing alone, and we can have a profound influence on others around us.

Ajahn Mun was one of the preeminent teachers who revived the Thai monastic forest tradition during the early part of the twentieth century, and there is an endearing story about his gentle yet persuasive Dharma. When he was among the hill tribes in northern Thailand, a people who did not have any previous experience or knowledge of meditation, the tribe members saw the meditation master move with great deliberation and consideration, back and forth, up and down along the path on a hill above the village. The villagers began to follow him, and because of the narrow width of the path, they formed a natural line behind the teacher.

When Ajahn Mun reached the end of his path and turned around, he had the whole village in front of him. The people were concerned, thinking that the senior monk had lost something because he was moving so slowly with his eyes cast to the ground. They asked him, "What are you looking for, venerable teacher? Can we help you to find it?"

Ajahn Mun replied, "I'm looking for the Buddha in the heart. You can help me to find it by going up and down on your own paths looking for the Buddha." Thus that hill tribe began to meditate and practice the Dharma.

In downtown Oakland, California, at the East Bay Meditation Center, we had a less dramatic but still similar effect during our practice of movement meditation.

The first location where the EBMC made its home was on Broadway, one of the busiest streets leading toward downtown. Whether it was a weekend or weekday, there was always a lot of traffic on the sidewalks and in the road. At EBMC we don't always have the space to accommodate everyone to do movement or walking meditation inside the facility, so we do it on the sidewalk—moving on the pavement in a slow pace that supports mindfulness.

During some of these sessions I would go across the street and watch the period of movement. It is not as if life in Oakland stopped around us to accommodate us: there are always residents and other pedestrians moving along the busy sidewalks to their eventual destinations with the manifest intentions of getting to where they need to go—whether they are rushing home during the time we held evening classes or were part of the weekend bustle in the city. If one were to film the front of the center, one would always see a blur of movement in all directions—that is, until the practitioners exit the center to begin their period of mindful movement.

As the practitioners move with the same deliberation and attention that Ajahn Mun of Thailand taught to his villagers, the people at EBMC slowed down the world around them. The city blocks on either side of the center were busy with the fullness of urban energetic activity. But on the block of EBMC, people walking on the sidewalk would slow down or pause; even the cars in the road would decrease their speed. It was as if the mindfulness practice of the EBMC practitioners for just a few moments allowed the rest of the world to settle and calm.

It was fascinating to watch people who were rushing to get somewhere on the block before the center slow down and observe the people moving and walking in silence and mindfulness. There was inevitably some curiosity, whether skeptical or interested, about what was happening. People who were in such a rush also slowed themselves down, and even if they sped right back up on the next block past the center (as they most often did), there was a little more tranquility and calm on the blocks around the center. We could actually begin to feel the effect of mindfulness on the people around us, whether we knew them or not. This is a small step toward bridging the inner sense of stillness and peacefulness to the external world that needs it so greatly—and it is important.

Our path through our spiritual practice is incremental.

Every movement we make, every moment of mindfulness, strengthens more and more our ability to be present and to pay attention with an open mind and clear heart. The journey we undertake guided by the Dharma is a way of communicating with and developing a new relationship with the world. One of the deeply moving things I learned while practicing in Thailand is that before a temple is built, the monastic and the lay communities practice movement, walking, and silent meditation on the land—because of the belief that meditation practice both purifies the land and the people who will practice on the land. The purification happens when, through practice, a relationship is developed with the land with an intention to respect the earth, our ultimate spiritual home. Even beyond Buddhist meditation practice, this resonates with the deep-rooted earth-based practices that underlie all indigenous and cross-cultural spiritual traditions.

In Western culture, which is inclined to define and create a culture valuing material objects, one of the conventional relationships that we have with land is to own it. One of the assumptions behind the cultural message of the American Dream is that land, whether we own it or rent it, is property that can be possessed. The "dream" of the dominant culture since the days of European colonization of North America has been an aspiration or "right" to own a piece of the land around us.

As we are thrust into the environmental complexities of climate change, our deepening collective practice in community can support a realignment of priorities and a recollection—itself a quality of mindfulness—of not only what our true nature is but what our true relationship with the earth really is. What is our relationship with this earth beyond the narrow condition of ownership defined by economics and politics?

There is a saying attributed to Crazy Horse, chief and leader of the

Oglala Lakota peoples: "One does not sell the earth upon which people walk."

The Satipatthana Sutta, the discourse on the four foundations of mindfulness, supports a direct relationship to earth:

> A Noble One examines and reflects on this very body in whatever position it remains or is placed, as composed of the primary elements: There are in this body only the earth element, the water element, the fire element, and the air element.

The invitation here is to deconstruct the experience of the walking and movement meditation into the four primary elements universal in the material world. This concept of the four elements bridges spiritual traditions across numerous cultures and belief systems. In actual practice, we direct our awareness into the sensations of the earth element—the tactile qualities of solidity—as we touch and make contact with the ground as the foundation upon which we tread. The water element emerges in the changing nature of pressure and weight as the body moves with fluidity. The fire element manifests as the heat, energy, and exertion in the muscles and temperature of the skin and flesh. The element of air is expressed through the breath and the movement and vibration of the body through space. We are invited to re-experience our relationship to the earth by breaking it into its most basic components. The four elements make up a rich practice to apply in movement—even if the range is nuanced and subtle, like the movements within stillness.

As compelling as it is for our larger culture, as easy as it is to associate our experience with land as property, our relationship with land is so much broader than our market economy reveals.

Truly, we don't own land. We don't work land. We don't use land, and we don't even exploit land. We *are* land. We are the same elements of which the earth is composed. We do not move and walk *on* the earth; we *are* earth that moves and walks with the whole—regardless of the extent of our physical abilities. This is the interdependence and interrelatedness—the universality—to which all great spiritual traditions speak. This is the invitation of mindfulness, in its truly global sense, to feel the organicity of our lived experience with the organicity of the earth around us.

We begin to see that all the ideas of our small self occlude the expansiveness of what we call life.

We cannot control the journey into awakening together. We use the tools of individual and communal mindfulness, yet even so our journey may not turn out to be the one we thought we would be taking, or wished we were. It may take more patience, time, and resources than we think we have to offer. And while we may not be the ones to complete the journey, we can contribute vitally to its development because we each contribute something worthy to this life.

In the case of developing and evolving the practice community for people of color, it took innumerable contributions from practitioners, leaders, and teachers, both of color and white, at their varying levels of ability. Some continue to be involved after decades of perseverance. Some were able to commit their energies for a certain period of their lives and then had to withdraw. Some are only able to support from the sidelines.

All are indispensible in creating the totality of the movement forward to offering the Dharma to diverse communities in this modern age.

Movement and walking are often regarded as the method by which the practice of spiritual pilgrimage or journey is enacted. A pilgrimage is movement through space and time to honor and respect the archetypical sacred sites of a tradition.

Another way of looking at pilgrimage is to see it as not about the places we visit or the physical locations in the world but about the inner places of our life that we touch, move through, and are intimate with. In this sense, pilgrimage is not so much about how faith, confidence, and devotion motivate geographic travels but about how faith and confidence motivate movement in our lives and motivate our travels even farther down the Dharma path.

The pilgrimage is right here, right now.

Each time you sit, you're visiting a holy site. Each time you move through space, whether through walking or by other means, this is a place of sacred activity. Pilgrimage represents that yearning, that aspiration of the heart toward freedom, and it happens one movement, one step at a time. It's incremental.

Reverend Dr. Martin Luther King Jr. writes, "Take the first step in faith. You don't have to see the whole staircase. Just take the first step, and then the next."

This is the journey we are on, whether we move, walk, sit, or lay still. This is the pilgrimage; this is the movement both individually and as communities toward freedom. Our inner freedom does not depend on any external condition.

Each time we practice in activity or in stillness, we move closer to becoming aware of who we are in this life. With each moment of practice, we begin to shatter the glass ceilings that confine our self-image and self-worth, which the unconsciousness of the larger society and our own internalized messages of self-judgment have imposed on us.

Each move we take in our mindfulness practice is a move toward collective freedom.

15

Consciously Creating Community

Reverend Dr. Martin Luther King Jr. wrote, "Our goal is to create a beloved community and this will require a qualitative change in our souls as well as a quantitative change in our lives." In seeking to create a Beloved Community for all of us, how do we make the qualitative and quantitative changes necessary?

When establishing the East Bay Meditation Center, situated in the middle of the vibrant diversity of downtown Oakland, California, one of the aspects we considered most important as a foundation of the multicultural community we hoped to build was forming as diverse a board of directors as possible from the very beginning. EBMC renamed this governing group the "Leadership Sangha." The change was to enforce the underlying principle that governing is a practice of community—both being in community and building community. Governance is not simply a management forum to coordinate tasks and roles for particular outcomes. As an organizational resource, governance is instrumental in creating community as opposed to imposing decisions upon community. In order to create community, the governing group needed to be part of the community and also operate with the same principles and values as the community itself.

In the first years after we opened our doors, the Leadership Sangha was composed of an African American lesbian; a white upper-middle-class heterosexual man; an Asian American straight woman; a white, gender-neutral, queer-identified, large-bodied person; an Asian American queer gay man (me!); an African American heterosexual woman; an African American heterosexual man; and a white lesbian parent. We had three members with limitations or differences in abilities due to physical and medical conditions including multiple chemical sensitivities (a form of environmental illness). Our ages (from thirties to sixties), level of education (from high school to graduate degree), and economic classes (from working to privileged) varied. Thus, we were pretty successful at creating diversity in our governance that reflected the community at large.

How great! . . . in theory.

The reality is that we disagreed much more often than not. All the issues of identity came up, usually embedded in differences of opinion and conflicts. Of course our differences went quite deep. We frequently disagreed—even those of us who had friendships prior to our working together at EBMC. We had innumerable disputes that were sometimes facilitated and mediated, and sometimes we had to "get along" (or not) by ourselves. We accused each other of being petty or egotistical and even unethical.

I believe all of us wished we didn't have conflicts. We certainly didn't enjoy the conflicts we had. And in reality, many times we just didn't like each other, plain and simple. We wished we didn't have to deal with each other.

Yet all of these difficulties are part of the refuge in building community—so rather than splitting apart over our differences, we held the tension of our differences together.

We did our best to hold those tensions because we knew we were creating something much more important than anything based solely upon our individual preferences or beliefs. We had, and continue to have, an aspiration that the whole be so much greater than the sum of its parts. This is despite the frequent worry that, at times, we feared parts of our EBMC experience could implode or self-destruct.

Our collective journey, which invites us into both personal and communal liberation of our minds and hearts, is not an easy one. We each traverse our own personal places of unconsciousness and injury, and we also need to navigate the unseen aspects and wounding of our communities and cultures.

Community-building as a spiritual practice is not an easy or simple endeavor. It always takes longer than we would like. It always takes longer than we think it should, longer than we think is necessary, and longer than we have the patience for. It always is more complex with more contradictions than we think possible. It always goes through difficult relationships, dynamics of conflict, and seemingly unresolvable differences.

Yet ultimately, it is not about what we think or what we like, but how we are with each other in life, in relationship. How do we practice—getting together, making mistakes, causing harm, being frustrated, experiencing disappointment and even disillusionment—without giving up the aspiration of our beautiful and Beloved Communities, difficult, challenging, and complex as they may be?

Ajahn Chah was a Thai forest meditation master who established more monastic communities than most contemporary Buddhist leaders and teachers—about 140 at the time of his death in 1992. Regarding this (as told by Ajahn Amaro), Ajahn Chah said, "Well, it is easy for me to go and be alone and be the fierce ascetic off in the forest. What is difficult is to be with other people, to learn how to spend time with others."

Luang Por Tong, who was my preceptor and abbot at Wat Chom Tong, the temple where I ordained, told me, "Building community is like putting volcanic rocks into a millstone. The rocks grind against each other until they are smooth and beautiful." Volcanic rocks rubbing against each other may not sound like a pleasant thought with pleasant sensations—and veritably, it is not.

It took us time at EBMC to realize our own experience in the inevitable manifestation of Ajahn Chah's and Luang Por Tong's teachings—this process of the volcanic rocks grinding against each other to polish and purify the practice jewel of sangha and community. At EBMC, we were conscious, even before we obtained a physical space in which to meet, that we were going to address an unmet need in the Bay Area. We had the vision of serving diverse communities that had not been on the radar or recognized by mainstream meditation centers. EBMC's mission statement is:

> Founded in a celebration of diversity, the East Bay Meditation
> Center welcomes everyone seeking to end suffering and culti-
> vate happiness. Our mission is to foster liberation, personal and
> interpersonal healing, social action, and inclusive community-

building. We offer mindfulness practices and teachings on wisdom and compassion from Buddhist and other spiritual traditions. Rooted in our commitment to diversity, we operate with transparent democratic governance, generosity-based economics, and environmental sustainability.

I feel that this is a powerful statement—not least because it places diversity in the foremost position.

All the initial organizers of EBMC had their own experiences with the range of meditation centers in the Bay Area. We each brought what we learned and how we were motivated to do things differently. We found from our own experiences that inviting diverse communities to participate in something as intimate as a collective sacred space must be done with a deep commitment to creating the conditions for inclusivity to flourish. We knew from our previous experiences with other centers that when only the intention is expressed, when people offer only lip service to diversity by saying that the doors are open to everyone, inevitably, not everyone shows up—and not everyone stays.

At EBMC, we saw how other meditation centers were not able to bring the practice of mindful awareness into relevance for diverse communities. Because many of us had ourselves experienced the impact of cultural unconsciousness, we learned both from our own personal experiences and from those of the communities we are close to how to bring multicultural awareness and mindfulness into the creation of our Dharma community from its inception. From the very early stages of EBMC, inclusivity of cultures was the highest priority.

Most mainstream Western Dharma centers were created without priority given to multicultural involvement from their beginnings. The usual pattern is that mainstream communities become conscious and aware of the need for diversity through a series of injuries or offenses unwittingly committed by staff, management, or teachers that marginalize practitioners, or because they begin to recognize a pattern of one-time, nonrepeat visits to their centers among people of diverse backgrounds. The call to advocacy typically comes from someone from one of the diverse communities affected, rather than from within the leadership of the community itself—with a few exceptions. (I think of New York Insight, EBMC, and Flowering Lotus as among those few exceptions.)

Once awareness is triggered by an initial event, centers struggle to begin to implement the work to retrofit into the organization multicultural, anti-racist, and anti-oppressive consciousness, sensitivity, and behaviors. In this scenario, the work is not only about raising diversity consciousness but also about reconditioning the patterns of cultural norms and unconsciousness already developed over time into unconscious habits.

For an organization like EBMC, by placing the issues of inclusion front and center from the very beginning, the organization has been able to create diversity without having to additionally overcome the encumbrance of entrenched patterns of collective insensitivity or harm—although this has not been easy.

Initially, EBMC began as a series of conversations among experienced practitioners and teachers in the San Francisco East Bay area. There were about twenty people at the very first meeting during the winter of 2000 at the home of a white Dharma teacher. I was one of three people of color among the twenty participants—and I was unsure of whether I belonged. I didn't see the relevance of the project to my life, and at the time I had other things to do that were much more connected to diverse communities.

In fact, I didn't return after that first meeting until a new incarnation of the steering committee had begun to take shape.

Over sixty people rotated through the initial steering committee, from both communities of color and European American communities. The main stumbling block seemed to be diversity itself. It was encouraging that it was such a prominent issue, and yet it was an issue among the group that no amount of training or processing could resolve. Differing compositions and iterations of the original group(s) debated over and over again whether the center should be in Berkeley or Oakland—a geographic indication of the racial and cultural fault lines that divided people during that initial organizational period. There was a white middle-class community in Berkeley interested in this project and multiple communities of color who wanted EBMC to make its home in downtown Oakland. During that nascent phase of EBMC there were fundraising events and infrequent one-off events, but the community could never get beyond the stalemate of where the center should be located, and how diversity should be implemented.

It is interesting that only when most everyone had left or became frustrated or disinterested in the project did a new leadership composition begin to take form. When I was asked to re-engage with the project, there were three people of color and one white male ally who had done a lot of personal work in cultural awareness. That change in the makeup of the group was critical for movement to actually happen. All of a sudden there were no stalemates or impasses based on what mission the center would serve. There was no disagreement that the community had to be geographically centered in diverse communities for accessibility. Regardless of the differences we brought with our own identities, we were all clear about the aspiration and vision of the project to benefit diverse communities.

Even with the confluence of our visions, none of us presumed to know how our visions would land in the communities themselves. As practitioners we had all been involved with mainstream meditation centers built on the power of the charismatic leadership of a specific Dharma teacher. These centers often assume that they know what is best for the community at large. The attitude might be described as one of "build it and they will come." Such centers have a certain quality of imposition: they were conceived without discerning what the needs of the potential participating community actually were.

At EBMC, even before we looked for a physical space to call home, we gathered in several community meetings to gauge not only community interest but also what the needs of the interested communities were. The data gathered from those meetings indicated to us that a downtown Oakland location accessible by public transportation was paramount. In addition, a majority of respondents felt the importance and need for culturally specific events to create both safety and community. Even before we found a permanent space, we had pop-up events and classes for communities of color and the LGBTIQ communities.

We analyzed the demographics of our practitioner audience and looked at how to include diverse participation from the moment we opened our doors. We designed programs that met the specific needs of specific diverse communities, thereby making the events and the teachings directly relevant to people who walked in the door. There were consciously programmed events that were culturally specific for communities of color and LGBTIQ-SGL communities (*SGL* stands for "Same-Gender-Loving")—with whom we have come to use the affectionate name of "Alphabet Sangha." As a symbolic gesture, we hung the rainbow flag in the meditation hall even before we installed the Buddha statue. It was critically important to give diverse communities the experiential sense that they were not only included from the inception of EMBC but also co-creators in developing the center.

The Alphabet Sangha group meets on Tuesdays. The Thursday night PoC group provides a dedicated spiritual space for communities of color. Every Body/Every Mind on Sunday nights welcomes differently abled persons of any physical or mental capacity. And the Friday Maha Sangha Group serves everyone from all cultural communities who are interested in the Buddha's teachings.

In addition, we have groups for young people and teens, families, and practitioners in recovery from addiction, as well as other affinity groups we call Deep Refuge groups. These include groups for men of color, queer men of color, folks who identify as multiracial, and folks who identify with the queer leather communities.

Again, the deep exploration of practice through different identity groups is not the end of the path, the final goal—but for many practitioners the experience of identity can be a threshold, an invitation to walk through a doorway or gate into practice. And the continuing invitation is not to be attached to the "door" of identity. As we explore what is beyond the door of identity using our spiritual practice, we begin to directly enter a landscape of experience that is expansive and not dependent upon how we identify in our lives. That is where ultimate freedom lies for all of us.

This inclusion and awareness of diverse communities from the outset were critical to EMBC's development, mission, and success in creating a place where it was truly possible for multicultural communities to gather and practice. EBMC has been called the most diverse sangha on the planet.

Awareness of the need for diversity itself is not enough to make a diverse sangha happen. In order to truly create diversity, awareness must be followed by actions and behaviors that actualize the intentions of multiculturalism. Otherwise the efforts toward diversity can feel like always "fixing a problem" rather than composing an art form or weaving a tapestry of building community—bringing together and valuing the multiplicity of our differences and connections. When we start with multicultural awareness, multicultural mindfulness, we have the possibility to prevent further reinforcement of the patterns of cultural unconsciousness in the larger society that lead to so much harm and oppression.

Issues of diversity or the lack of diversity within mainstream Western meditation centers have deeply affected how the Dharma is experienced in the West for a long time, and it has been challenging for predominantly homogenous or monocultural Dharma communities to transform themselves into truly multicultural fellowships. This reflects the similar conditions and larger dynamics in our wider society when spaces, environments, or communities have been mainly focused on serving the needs of the dominant culture.

The hurdles in diversifying or retrofitting already-formed homogenous groups include, but are not limited to, elevating multicultural awareness; understanding the dynamics and impact of current and previous patterns of oppression; understanding and changing current practices that are discriminatory; initiating restorative rebuilding of trust and relationships due to previous injury or harm caused; dealing with resistance and denial of the importance and reality of diversity and culture; dismantling systems in place that keep white hetero-normative values and assumptions in control; progressively revealing layers of unexamined privilege and entitlements of members of the dominant culture; recalibrating power and authority that are not accountable and often hidden, which can reinforce unconscious privilege; developing tangible strategies of inclusivity across all levels of leadership and participation (including teachers and governance); and transforming attitudes and behaviors to recalibrate, value, and incorporate different cultural experiences in living together as a community.

It is no wonder that it is extremely difficult for any group to realign cultural values, norms, behaviors, and actions once they have formed and already been conditioned over time. The longer they have been conditioned with the norms of the dominant culture, the more challenging that process of change can be. As many predominantly European American–centric Western meditation communities have found, it is extremely difficult and frustrating to retrofit multicultural experience into a community that has already evolved and developed, conditioned by mainstream cultural values and patterns.

Once EBMC successfully invited in diverse communities, we realized that there would need to be progressive efforts to keep the environment safe enough for multicultural communities to unfold and flourish. In other words, we needed to follow up our invitations with actions that supported our vision for inclusive diversity. Very quickly in its development, EBMC designed a registration system that could balance the demographic numbers of our diverse communities in the meditation hall for any one event. We found that the single most dramatic factor in creating a welcoming and inclusive space is to have a large portion of the participating audience be diverse from the beginning. This means that our goal for most, if not all, of our events was to create a space in which 40 to 50 percent of participants were from communities of color. This is a structural and institutional method that EBMC has used to support the full participation of communities that have not received previous attention or care. The implicit message is that diverse communities are equally valued on an equal playing field, regardless of the external conditions of our society, which still promotes disparity and inequity. And it communicates that EBMC is willing to go against the presumed mainstream norm that "more is better." More people in the space brings in more income and more visibility, but this is not the highest priority for EBMC; the highest priority is the quality of diverse cultural experience.

EBMC's demographic consistency deeply contrasts what one experiences at mainstream meditation centers, where most of the time only a handful or less of people of color appear in a room full of European

Americans. This is still the standard for most of our Western Buddhist communities, giving further credence to Reverend Dr. Martin Luther King Jr.'s observation of more than half a century ago that the most segregated hour in North American life takes place in our places of worship.

Recalibrating the racial and cultural demographics of the meditation hall gives rise to an opportunity for increased collective mindfulness simply by changing the usual pattern of our social interactions. When the dominant European American pattern is reversed and when there are at least equal or more people of color in the room, the cultural, social, and interactional dynamic within the group changes. As soon as people walk in the room like this, whether they are European American or a person of color, there is a sense that things are not business-as-usual. Regardless of whether anyone has gone through diversity training or multicultural education or cultural competency work, an incipient awareness is heightened. People are more mindful that things are different—and this is not a bad thing. People have the opportunity to be more attentive of what they say, what they do, how much space, time, energy, and attention they take up, and how they impact others.

This is certainly not a guarantee that harm will not take place. Just because the cultural balance in the room is different does not mean that there is enough awareness or skill to prevent racism, injury, or unconscious privilege from arising. Realigning the demographics of the room does not preempt cultural training and education, but it does provide an opportunity to be experientially aware in the moment of multicultural experience, which likely would not occur in a predominantly white space. Changing the demographics can provide a safer space for marginalized communities. It also may provide a counterbalance to the assumption or imposition of mainstream cultural values onto different groups who hold diverse norms, opinions, and feelings emerging from their different lives.

The residential retreats I mentioned in chapter 6, which were held over the Martin Luther King Jr. holiday weekend, are another example of this conscious method to shift the demographics of meditation experiences. Those residential retreats also used a registration system to create a balance in the room with at least 40 percent people of color, to gather needed additional financial support for the participation of diverse communities, to tailor outreach and marketing of the events, and to train staff to be able to meet the needs of diverse communities.

Efforts were then made to build upon what we learned, and a mainstream meditation community offered a ten-day residential retreat in the deserts of Southern California with the theme of "Sacred Tenderness: Exploring the Energies of Our Heart." Some thought we would not be able to fill all 140 registration slots with mixed demographics for such a lengthy residential retreat (always an underlying organizational business concern for meditation centers) and that it might lead to a financial loss. And yet, with a diverse teaching team and outreach to diverse communities, we were able to keep the demographic ratio of the meditation hall at 40 percent from communities of color, all the while filling the retreat with an additional waiting list of over 150 people. Evaluation surveys are usually emailed to participants when they return home at the end of the retreat. This retreat received the highest survey return rate of any previous retreat ever done. The return was 66 percent with 100 percent of those returned surveys commenting favorably about the intentional diversity of the retreat.

It is possible to hold inclusive and culturally diversified retreats.

They take focused intention and concentrated attention to learn what communities need in order to feel welcomed. One possible next stage of development for these residential retreats will be to create an entire teaching team composed of teachers of color who will offer teachings at a mainstream retreat to which all communities are invited to attend. It has taken us this much time in the history of Western Insight Meditation to develop and nurture enough teachers of color to offer this variation of demographics on a teaching team.

Ultimately, it's important to recall that diversity and inclusivity are not just to benefit communities of color; they are illuminating, liberating, and awakening for the mainstream audience as well. They are fundamental to the very essence and existence of the Dharma.

The difference between EBMC and mainstream meditation organizations is the consistency of the learning curves. While the combined efforts for the Sacred Tenderness retreat produced wonderful practice opportunities for that specific ten-day retreat, it takes prolonged and ongoing efforts over time to change the demographics of the meditation hall in the long run. Unless it is a consistent priority that has allocated resources and attention, the demographics will default quickly back to the mainstream homogeneity that is the unconscious norm.

The Sacred Tenderness retreat has not been scheduled again for a variety of organizational reasons. Nonetheless, that retreat has indicated what could be possible if only efforts were sustained consistently as a priority over time.

EBMC also used additional strategies to work toward creating truly inclusive communities. We remove as many financial barriers as we can to accessing any of the teachings and dedicate as many resources as possible to offering teachings to diverse communities. In Buddhist practice we use the Pali word *dana* to refer to the spiritual practice of generous giving. When the Buddha taught in a new geographic region, he actually shared the teachings of generous giving as one of his first teachings, because he knew that if the teachings were not supported by the community they served, the Dharma would be unable to survive or continue into the future.

Over the past two and a half millennia the Buddha's teachings have survived migrations across continents, across cultures, across oceans, all through generations of practitioners generously supporting the momentum of the teachings as they were preserved and passed to each successive generation. Generous giving is not only a beautiful teaching, it is an essential teaching for the survival of the Dharma into the future.

In the current status of Dharma in the West, it is still not certain that an organization-wide, all-*dana*, all-donation–based economic model is sustainable amid the instabilities and competing demands of our market economy. However, we have found that generosity toward diverse communities does inspire participation from those communities. The removal of financial barriers of cost, fee, and price from events is very relevant to multicultural communities because it allows them full access to the teachings. It really welcomes everyone through the doors of the Dharma to experience how the teachings can be meaningful for their lives and their paths toward happiness. This is the direct impact of generous actions toward inclusive collectivity.

Through these and other simultaneous strategies, EBMC has been extremely successful at attracting diverse communities and people into our sangha. EBMC also found that we could not rest on the laurels of any past efforts. Creating a space where people can come does not necessarily mean that it is a space in which people will *stay*. It is a deepening of collective mindfulness and spiritual practice not only to invite people through the doors but also to build community together. EBMC explores what would allow people who may have very diverse backgrounds to invest in practicing and creating spiritual community together. We knew from experience that when differences arrive in the room, the volcanic rocks begin to rub against each other.

In many of EBMC's events, not unlike other Dharma communities, we have Dharma discussions as part of a class or daylong event. We noticed immediately that people who were from the dominant culture of white, male, hetero- and gender-normative backgrounds generally dominated the interactions in all forms of communication: one-on-one dyads, sharing in small groups, and discussions in larger group as a whole. The participation of folks from more diverse backgrounds tended to be quiet and passive, with nonverbal cues of restlessness, distraction, even departure from the event. Frequently we would get feedback from folks after the fact through event evaluations that there was no "space" for their participation, and that others "took up all the airtime."

We realized that one of the skill sets and practices that we needed to offer in order to maintain, sustain, and grow true participation of multicultural communities was the experience of relational, respectful communication. Often, not only do cultural significance and values get expressed through verbal and nonverbal interpersonal and group communications, but a community's relationship to other communities also gets expressed. Cultural norms of assertiveness or humility, competition or sharing, providing answers or providing support, and even dominance and marginalization can be expressed and reinforced over and over again through how we communicate, as well as through what we communicate in our content.

When diverse communities come together, we bring all those relationships into our interactions. Unless there is an intentional awareness aimed at developing skills together in communication, things may default to patterns favoring the dominant culture. This default serves to continue the experience of marginalization for nondominant groups. Voices that are the loudest are usually the ones that will be heard. Voices that express themselves indirectly will usually not be given the time to be fully understood. In order to prevent this, EBMC works with a set of Agreements for Multicultural Interactions to improve and build skills for the members of all our communities so they can live together. These agreements appear in Appendix 3 at the back of the book.

Two EBMC Dharma teachers, Kitsy Schoen and Mushim Ikeda, took a set of multicultural communication guidelines from Visions, Inc.—a consulting group long known for its demonstrated and distinguished expertise in diversity and inclusion work—and modified them for their teachings in EBMC's multicultural, spiritual, and Dharma context. Over time, because of the demonstrated effectiveness of these agreements in creating safer spaces and in developing relationships among multicultural individuals and groups, these agreements have been expanded from use in solely teaching events to their ongoing use in organizational work, committee meetings, and interactions with communities at large—and they have been woven into the fabric of EBMC culture and support the continued growth of multicultural participation in the evolution of our entire community.

The creation of community is an act of consciousness and an actualized awareness of the fact that we ourselves are not designed to walk this spiritual path alone.

Our Western mentality is often inclined toward individualism and the personal goal of healing or attainment of some achievement, whether spiritual or material. This can produce the belief that we should be able to awaken on our own, that we would awaken on our own given the right conditions, and that if we do not awaken on our own, something is wrong or broken with the teachings, the teacher, or ourselves.

Yet the teachings of community and sangha invite us into the experience that not only are we not supposed to do this alone but actually we cannot do this alone.

We can only awaken within the compassionate arms of our communities together, in solidarity.

For Reflection

As you reflect and sit with the Multicultural Agreements from EBMC, how do they feel to you as a whole? Are they supportive? Is there any resistance from your inner experience? Is there any resistance that you can imagine coming from your community or organization?

Go through the agreements, and feel which ones are easy for you to commit to, both individually and as a group (whatever your group or community experience might be). Which ones are difficult to commit to on an ongoing basis?

Can you imagine not being able to fulfill one or more of the agreements? How does that feel? What might your response to that inability be?

What are other methods or practices that you would use to consciously create community?

16

Breaking Together

B EING SKILLED at inviting diverse people through the door and build-ing skills to be in relationship with each other are initial steps to creating a larger sense of community. "Living together" in community is not simple. Complex needs inherently emerge, converge, and even diverge when diverse communities assemble.

One of the first places this becomes apparent is in the demographic composition of teachers in any community. Again, part of making a center accessible to diverse communities is to reflect and model those communities and their identities in those who assume the teaching role. To see oneself reflected in and reflecting the teachings and teachers is a powerful experiential validation that allows practitioners to feel that they belong in this practice and community.

When East Bay Meditation Center first opened, many white Dharma teachers from mainstream Dharma communities were interested in teaching at EBMC because of the opportunity to share with and teach communities with whom they had previously been unable to interact. Some of them were quite well known and would surely have drawn high numbers of attendees. Yet it became very clear as we struggled to weigh the needs of the community with the interests of the teachers that the needs of the community had to be paramount. Ultimately, we concluded that the risk was too great that promoting events with mainstream teach-ers who had no experience teaching in multicultural settings would alienate our diverse communities and diminish the sense of trust they were developing with EBMC.

Training teachers, especially infrequent guest teachers, is a challeng-ing task. The programming policy that was developed was that white teachers new to EBMC are usually paired with teachers of color, even when that was not in the original proposal for the teaching event. This inevitably caused some tension among experienced white teachers who were accustomed to being accommodated due to their experience and popularity. It was an awkward situation. It was also an important instance of recalibrating the privilege associated with dominant cultural teachings to bring them more into alignment with the needs of diverse communities.

Those white teachers who have engaged with EBMC's policies have had the opportunity not only to serve diverse communities with whom they may not have had frequent contact but also to avail themselves of the chance to teach and learn from a place of cultural humility. Others withdrew their interest in teaching at EBMC or expressed their continuing disappointment that EBMC did not treat them with the same deference other centers gave them. Some prominent white teachers, when asked to co-teach with a teacher of color, simply never responded to EBMC. Some expressed that their feelings were hurt in the process of defining our communities' needs.

The needs of one community may not be congruent with the needs of another. This always promises to be complex.

The level of complexity increases when the needs of one community are not only incongruent with the needs of another but may even harm them. Women may experience recalibrating the male-gendered language that exists within very masculine-dominated traditional Buddhist texts as a healthy realignment and healing change, but those who do not identify along binary male-female cisgender lives may continue to feel invalidated by even this alternate language. It must not be just the responsibility of gender-queer folks by themselves to connect the dots between gendered experience and gender-nonconforming identities. We must all be responsible for holding the complexity of the issue. Just as for any who have a marginalized cultural experience, it is not the sole responsibility of the marginalized community to translate dominant cultural experience into their own, especially when all the resources and attention are usually focused on supporting the dominant view. The structural question for the meditation center was how to provide access to the teachings, which in this case meant creating the language of accessibility for nongendered, inclusive communication, and making it the norm for community gatherings.

Another example of the complexity that faces diverse communities are the medical- and physical-based needs for a fragrance-free space on the part of those who experience multiple chemical sensitivities (MCS) and environmental illness (EI) and how those needs may conflict with the needs of diverse cultural communities who use fragrance and different scents as a form of cultural expression and identity. The National Academy of Sciences estimates that up to 15 percent of the general American population is affected by chemical sensitivity. The same study shows that 13.2 percent of MCS/EI-affected folks identify as African American and 5.3 percent as Latinx—and it is often the white population who are more likely to speak out about being impacted by this medical condition.

When the EBMC community was in its second year, I taught a daylong retreat registered to full capacity. Even before the retreat had begun, it was clear that there was little room in which to navigate the physical space. The retreat manager and I were attempting to protect pathway and corridor space to ensure access for people with physical limitations or those using wheelchairs to allow the broadest access of the space to all communities.

As I was turning to begin the retreat, a white woman, similar to me in age, asked for my attention. She shared that whenever she went to EBMC she either had to move or leave the space because even though we had a fragrance-free policy, the space was not fragrance-free. She was always the one who had to accommodate others by moving or removing herself. It was painful to hear about her experience and distress, and it was painful to hear her say in the end, while pointing at a group of young women of color, "It feels like you are choosing them over me!"

The pain in that short exchange emerged from the complexity of not only different but often contradictory needs that arise when communities are truly diverse. There were, of course, other folks who had a perspective opposite to that of the woman above. This group of people was frustrated because they did not understand EBMC's fragrance-free policy, which they felt excluded them as folks of color. They felt that people with MCS should not force others to change and they should practice in the privacy of their own homes if they were reactive to or averse to the center. Some people identified their use of scents as a spiritual expression and felt that they were being asked to conform to the ways of other cultures.

Part of the skill of creating truly inclusive communities is bridging the false splits between us. By taking care of all of our collective physical and medical needs, we take care of something very basic. We know that we will be included and not forgotten when we are physically limited or restricted—as we all will be at some time in our lives. By acknowledging the cultural component fully, we can acknowledge that medical necessities know no cultural boundaries and that diverse communities are just as impacted by environmental illness as other mainstream communities are.

Every EBMC event now announces the importance of physical accessibility and maintaining a fragrance-free space, even in weekly culturally specific practice groups. Every community realizes that other communities might have needs that are different than their own and that all of them need respect in order for us to be inclusive together.

Where a community is most vulnerable, tender, even injured is where that community might need the most attention and care. And if our vulnerabilities within different communities are also different from each other, how can we support each other's vulnerabilities where we might feel some strength? How can we watch each other's backs together through the injuries of life? My dear friend, colleague, and teacher Sylvia Boorstein when teaching that we are all vulnerable and prone to injury, then asks, "What if we and all the world were able to be with our vulnerabilities? How would we live our lives with each other? How would we relate to each other?" The answer can only be with tenderness and loving awareness.

We know that raising the collective consciousness of multiple communities (and therefore multiple worldviews) with respect to complex issues cannot be done overnight, even if our needs feel like they must be immediately met. Like any educational process, raising consciousness occurs over time, over the span a community lives together.

In the first decade of EBMC's existence, the vision and mission of inclusivity have broadened so that the communities toward which inclusivity is directed are not limited and few but expansive and multiple. Community-based inclusivity is the template with which we learn to live with all beings with tenderness and openness, in all directions of our identity and experience.

In the unconsciousness of our larger culture, when differences become strong, the predominant conditioned pattern is to fragment and scatter into our respective corners, spaces of comfort, familiarity, and safety, quickly polarizing into adversarial stances. And it's worth noting that this dynamic is, ultimately, the one through which all wars are begun. It is so easy in the face of both our individual and collective unconsciousness to believe that the "problem" or source of the conflict is with the other person or other group, and not with "me" or "us." However, the spiritual practice of community awareness is to instead ask, "How do we stay in the room and in relationship with each other regardless of what arises, rather than split apart?"

What would it be like, even amid all the complexity, even in the face of injuries, even in the face of harm, to break *together* rather than break apart? Could we stay together even as we experience our differences and the hurts caused by them? What would it be like to hold our hearts open toward the injuries caused by our seeming adversaries as best we can? How do we stay in the room with each other, stay in relationship with each other, even when the unconscious, reactive mind—or even the conscious one—wants things to be different from the way they are? We have all been guided, whether by the formal teachings or our own intuition, to know that there is a higher place to which we all could go. We may not have the skills yet, nor the awareness, nor even the kindness, but those can gradually come if we have the intention of not leaving the room and of not leaving the relationship.

In 1964, Jean Vanier, a French Canadian Catholic theologian and humanitarian, founded L'Arche, an international association of communities supporting people with developmental disabilities and those who assist them throughout more than thirty-five countries. He also has a most elegant passage describing community. He says that "Community

reaches its height in celebration and its heart in forgiveness. Community is the place of forgiveness." In this way, community becomes the
container and sacred space for relationships to occur in both happiness
and pain. Moreover, remaining in community is an ongoing process and
action involving all our personal and collective joys and sorrows. This is
the broadest scope of community and also its deepest potential—that
community is possible no matter what the conditions are, because none
of us lives this life alone.

In July 1962, during one of the times that Reverend Dr. Martin Luther
King Jr. was imprisoned, he used that time to refine one of his most powerful sermons—"Loving Your Enemies"—and speaks to the forgiveness
that is continually asked of us when creating relationship and community, even with harms of such a scale that we might apply to them the
label "evil":

> First, we must develop and maintain the capacity to forgive.
> He who is devoid of the power to forgive is devoid of the power
> to love. . . . Forgiveness does not mean ignoring what has been
> done or putting a false label on an evil act. It means, rather, that
> the evil act no longer remains as a barrier to the relationship.

Without the ability to be in relationship, without the capacity to live
together in both harmony and disharmony, we do not have the chance to
live fully into our potential as social and relatable living beings—which
is to say we do not have community.

The Harvard Grant Study, begun in 1938, is one of the longest-running
longitudinal research studies of the medical and psychological profiles
of a human life. One of the core subjects of inquiry in the study is the
question of what creates happiness throughout our lives, and how that
relates to what we hold as valuable. All the data and information the
study has collected thus far indicates that by far the strongest predic-
tor of happiness is the ability to be in strong and caring relationships.
Moreover, in addition to being a predictive indicator of psychological
fulfillment, it is also one of longevity and physical health. In our very

bodies, hearts, and minds we are programmed to be in relationship and community together.

Breaking together means, when community gets tough, we can feel how much difficulty, pain, and suffering there is in the community. We break together because we all know what suffering feels like. We break together because none of us wishes to add one more drop of suffering to this world that already suffers so greatly. And we break together to continue, from the sum of our individual selves, to create a larger whole that all of us can be a part of and contribute to—a larger whole whose only destiny is evolution, becoming ever more fully human.

In this way, we aspire toward freedom in the midst of the many forms of suffering, in the midst of the first noble truth. We may not be able to become fully awake in this lifetime. We may not be able to create a perfect, enlightened world in this lifetime. But we *will* create a better world now when we honor the diversity of our differences, tend, care, and restore ourselves when injury and harm are inflicted, and humbly bridge and connect across our irreconcilable perspectives.

Peace begins with these efforts of dialogue, kindness, and staying in relationship—when we are able to break together, when we are able to shift our consciousness and live in our differences together, and when we are able to awaken together.

When we work with people who hold different views and come from different life experiences, change often takes longer than we think it should, longer than we think is necessary—and includes more contradictions than we would like to deal with. Most of all the work of creating community is not about what we think or what we prefer; it is about how we treat one another and *how we are with each other*.

There have been substantial strides made, including twenty-plus years of retreats for communities of color within the Insight Meditation community, increased participation in multi-year Dharma study programs by diverse communities, and the current efforts to empower people of color into full residential teaching status and positions of spiritual leadership. However, individual leaders and teachers of color still do much of the work, unsupported as yet by any ongoing organizational structure to continue moving the effort into future generations of practitioners and communities. When people of color step back or take a break, the collective conditioning often "rubber-bands" back into its former unconsciousness.

Sometimes it seems that the collective dominant cultural experience often cannot absorb or retain what was learned from the interaction with multicultural communities. The conversations and negotiations for a leadership training program for teachers of color have taken almost four years to debate, argue over, and negotiate. Something that seems to be such an assumed benefit, given the explicit need for diverse leadership in all communities, was frustratingly difficult to create within existing systems still enmeshed in unconscious patterns and resistance.

People ask me why diverse communities don't just do it "on our own." "Just train your own teachers," we're told. "You don't need the mainstream organizations."

It may be that this is sometimes what is needed, at least as one option for teacher empowerment and spiritual leadership. And I don't believe that diverse communities do not benefit from mainstream ones, and I certainly do not believe that mainstream communities do not need diversity. We need each other to continue to bridge our collective places of unconsciousness, the voids of our disagreements, and our inabilities to resolve conflict. It takes all of us to see the whole picture.

As another example, despite the multiple differences and conflicts and injuries that have occurred among us at EBMC, as they inevitably do, we have created an incredibly beautiful and so far unique center for practice communities. Harm and transgression still occur, but by going through the suffering together over and over again, we actually grow more skilled at not only getting through suffering but living together.

Whether it is through the connective practices of forgiveness, or of working for restorative justice, or of engaging in anti-oppression awareness and skills development, we break through the judgments of thinking that we cannot do this, or that we are not good enough to deserve this, or that we do not have enough resources to create this. And we do it by living our diverse lives with mindfulness and kindness, for ourselves and for others, and for awakening together.

Breaking together means not pushing conflict away for some hoped-for, more pleasant, more peaceful experience that is not happening in the present moment—or pushing conflict away to be dealt with by some other group. Breaking together with conflict is the process by which we create peace. When we break together and live relationally with conflict, resolved or not, we create peace. We must continually call ourselves back to our higher aspiration of breaking together in order to transform our world together.

For Reflection

When have you felt tensions in your community?

How do the tensions feel in your body? How do the tensions express themselves in the collective experience? What are the feelings of conflict or disagreement? What range of feelings and experiences in the community can you sense?

By what methods is it possible to hold such tensions with awareness and compassion?

How do you navigate through the complexities? Does the community go around or bypass any of the issues? How does the organization become as aware as it can be to all the tensions involved? Are as many of the differing needs as possible taken care of enough? If so, how is that accomplished?

17

Supported on Each Other's Shoulders

MY OWN INVOLVEMENT in the issues of race, culture, and diversity in Dharma practice emerged from my own life experiences and struggles—and from the meaning that such experiences with identity and culture have given me. These meanings are also the reasons I became a social worker, activist, psychotherapist, and diversity change agent. Such reasons are not unlike the reasons any of us get involved with work we feel to be worthy in the world—one feels that it is beneficial and fulfilling to be of service, but it also touches and deeply resonates within our own hearts and lives.

We are not disconnected from our own histories and what we have gone through, and our lives are not only about ourselves or about our own experiences. I have a sense, now more than ever, that my work, my livelihood, and my teaching do not emerge solely out of my own efforts for personal development. I am able to do what I do because the ground has been broken before me by practitioners and leaders who had their own concerns and their felt need to diversify and have more inclusive Dharma communities. Cultural transformation of a community is no small task and always requires the many, more so than the efforts of individuals. In this chapter, I want to offer some of the history of this work as it took place at Spirit Rock Meditation Center in northern California, in the hopes that knowing our efforts and struggles will be of value elsewhere and in the future.

We all are supported by and stand upon each other's shoulders to move the work to higher and higher levels of awareness, multicultural mindfulness, and actualization of inclusivity. We have as our foundation the efforts of those who have come before us—the work of those who, over time, have made contributions and have left behind their work, communities, and practices. And, of course, we have as support all our peers and allies who continue expanding the Dharma into broader and broader cultural arenas.

Working at a time when there was minimal collective and organizational awareness among Western Insight Meditation communities, some practitioners and teachers were pioneers in recognizing the priority of bringing multicultural awareness to how the Dharma is offered. From the early daylong retreats for people of color in the 1990s organized by Ralph Steele, Michele Benzamin-Miki, Margarita Loinaz, Marlena Willis, and Marlene Jones to the formation of the Interracial Buddhist Council (involving Ralph, Marlena, Marlene, Linda Velarde, Lewis Woods, Jack Kornfield, and Julie Wester), these leaders and the events they organized repudiated the prevailing dominant cultural belief that meditation and Dharma practice are not of interest to diverse communities.

As the Interracial Buddhist Council transformed into the first iteration of several groups working on diversity (with Marlene Jones as its first chairperson) over the next two decades, pressure grew on the mainstream meditation community to turn its attention toward cultural experiences outside of the dominant white culture. By 1999—with Marlene and Margarita forming the first sitting group for women of color in Marin County, with Ralph obtaining foundation grants for several of the first residential retreats for people of color in different meditation centers, and with myself having initiated a scholarship program for practitioners of color—all these efforts began to support further residential practice for people of color. It takes a collective effort from many directions to create conditions that change the unconscious assumption that all the retreats that had been conducted to date were truly welcoming of all communities.

But the work of diversifying Western Dharma was only just beginning.

When I began practicing in Western white Dharma communities, it was challenging to experience the seemingly small yet impactful injuries and exclusion that I felt. It did not help for me to be asked within Dharma communities questions that were insensitive, at best: "What Asian country do you come from?" "Why do you come here as opposed to the Chinese temple in San Francisco?" "Oh yes, we have been to China—it is just so *dirty* there, don't you think?" The brilliantly incisive comedienne Margaret Cho shares on her album *Revolution*, "Living as a minority in America is like dying of a thousand paper cuts." That is the toll that marginalization and microaggressions have upon the lives of people in diverse communities.

Because of those kinds of microaggressions, though I never doubted the teachings, I spent more than a few years doubting the community. I not only questioned whether I belonged, I also questioned the extent to which people were truly practicing mindfulness if such remarks were being made—even with harmless intentions.

A spiritual community can't help but reflect the pain and suffering of the external world's racism, discrimination, and unconscious privilege. I decided that if nothing was exempt from mindfulness and spiritual practice, then I would also make this my awareness practice: to bring a reflective observation and compassionate attention to these experiences, rather than only wanting the moment to be different than it was. But at that stage in my practice there were no teachers who could offer guidance around this.

I did the best I could to stay with the physical sensations in their totality, to observe my judgments without judging them any further and feeding them, to try to open to the experience of "other" or even "oppressor" with the compassion of knowing that they too were imperfect beings on this human plane of existence, and to experiment with letting go. Practicing in this way is a component of forgiveness that helps restore interrelatedness.

From that internal noticing, I began simply by using the most basic tools of grassroots community-building. I wrote letters that expressed my experience and advocated for the unmet needs of different communities. The letters went mainly to the board of directors—even though I was still on the periphery of the community and didn't know any of the board members personally. I did know that shifting organizational attitudes needed the inclusion of governing and managing groups. After several letters, I heard from someone that one of the board members had said, "If I receive another letter from Larry Yang, I will leave the board."

I knew from that comment that I wasn't getting through. I couldn't discern whether I was failing due to my own lack of skill at expressing myself in a way that white people could hear or because the external unconsciousness was so intransigent and defended that it was simply overpowering the gravity of the issue.

For my practice, I saw this as the internal and external mindfulness practice articulated in the Satipatthana Sutta showing up in the complexity of community in general, and even in the complexity of *spiritual* community in particular. Organizational change agents know that transformation of an organization can happen due to work on the inside of the organization (internal change) or pressures coming from outside the organization (external). It usually takes both.

In order to change the deep conditioning of an organization, one must know how that organization operates. In order to change the rules of a game, one first needs to know the rules. There is a dance between external forces of change (like my letters to the board) and internal ones (like working to become a board member). A sort of blindness can occur when one is on the inside all the time, when an organization is solely self-referential to the exclusion of the communities around it—just as an individual can get caught in self-preoccupation to the exclusion of other people around them. And so I began participating actively in different committees that were exploring how to fulfill multicultural needs within the Sangha.

After two years, an overarching diversity initiative was crafted at Spirit Rock that got approved by the circle of Dharma teachers as well as the circle of board governance. The document had around twenty authors. Fifteen years later, it is still relevant to our present conditions. It states in part:

> Our purpose is to ensure [this community] is accessible and welcoming to all people who wish to participate in the sangha regardless of ethnic origin, race, cultural background, socioeconomic class, age, gender, sexual orientation, or physical ability. Our purpose is to awaken and sustain an engaged exploration into the many levels of seen and unseen separa-

tion among [this] community using the fundamental ground-
ing of our Dharma practice.

Separation occurs in innumerable forms, however in North
American society a most difficult and deeply profound wound
is that of race. We have embraced the following priorities: (1) to
address the separation in regards to race with compassionate
honesty and diligent effort and (2) to cultivate attitudes, processes, and methods by which to develop freedom and healing
from the *dukkha* of racism and oppression.

The organizational time and energy required to maintain the intentions of this first Diversity Initiative are enormous. Over the next fifteen
years, the Diversity Council went through three cycles of formation and
involved almost thirty people of color and over twenty "white allies" with
varying lengths of tenure.*

It was and still is a collective effort because the organizational change
is so much larger than any of our individual intentions or efforts. Among
other things, the current council has worked on and successfully passed
a Spirit Rock community-wide Diversity, Equity, and Inclusion Policy as
an update to the Diversity Initiative of a decade and a half ago. Diversity
and inclusivity is a living process that changes and morphs as the communities around the efforts do.

And yet, thus far, only four white Dharma teachers have participated
for any length of time in these diversity working groups over fifteen
to twenty years. The level of enthusiasm from spiritual leadership has
always been noticeable, but even that absence has not prevented change
and progress from happening.

Over the last decade, there were efforts to expand diverse programming and retreats to communities of color and other marginalized

---

*The term "white allies" refers to people who self-identify as white or European Amer-
ican and who make tangible, ongoing efforts to involve themselves in anti-racism and
transformation of oppression within the larger culture. They do their own internal work
and support the external work with communities of color and other white allies. The
most effective allies are involved on issues for communities of color as much as people
of color are.

groups, like the LGBTIQ communities. For the first six years of retreats for people of color, attendance was always regarded as low and economically unsustainable. However, there were indications that the audience was available if only the right conditions could be created.

In 2002, Marlene Jones coordinated the groundbreaking African American Dharma retreat, and conference people still mention it as a defining experience with teachers such as Rachel Bagby, Thulani Davis, Gaylon Ferguson, Joseph Jarman, George Mumford, Ralph Steele, Sala Steinbach, Bhante Suhita Dharma, Alice Walker, angel Kyodo williams, Jan Willis, and Lewis Woods. The retreat was oversubscribed and filled to capacity—clearly there was an audience for the teachings.

In 2004, Mushim Ikeda, Michele Benzamin-Miki, and I led the Asian American retreat and conference including an equally diverse array of teachers: Arawana Hayashi, Ryo Imamura, Tenzin Kacho, Jakusho Kwong, Kamala Masters, Minh Thien, Mayumi Oda, Rina Sircar, and Viveka Chen.

After teaching in 2005, my colleague and dear friend Gina Sharpe, the guiding teacher from New York Insight for its first twenty years, and I proposed and advocated that the PoC retreats become completely donation-based to eliminate any financial barriers to participation. We proposed this because we realized the costs and fees for residential retreats were obstacles to access for many people of color as well as people from working-class communities, making retreat practice basically into a luxury experience. Rather than the "Middle Way," high-fee-based retreat centers are referred to facetiously as practicing the "Upper-Middle Way."

The first resistance Gina and I met, of course, was the inability or unwillingness of the organization to raise the needed funds to support the initiative. So Gina and I raised the funds from private donors. Even this did not solve the problem because the pledged funds were initially turned down by the organization on the basis that "conditional-use funds" were unacceptable and set a poor precedent in fundraising. We wondered if similar funding would have been turned down if it had been for mainstream programming for "everyone." Eventually though, the center conceded and accepted funds dedicated to communities of color. The experience was an early hint that although the public stance was that diversity was "a good idea," the actions needed to accomplish change would always prove to be a complex struggle.

The registration for the next PoC retreat subsequently went from less than half full to long waiting lists, with scores of practitioners of color eager to gain experience in the Dharma. This turnaround was a benchmark in programming and outreach to diverse communities, but it was not an obvious solution to the mainstream organization. This is yet another part of the collective unconsciousness that needed to be questioned—requiring awareness, discussion, education, and subsequent realignment.

In the years after the approval of the Diversity Initiative, the Diversity Council began to meet with the teaching and governing groups to develop relationships and multicultural training programs in order to elevate the practice of awareness into the realm of culture and diversity, thus expanding the organization's experience in multicultural mindfulness. The need was not only to develop awareness but to bridge education and intention to tangible actions, behaviors, policies, and programs in which diversity would be a lived experience, not just a hoped-for ideal. In other words, we needed to organizationally walk the talk.

Organizational learning, like mindfulness practice, needs incrementally structured training. Like the capacity to return to the breath or physical sensations, the capacity to return to the intentions and issues of diversity requires training. And like any aspect of the mindfulness practice, it is so easy to grow distracted from, frustrated with, or averse to the training itself.

Over the years, there were several diversity trainings offered by seasoned professionals and experienced practitioners within the Sangha. Despite best intentions, the patterns of resistance arose as extremely defensive expressions. We heard things like, "This doesn't have relevance to my community"; "The trainers are not Dharma practitioners, they don't know where we are coming from or who we are"; "I was trauma- tized by the last diversity training"; or "There was so much anger in the room; that was so unskillful and unbeneficial and not about what the Dharma really is."

Unfortunately, collective resistance such as this is a common obstacle to organizational awareness.

We all know it requires challenging and often difficult effort to pierce and dissolve our individual unconsciousness. This is even truer with the cumulative experience of whole groups of individuals who may not have ever turned their attention and awareness practice deeply toward our collective experience with cultural diversity. When people routinely do not pay attention to the lack of diverse practitioners in the meditation hall and what conditions have caused that to happen, that lack of atten- tion itself becomes the collective default condition and organizational baseline from which the center operates. If this turns into the normal operational mode, lack of mindfulness solidifies into an ignorance that prevents one from seeing that there is ignorance. The power of collective unconsciousness as a whole is often greater than the accumulation of ignorance in an individual. In this case, the impact of a whole commu- nity's lack of diversity awareness is much greater than the sum of the ignorance of any of the individuals involved.

The counterpoint to this collective unconsciousness is the practice of community—our practices together, in order to become aware together, of just what the unseen conditioning and patterns we do not pay atten- tion to are. Such efforts require the support and attention of all of us, as a community.

I have heard that some teachers, in particular white teachers, would like their primary personal legacy to be how they have contributed to diversity in the Dharma of Western communities. I personally cannot accept this attitude. This work is not for anyone to own as *their personal legacy*. It is so much more than the efforts of individuals; it goes beyond ownership. It is our collective path and not dependent upon any person- ality or singular effort. It can't be dependent upon individuals, because it has to be available to all of us. We are supported on each other's shoulders and never do this work alone.

Just as unconsciousness is a collective experience, so is consciousness.

During one residential retreat for people of color, I led a modified movement/walking meditation as a collective experience. From the meditation hall we moved and walked mindfully, forming a single line, exiting the space. We deliberately and consciously walked together noticing the internal experience of the bodily sensations and also the external factors of not colliding with each other and maintaining an equal distance between everyone. As a single file line, we wound our way across an open plaza. There, overlooking the grasses and trees of the valley below, we opened up to the glory of a brilliant summer's day with the warmth of the sunshine and the cool breeze from the woods behind. I invited the meditation practitioners to physically open their arms, stretching from their torso into their fingertips and extending their bodies into the landscape that lay before them.

We did a Tibetan practice of bringing the breadth and depth of the sky into our awareness and envisioning our minds to be as spacious as the sky itself, breathing in all that expansiveness through every pore of our being using all of our five sense doors. As people connected with the earth and elements, we continued to invite this spaciousness as we returned from the collective movement practice and spiraled our mindful ways back into the plaza. As people re-formed into a circle, we bowed to each other deeply, drinking in the earth, the sun, the sky, the wind, and each other.

At the end of the meditation, I was standing in the lobby of the meditation hall and one of the women of color who participated in the movement and walking motioned to connect with me. We chose a secluded corner to talk and she queried, "Can I ask you what your intention behind that exercise was?" I replied that my intention was a merging of mindfulness in movement methods, including variations of movement and walking meditation in a single file line with principles of yogic movement practice and the Tibetan practices of expansive sky visualizations. I told her that the invitation was to bring movement practices together in order to experience mindfulness, not just in the stillness of sitting but in the motion of activity.

After a pause, the practitioner responded, "Well, you know, whenever you get folks of color into a line, you can get a different experience." She continued, "What came up for me were images of the Trail of Tears, the Diaspora of the Middle Passage, and the queues of immigrants at Angel Island."

As she described her experience, I could feel the historical and generational trauma behind her words. Not only was she feeling it, but it also triggered the cultural impact that oppression has had on my own experience and that of my family. I could feel the constriction in my body, and the feelings and thoughts that were arising.

In the next pause, as I simply held the space for her to continue describing her experience without needing to judge or have any opinion about where she "needs to be" in the retreat or her practice, she further revealed, "And then, it was different. And then, somewhere on that hill, I felt completely in the present moment. I deeply knew—more than 'knew' but *felt*—that the present moment is not what I 'think' it to be. And there was a letting go—of thoughts, of images—and there was some freedom."

For this practitioner, there was a moment of insight, a moment of wisdom, and a moment of letting go of suffering. When this was shared in the larger group at the end of the retreat, her moments were of such relevance and meaning to others.

We are able to access a tremendous healing in the expansiveness of our awareness. We often think of "letting go" as something we have to do or some task we need to accomplish. Instead, we can allow "letting go" to emerge moment to moment with each moment, to develop a momentum that can change our life. Over time, the mind will incline itself toward nonattachment and learn how not to attach to things.

Ajaan Fuang Jotiko, another of the great teachers from the Thai forest tradition, writes in *Awareness Itself*:

Whatever you experience, simply be aware of it. You don't have to take after it. The primal heart has no characteristics.

It's aware of everything. But as soon as things make contact, within or without, they cause a lapse in mindfulness, so that we throw away awareness, forget awareness in and of itself, and take on all the characteristics of the things that come later. Then we act out in line with them—becoming happy, sad, or whatever. If we don't want to be under their influence, we'll have to stay with primal awareness at all times. This requires a great deal of mindfulness.

We not only collect these moments of freedom and insight in our personal practice, but we collect together our experience of insight and wisdom. We move through historical trauma and injury together, becoming stronger as a community—even when patterns of oppression re-emerge.

Over the past decade, opportunities and accessibility for communities of color, LGBTIQ communities, and other expressions of diversity have increased—though of course, patterns of continuing unconsciousness persist even as progress is made. As we do the work to dissolve racism and oppression, we do it in a society that still is racist, which is why the work is needed.

As any organization moves into another cycle of multicultural awareness training and commitment, comments and attitudes of resistance that are remarkably similar to those from a previous period, a previous iteration, appear again. I hear from people that they "can't go through what they went through last time." Letters that come in from practitioners of color mirror almost exactly the initial letters I wrote to the board about diversifying programming, staff, teachers, and leadership over fifteen years ago.

And yet, amid such similarities, things are also different.

In my Dharma communities, we have many thousands of practitioners from communities of color who have accessed the Dharma over the past fifteen-plus years. The retreats for people of color are no longer questioned for their worth by the organizations as a whole (even if some individuals might continue to question them). The retreats for LGBTIQ folks have expanded to more meditation centers. There is currently more diverse participation on boards and governance committees than ever before. Despite institutional challenges, progress has been made through policy initiatives, expanding programs, and yes, even failed trainings, because there was at least a collective intention to keep returning to the effort.

It can seem that both the process and transformation around race and diversity move at a painstakingly slow pace, taking so much longer than any of us would like. But in hindsight we see that within recent years thousands of new practitioners of color have indeed been impacted by the teachings, and white-dominant communities have also felt the impact of that inclusivity. This is the fruit of our ability to practice and awaken together.

What we do in our Dharma and mindfulness practice is critically important.

There is a direct connection between how we build our Dharma communities and how we are in the world. The creation of less suffering and more freedom in this world that so desperately needs it is no different than the creation of freedom within our own spiritual communities. It has never been so urgent to learn the teachings more deeply by actually practicing them within our own sanghas and communities—in order to practice with all sanghas and communities.

For Reflection

Regardless of what cultural background(s) you identify with, what are the different histories within your community or communities involving the Dharma?

What is that history of your community for you?

What are the conditions, efforts, and complexities of how the Dharma arrived into your community?

How might awareness of those histories influence the development and governance of your community in the future?

18

Manifesting Diverse Spiritual Leadership

THE ROLE of spiritual leadership and Dharma teacher in the West is quite complex and interwoven with differing understandings and needs. For some practitioners a clear line of authority and sense of hierarchy provide a beneficial context to receive the teachings, producing a sense of allowing and surrendering to the guidance and methods of the lineage. For others, especially those inclined to the democratic values of Western culture or who have been harmed by the rigidity of different faith traditions, there may be a need for less authority and more permission for self-agency and self-determination.

Unlike other spiritual traditions that might use different terms and definitions for leadership (for example, priest, reverend, etc.), and because there is no formal terminology that exists in Western Insight Meditation for spiritual leadership outside the monastic roles of nuns and monks, the designation of "Dharma teacher" has become laden with complexity.

The spiritual and psychological aspects projected onto Dharma teachers can sometimes come in the form of an unspoken assumption that teachers have achieved something practitioners have not—some level of enlightenment or at least some attainment of insight or compassion. Adding the layer of diversity and race to these interactive dynamics adds to the complexity in relating to spiritual leadership. If there is a dearth of teachers of color, what subliminal message does that send about the cultural disparities involved? Does it mean that people of color are not capable of developing as Dharma teachers or spiritual leaders?

As has been stated, it is difficult and challenging to find a spiritual home and comfort when very few people look like you and the forms and expressions used to offer spiritual teachings are different than those from your own culture of origin. Having exponentially expanded the numbers of Insight Meditation practitioners of color in the last fifteen years, it has become vitally urgent for the community to cultivate Dharma teachers who are culturally congruent to the practitioners themselves, that is, to develop Dharma teachers of color. While the presence of leadership of color does not eliminate racism or disparity, it helps to dissipate the seeming limitations held in place by our cultural assumptions—the ones that suggest that this practice is not for people of color or non-mainstream cultures. And, of course, leadership of color helps to create an inclusivity in the room that reflects the diversity in our larger culture and human lives.

In addition to being valuable to practitioners of color, leadership of color is equally if not more important for the white dominant culture to experience leadership from communities of color. Everyone, every community benefits from the experience of the expansiveness and diversity of life—and only with diversity fully visible is there a possibility to shift from the dynamic of white culture as the defining template and standard against which everything is measured. It is critically important to the breadth of the Dharma teachings that white European American practitioners are offered teachings from teachers of color and from other diverse backgrounds. When the Dharma is taught through diversity itself, the second-guessing of whether diversity is part of the Dharma will fall away. Only then will there be truly inclusive and broad teachings that will reach a diverse audience through diverse voices.

This is quite difficult to accomplish at the moment. For instance, in the tradition in which I practice, there are only eleven teachers of color among three hundred-plus trained Dharma teachers in the Western Insight Meditation community. There have been some small attempts to cultivate individual teachers of color in the past, yet teachers of color have been and remain exceptions to the rule—specifically, the unspoken rule that everything including leadership is measured by the standards of the dominant white culture. The few existing teachers of color have managed to make it through a system that continues to favor white, hetero-normative, able-bodied, upper-middle-class candidates for roles in spiritual leadership.

For years, leaders and teachers alike in my tradition have been saying to each other that they were interested in training more teachers of color, but no people of color had the qualifications and practice experience necessary to be trained. This passive, naive attitude that people of color are unavailable demonstrates just how inattentive the whole community has been to the needs and circumstances of communities of color and other forms of cultural difference.

I am often asked, "Where are the teachers of color? Do you know of any?" While it might seem like a straightforward question, the answers are much more complicated. The question is rather simplistic because it reduces the development of leadership to the expectation of having it emerge in front of us without preexisting conditions, as opposed to inquiring whether the causes and factors that will engender leadership of color to flourish actually exist. No community can expect fully formed leaders and teachers to show up by happenstance.

Dharma teachers and spiritual leaders require the time and opportunity to develop and grow. More than a few decades ago when my father was chair of a university department, the university administration was interested in diversifying academic faculty, particularly in tenured faculty of color. "Why doesn't the university receive more applications from candidates of color for these tenured positions?" they asked.

The institution had to learn that professors of color qualified for tenure don't just show up on one's doorstep. It was incumbent upon the institution to be part of the social change that would lead to that outcome from the very beginning of the education system. The effort needed was to create educational opportunities for kids of color in elementary school, nurture and develop their talents and strengths in primary and secondary education, deepen their learning and skills with undergraduate and graduate experience, and provide teaching opportunities so that they might train in skills they could bring to that tenure review. There needed to be a change in the entire system to create truly inclusive leadership, not passively wait for exceptions to the rule to appear.

This process is still something that most mainstream Dharma communities do not recognize, do not realize, and do not pay attention to. The norms of the dominant culture, specifically within teacher training, do not support diversity beyond stating verbally that they do so—that is, they offer mere window-dressing. There is nothing in the training system that encourages the flourishing of diverse teachers. There is an implicit pressure to conform rather than to be diverse. In my opinion, we eleven teachers of color were unplanned at best. We are unusual, as individuals, in that we made it through the existing system.

And at times, I harbor doubts about whether or not the system wants us.

To develop fully empowered Dharma teachers of color, we need to create a pipeline specifically to engender multicultural leadership—and this is what some of us have attempted to do for Insight Meditation communities over the past two decades. There has been a concerted effort by a few teachers of color, even while concurrently developing our own leadership and teaching skills, to cultivate and nurture the development of future teachers. While this might be an added responsibility for teachers of color to accept (being newer teachers themselves), it is also a necessary reality.

One aspect of leadership that the dominant culture does not adequately attend to is succession of leadership and the ongoing archetypal role of Dharma teacher beyond a single person's lifetime. Succession is of indispensible importance to consider when there is any discussion about building diverse spiritual communities—and it is never too early to consider and support the development of succession in leadership. This is vital to the survival of diverse communities.

In a certain way, the dominant culture doesn't actually have to worry about succession. The dominant white culture is able to depend upon the expectation that its own culture will be able to continue. There will be always another person from the dominant culture available to continue that culture's dominance. White teachers are not the exceptions to the rule, they *are* the rule—because it is their culture that determines the rules of engagement.

Meanwhile, the reality among diverse communities is that as soon as a community forms, we begin to think about who will come after us and continue the work that we have started. For teachers of color it is not a choice or a luxury to train their successors as teachers of color; it is a necessity for survival and an obligation to the future of the community. One of the key issues that diverse communities face on the journey toward diversification of Dharma communities is the need to develop diverse teachers and leaders not just for the present but for the future, for the long-term sustainability of our communities—or within indigenous terminology, for the next seven generations.

In my Dharma communities, much has been done to clear the fields, plow the terrain, and till the soil to allow and invite entry-level practice for people of color and other diverse communities through daylong retreats, sitting groups, and classes. The meadows and pastures have been seeded and watered with the encouragement and support of residential retreat practice to deepen the experience of diverse communities with the Dharma.

Emerging Dharma communities and practice groups of color have fertilized and nurtured the garden with their participation in yearlong and multi-year practice programs to further deepen the channel of the Buddha's teachings into diverse lives. Teachers and leaders have begun to emerge from the growing depth, concentration, and dedication of contemplative practice over time.

It's worth noting that Dharma teachers are created not solely from their own personal aspirations—although that is a component. Accordingly, we have begun to see the fruit of leadership ripen on the branches of diverse practitioners over the past twenty years.

Within the Insight Meditation community, since 1997 the Community Dharma Leadership training program has provided initial training for hundreds of Dharma leaders and teachers within community settings. For the first ten years, the program had a participation of less than 7 percent from communities of color. Over time, with the growing depth of practice from practitioners of color along with the anti-racism and diversity advocacy being done to change the organizational culture, the program has come to sustain a participation rate of over 35 percent from communities of color. Those demographics change the room in which the training takes place; they change the way the curriculum is offered; and they change how our spiritual communities will be led.

From among these community Dharma teachers and leaders, some will be selected to receive the final stage of training necessary to become fully authorized Dharma teachers who are empowered to teach intensive residential meditation retreats. This will require a four-year training of selected candidates who meet multiple personal and practice-related criteria, including having practiced for extended lengths of time of multiple months without interruption.

We are now on the cusp of supporting a significant number of full Dharma teachers of color in the Insight Meditation tradition in order to ensure the continued expansion of the Dharma in multicultural communities. This is not an insignificant process.

Please do not take this fact for granted. Please do not assume that any of us (PoC or white) are entitled to it, or that it will always be here without our continued maintenance, advocacy, and effort. Cultivating diverse teachers is a fragile process within the restricted confines of a white mainstream culture that still tends to unconsciously dominate even in the leadership development process.

This is the complexity of working within a system that is not fully awakened.

This is the complexity of dismantling racism within a system that is not completely anti-racist or free from oppression from the dominant white culture.

And this is a microcosm of life in our larger world. Just because we have had an African American president does not mean we will continue in the same trajectory toward cultural transformation into even greater equity.

One might ask, "Why not train teachers of color independently or outside the constraints of mainstream centers?" This points to the classic inquiry into whether one attempts to manifest cultural change from within the system or from outside of it. This is precisely what many social activists find they must choose between—and of course, its resolution depends upon all the surrounding conditions including obstacles and opportunities. The resources and accessibility to infrastructure offered when one works from within the system provide great opportunities, and they should not be undervalued. Teachers trained within a lineage or group of practice centers have access to those centers to teach retreats—a huge advantage, considering re-creating the infrastructure to manage and hold retreats is an enormous investment. And, of course, existing organizations have staff or volunteers to support the teaching of retreats and the networking of teachers.

Regardless of training, people of color are often unconsciously expected to perform better than their white counterparts in order to prove themselves worthy—perhaps even to prove that they have reached some level of attainment. While discussing the issue of diversity and teachers at a regional Dharma meeting, someone publicly asked, "Are there any *good* teachers of color?" The question was answered with a silence that indicated the larger group's reply. This disparity of credibility between white and nonwhite teachers can place teachers of color who are independently trained without the backing of an institution at even greater risk of being marginalized.

This questioning of the credibility of teachers of color—that they are somehow unproven against dominant culture standards—pushes diverse communities to create their own organizations and structures, to find their own venues to teach in, and to find a different means of sustaining the Dharma. It isn't impossible, but it is an added burden that white teachers in most instances do not have to take on.

The unconsciousness and racism embedded in any social organization and community remain even as we endeavor to train a new generation of teachers and leadership. It is a worthy intention to train future teachers to enter a less hostile, more hospitable environment, but the reality is that social disparity, cultural oppression, and white supremacy do not go away immediately, even as we work toward their transformation and dissolution.

Whether collectively as communities or separately as individuals, we are all imperfect beings hopefully working our way toward a less imperfect world. This is equally true with respect to the role and archetype of spiritual teacher—and I would add that the mantle of spiritual leadership speaks less to the attainments or accomplishments of the individual than it does to the dedication to the journey and progress they have made.

Teachers teach what has worked for their own practice and lives. Their teachings emerge from their own direct experience with life, spiritual and otherwise. And great teachers are able to inspire others to find their own ways of actualizing freedom. But all teachers are invited to teach beyond their personal experience—to reach cultures, genders, and orientations different than their own.

One of the finest things that my father taught me was that, as a teacher, he gauged his success by how well his students were able to supersede him. This is a role modeling that I will never forget. And I have come to feel that the best teachers create a kind of alchemical process of learning that invites the student to surpass the teacher—a refined skill to inspire learning *beyond* the level of the teacher's own practice. If a teacher is only able to teach to the level of their own practice, then the teacher becomes a limitation. But with humility, the teacher can invite and encourage students to surpass them.

Indeed, there are examples of this beautiful dynamic, such as with Anagarika Munindra, an important teacher of many of our Western teachers, who taught Dipa Ma to access states of mind that he himself did not access. The humility of teachers bringing students beyond where they are as teachers is visible in all our lives, when a coach mentors an athlete, when a professor advises a graduate student, or when a parent raises their children. We all support them in whatever ways we can to go beyond where we ourselves have gone.

Humility in the teaching role is crucial because it balances two other aspects of the teaching role that are needed in leadership: authority and power. Outside of organizational authority, which is usually an imposed structure of hierarchy, spiritual authority comes from the teacher's own direct realization of how the Dharma can change lives and transform the world around us. There is a real authority that develops from our depth of practice and dedication, and this authority emerges equally from a communal sense of trust that the teacher supports the needs of the community with integrity and care. There is also a way in which spiritual authority is granted to teachers by the community itself. Both these internal and external characteristics of authority allow the Dharma teacher to skillfully use power.

Power, like other resources such as wealth or opportunity or privilege, has no inherent positive or negative valence to it; it is not good (or bad) unto itself. The impact of power, whether it is beneficial or not, depends on the intentions behind the energy, how it is used, to what ends, and how the impact is experienced by those who receive it. I find it helpful to think of power paired with another core teaching of the Buddha, that of *dana* or generous giving. This is what invites power itself to become a practice of the Dharma.

Power becomes dangerous and potentially harmful when attachment, conscious or unconscious, is involved. This will inevitably create suffering. But when power is fluid and offered and released freely, rather than only empowering individuals, it is a force that can elevate entire communities. The skillful use of power is to offer it in a spirit of generosity, judiciously and with wisdom—and without needing anything individually in return.

Moreover, when we give power away, we do not ourselves become less powerful; rather we become more powerful through the force of generosity of our heart and the integrity of our practice. This may contradict the zero-sum conditioning of our larger culture that tells us in so many ways that "more is better" and "most is best." This view is born of an economics of scarcity, rather than of generosity.

Within the terminology of social psychology, the University of California Berkeley professor Dacher Keltner outlines very similar "power principles" in his book *The Power Paradox*. His articulation of power goes beyond the conventional definitions of power rooted in obsolescent Machiavellian definitions that portray power as simply coercive force. Keltner vitalizes a new understanding of power, describing true power as the energy and ability to make a difference in the world for the greater good. Two of his principles concerning power are:

(1) Power comes from empowering others in social networks.
(2) Enduring power comes from giving.

This is so relevant to the cultivation of teachers and future leadership for our diverse spiritual communities. It is imperative that power is fluid and flows in the training of new teachers. If the older, more experienced teachers are attached to power or hold on to it for whatever personal or impersonal reasons and do not let power flow to the next generation of teachers, the training of future teachers will be immediately impaired. Partial empowerment is insufficient and produces only a weakened future leadership that remains dependent upon existing patterns of decision-making and uses of power. The unconscious byproduct is that the skills and achievements of teachers from one generation become the limitation and boundary for where future generations of teachers are able to go.

It is critically important to pay attention to this flow of power in multicultural contexts. Because existing Dharma community organization and development have only focused on developing white leadership and teachers, diverse communities will only be able to live within the replication of inherently racist, oppressive conditions that continue patterns of disparity and white supremacy unless and until we can fully empower leadership and teachers of color. It is incumbent on current white Dharma leadership to offer support and resource programs to transfer and offer power to diverse leaders and teachers of color, empowering them fully. This is a necessity if diversity and working toward an inclusive, anti-racist society is truly our collective aspiration.

It is not necessarily the obligation of white leadership to lead, teach, or determine what those programs of empowerment are. As communities of color practice more and more deeply with each other and with white mainstream communities, what is needed for leadership in communities of color will become clear to the members of those communities themselves—and this clarity may not develop within white unconsciousness in the same time frame. The nature of white privilege and unconsciousness is that white folks often do not know what they do not know; they do not realize the privilege that surrounds them. White leaders often are not aware of the power and privilege that they have, nor do they understand the impact upon folks who are not white, privileged, or part of the dominant culture. For this reason, part of the experiential practice of inclusive diversity and anti-racism for white people is to trust that communities of color know what they need in terms of leadership development.

Another aspect of the EBMC Multicultural Agreements (Appendix 3) that is implemented collectively rather than individually is "move up and move back." In collective application of these principles, the larger mainstream community provides the same resources its own leadership has been able to avail itself of and makes that offering for communities of color to move up into their empowerment. This also means that those same mainstream communities move back to create space for the expression of that leadership empowerment. In order to create a larger sense of wholeness for all communities in the longitudinal course of the Dharma, there must be conscious and intentional movement of power between communities.

In creating the next generation of diverse Dharma teachers for all communities, we cannot rely on simply training residential retreat teachers as we might have in the past, nor depend upon training Dharma teachers for a particular community (which is what dominant cultures have functionally done). Rather, we are creating the empowerment of a community of spiritual leaders to hold and be of service to all our communities.

Leadership is not a process of individual development or attainment. That view arises out of a competitive model focusing only on personal achievements of the individual, and it does not account for the collective needs of the community. Nor does that view serve the future generations of communities.

Leadership is the responsibility, obligation, and cause of all of us—even those of us who never step into that specific role ourselves. We all collaborate in order to manifest the leadership all our diverse lives need. If this is not so, leadership will fall only to those who have the resources, privilege, and power to obtain it—because the playing field continues not to be level in our culture.

Leaders from diverse communities may need encouragement to come forth and teach. And in fact, the Buddha was like this too. After his awakening, he felt the pull into the privilege of using his insight solely in the service of his own liberation. Initially, although he saw how much suffering there was in the world, he felt there was no point in offering the teachings that would be the antidote to that suffering because most people would not understand them. The Buddha had to be asked multiple times, entreated by one of the celestial devas, to offer his insight and compassion because there were some beings with "little dust in their eyes." So too with the Buddha, spiritual leadership is a collective work.

If the Dharma is to do more than simply survive into future generations, if it is to fully actualize the human potential for freedom, practitioners cannot be expected only to practice to the level of their teachers; they must be invited to expand our collective consciousness as overall spiritual leaders, not simply Dharma teachers of a certain meditative form. We cannot evolve or mature into our humanity if we are solely dependent on specific teachers. If current Dharma teachers become the upper limit of awakening for each successive generation, the collective awakening in each era will diminish, and the Dharma will incrementally fade—as some ancient texts have predicted.

However, if as individuals and communities we aspire to a higher vision of what we can be, and if collectively we develop and support the continuing spiritual leadership that can serve that vision, we can raise the communal level of our consciousness together.

If we can do this, the power of spiritual leadership would flow from individual into community, and beyond, from generation to generation—and the Dharma's longevity will be guaranteed.

This is indispensable in how we awaken together.

19

Integrity: A Challenging Practice in Challenging Times

EVEN IN THE confusion and complexity of our times, there is still wisdom that underlies our experience from generation to generation. One of these aphorisms state, "Integrity is doing the right thing, even when no one is watching."

Without integrity, mindfulness is morally meaningless. Without integrity, metta is either wishful thinking or a spiritual bypass. Both mindfulness and metta require the actions of conscience motivated by an ethical barometer.

We see many forms of this lack of integrity present, even with mindfulness. One subtle form of this is our cultural conditioning in our market economy to get away with as much as we can, while giving as little as possible. A more acute form of this dearth of morality is our ever-quickening slide into a post-factual, post-ethical world, where truth is not respected and deliberately made to be confusing and obscure.

When there is less or zero external accountability in our larger culture, there emerges an indispensable spiritual imperative to redouble our internal efforts and concentration to have a moral barometer: this is the *integrity of mindfulness*. The integrity of mindfulness requires we be of benefit to our collective humanness, not simply to our personal being.

I would broaden the scope of integrity:

- Integrity is doing the wise and compassionate action when no one agrees with us.

- Integrity is walking our highest path, even if it is painful and arduous and long.

- Integrity is acting on behalf of others when we do not have to because we have some benefit, privilege, power, or entitlement that protects us.

- Integrity is standing actively (and not "bystanding") in solidarity with those whose voices and abilities have less volume or impact than yours.

- Integrity is being kind when everyone and everything around you is not kind.

- Integrity is loving when you do not feel loved yourself.

- Integrity is having ethics in unethical and amoral times—having a moral compass when others around you do not have a clue to what that means and/or disparage the very intentions of ethical behavior.

- Integrity is placing a higher value on the greater good of all, rather than the gain of an individual or selected individual groups.

- Integrity is holding to these principles, even when there are an infinite number of distractions, seductions, and judgments that seek to weaken and obliterate those principles.

In sum, integrity provides the vision, the aspiration, and the guide to any actions of mindfulness and kindness.

Where is your moment-to-moment practice of integrity in a world that wants us to compete primarily to benefit the gain of the privileged, the powerful, and the lucky few, instead of working for the equity and elevation of our human condition for the many? Where do you stand when $21-billion walls of fear, fueled by racial bitterness, are being designed to separate nations, instead of creating bridges of understanding and actions fed by common human connection? When $21 billion can buy enough food to feed 7 billion starving mouths, when $21 billion can create twice the clean water for every person living on this planet, when $21 billion can buy more than eight months' worth of medication for every HIV patient in the world, when $21 billion can compensate more than a half million public school teachers with a full year's salary—what choices would your integrity make? And what does your integrity ask of you when our government of the people, by the people, and for the people is based purely and only upon the self-interest and self-defined alternative facts of those few individuals and groups in positions of power?

Reverend Dr. Martin Luther King Jr. reminds us, "There comes a time when one must take a position that is neither safe, nor politic, nor popular, but they must take it because conscience tells them it is right."

Integrity is not just a personal practice but a collective one that transforms our communities and our world. Only in an ethically wholesome society can we create a healthy system of social, economic, and political justice, not to mention spiritual freedom. And since society is made up of each of us, because each of us is part of that experience of being human, that ethical transformation begins here—with all of us awakening together with integrity.

Epilogue

A Long and Winding Road

N ONE OF THIS is easy or simple. Awakening together in community is both an inspiring and frustrating process with all our collective imperfections and inevitable unconsciousness. It's not linear, and it's not always clear what it is that will support the process of raising our collective consciousness. There will be obstacles, injuries, missteps, harm, and even failures on our parts both individually and collectively. What happens when our delusion triumphs over our mindfulness and our social fabric is once again torn apart by hatred and injustice? Clearly, we are not an enlightened world.

What would the Buddha do? What did the Buddha do?

I do believe that the Buddha did the only thing he could do.

We usually speak only of the Buddha's attaining enlightenment underneath the bodhi tree. However, it is said that the Buddha did not awaken just through his efforts in only one lifetime. It took him innumerable lifetimes to awaken, practicing in different livelihoods, different relationships, different communities, and even as different forms of life (human, animal, and deva, for example). What happened in those multitudes of lifetimes that he did not awaken fully? What happened when he realized in a particular lifetime that he was not going to awaken? And what did he do when he realized the insight of his *not* awakening, over and over again, lifetime after lifetime—despite his best efforts? After all, isn't that what we are all doing—making our best efforts, doing the best we can? Did he linger in doubt or despair? If he was human, did he go through all the human feelings of grief over the loss of enlightenment's potential in that particular lifetime?

In the midst of his humanity and human angst, I believe the Buddha did the only thing he could do. He returned to the practice. He returned to developing the awareness practice to go beyond where he had previously reached. This meant turning toward the first noble truth of suffering of his own life and of the world—not turning away from it in despair or hopelessness—and it meant to return to the aspiration of extinguishing suffering with gentleness and care.

The failures of the previous lives of the Buddha are a teaching in and of themselves.

We will fail, and we do fail. But we return over and over again to the path leading to freedom—this is the work of social and collective awakening. Just because the 1964 Civil Rights Act passed doesn't mean that racism is dissolved. Just because same-sex marriage is now legal in the United States doesn't mean that homophobia is not thriving. The lack of awakening in our society is even more apparent after our electoral cycles prove to us how fragile any gains toward freedom can be.

Reverend Dr. Martin Luther King Jr. has written, "We shall overcome because the arc of the moral universe is long, but it bends toward justice." The profound subtext here is that justice, as worthy a task as it is in our lives, will take a longer time to fulfill than any of us would like or even might have on this earth.

Justice will require the efforts of the multitude and the many, rather than the individual and the few. Justice doesn't only concern itself with the political work of equity, it must respect the sacredness of life within each community and each individual.

There is tremendous injustice and unfairness in our cultures, our society, our nation, and our world—and there is freedom. This freedom is not dependent upon life being fair or just. True freedom does not require we be in a place where there is no problem, struggle, or oppression. True freedom means being in the midst of any or all of those things and still having *clarity* in our minds, *tenderness* in our hearts, and *integrity* in our actions. True freedom allows us to move through even our most difficult struggles for the benefit of us all without re-creating cycles of suffering or abuse for others. True freedom brings true happiness. This is the kind of happiness and freedom that we seek together.

This is how we awaken in community and awaken together.

In the chaos and despair of violence, senselessness, carnage, and oppression of our recent times, we can still take care of each other. We can hold each other with the most precious thing we can offer: our compassionate attention. Unwavering, we can love one another without questioning or second-guessing any aspect of that love, anyone's life experience, or anyone's identity. There is great power in this coming together—from whomever or wherever we are. In that solidarity with the deepest of places of our tender humanity, we begin to live the truth spoken in every single spiritual faith tradition across our history of human existence, embodied in these specific words of the Buddha:

> Hate never yet dispelled hate.
> Only love dispels hate.
> This is the Truth, ancient and inexhaustible.

From this wisdom, we create justice in the only ways possible—through just means—and doing so is an act of love. I offer this verse:

> Instead of justifying the oppression or injury of one,
> for the oppression or injury of others—
> instead of focusing attention and efforts for freedom
> on narrowly selected groups—
> instead of creating a hierarchy of privilege and misguided
> false freedoms—
> We endeavor to dissolve and transform all oppressions,
> for the justice of all communities,
> for the freedom of all beings.
> We can only create justice through just means—
> that is also the Truth,
> ancient and inexhaustible,
> this is the truth of awakening together.

Appendix 1

Steps to Take Now

HERE ARE some additional points and further reflections for existing Dharma communities to practice diversifying their communities and organizations. There are no easy answers or simple solutions. Perhaps that is the first point: be prepared for both the complexities and subtleties involved.

- Do whatever it takes to allow, invite, and encourage one's culture and identity as a spiritual exploration worthy of the practices of deep insight and boundless compassion. Train teachers to teach the Dharma through this lens.

- Humility. Humility. Humility. Value this value. It is a norm from the Dharma's cultures of origin. It is infused in the spirit of the teachings. How do we infuse it into our contemporary multiplicity of cultures—particularly when it is not so highly valued in the West?

- Develop your experience of spiritual practice and Dharma study together collectively as a community, rather than as isolated individuals. Take seriously—and do not take for granted—the third refuge of Sangha. Sangha might be listed third in the sequence not because it is less important that the first two but because it is the most difficult to manifest. Being in relationship with each other is an advanced practice.

- As you turn mindfulness practice toward community, explore questions such as: How does an organization be aware collectively of their internal experience (norms, values, and procedures)?

How do they become aware of the external needs of the community wanting to participate in the organization? How is the organization aware of the impact of their internal process on the external communities of practitioners?

- Explore how your community (or communities) experiences the teachings through specific cultural perspectives, including those perspectives of the dominant culture—whether that means white culture, patriarchal culture, abled culture, or heterosexual culture, among many other facets. Be conscious, aware, and mindful of those differing lenses and the impact on other cultural experiences. Turn mindfulness and *sati* toward cultural experience—both dominant and nondominant.

- Developing, building, creating, and nurturing a sense of diverse communities is a lot of hard work. Period. It takes more effort that you think possible. It takes more time than you might have. It takes more resources than you would like. What will support you and your community in this process for the long haul? How do you strengthen perseverance, stamina, effort, determination, and patience?

- Creating a space that is safe enough to feel as if one belongs requires more than just the intention to do so and a few words from the community. It requires a set of actions, behaviors, and attitudes that support those intentions. It means creating a space that people will not just feel invited into but feel connected to and can fully participate in.

- Do not assume that you are welcoming simply because you intend to be welcoming. Go into the community and get firsthand input from practitioners about what their needs are. Then demonstrate that you are working to fulfill those needs. Do not assume that you know what the community needs or that you know what is best for the community. Do not assume that your good intentions are enough. Listen deeply to your communities, and follow up that deep listening with authentic action.

- Support practitioners from diverse communities as they enter practice. Continue to support them as they go deeper into the Dharma. From the group of senior diverse practitioners, cultivate and support the development of leadership. Create a pipeline of support for practice across the spectrum of diverse life experience and across the timeline of spiritual development. Create a pipeline of practice for diverse communities from beginning, entry-level, experienced, through deepening study and intensive practice, into leadership, governance, and teaching roles.

- Create different demographics in the room if possible. Create a consciously balanced demographic in the room for at least certain events. That will change the dynamics even though it is not enough to prevent harm. If the demographics are different enough, everyone will be more aware, even if they may not be more skilled, in that moment.

- Train your teachers in all of this. Train your white teachers to collaborate with teachers of color. Require some involvement in team teaching with mixed demographics.

- Train your staff and volunteers in all of this.

- Offer trainings to your community through your programming.

- Financial accessibility is important across lines of culture. Make sure that cost and fees are not barriers. The generosity of the organization toward the larger community will be returned back to the organization. It will also demonstrate the commitment to people from many different backgrounds and experiences.

- Seek to diversify your governance, your staff, your teachers, your volunteers—and your community will also necessarily reflect that commitment. Empower diverse members of your community— it will be mirrored in the communities' trust of the organizational intentions.

- Create safety as much as possible—create communication agreements, develop conflict resolution processes, and design pathways to restore relationships.

- Hold the tensions of the relationships, the room, and differing communities. Hold the tensions to break together instead of breaking apart. When difference is present, the conditions of unconsciousness predispose us to fragment and coalesce around similarity rather than hold the diversity.

- Be generous with power. The highest power of all is the power to give it away. Offer it freely and wisely without needing anything in return, and what will be returned is the empowerment of a whole community.

- It is never too soon to cultivate your successors in leadership for the future generations of practitioners. Seed the conditions for circumstances in your community to be more diverse than it is currently. Practice the transition of power with love and ease. Practice it now—not later, when it is absolutely needed. Power is meant to be fluid energy benefiting everyone—not merely the ones who are closest to it, or have the most of it, or have been given it.

Appendix 2

Learning Points from East Bay Meditation Center

Tʜɪs ʟɪsᴛ is an expansion of learning points that EBMC has offered to other mainstream meditation centers as a way to support them in their evolution beyond cultural unconsciousness. These learning points were written primarily by white allies formerly or currently in leadership positions at EBMC at the time of this writing. My deepest gratitude goes to the collective wisdom of the EBMC community.

EBMC Lᴇᴀʀɴɪɴɢ #1:
Iɴǫᴜɪʀᴇ ᴡɪᴛʜ ᴄᴏᴍᴍᴜɴɪᴛɪᴇs ᴏғ ᴄᴏʟᴏʀ ᴀʙᴏᴜᴛ ᴛʜᴇɪʀ ɴᴇᴇᴅs.

Then, with people of color, collaborate in creating or altering organizational practices, and design or redesign the organization, based on those expressed needs, rather than expecting everyone to fit into the organizational and interpersonal norms of white culture. Avoid questioning whether the expressed needs are "legitimate" or "reasonable."

EBMC Lᴇᴀʀɴɪɴɢ #2:
Sᴛᴀʀᴛ ᴡɪᴛʜ ᴛʜᴇ ᴍɪssɪᴏɴ sᴛᴀᴛᴇᴍᴇɴᴛ.

EBMC's mission statement begins with, *"Founded to provide a welcoming environment for people of color, members of the LGBTQI community, people with disabilities, and other underrepresented communities. . . ."*

All organizational principles, practices, and procedures should flow from the mission statement. If an organization truly has a commitment to diversity, equity, and inclusion, it should be reflected in the mission statement.

EBMC LEARNING #3:
CREATE SAFETY FOR PEOPLE OF COLOR.

3a. Events reserved for people of color

At EBMC, one weekly sitting group and a number of retreats and classes are reserved for people of color.

Many people of color, in mixed environments, feel the need to "keep their guard up," to protect themselves from the effects of the micro-agressions of expressions of (often unconscious) bias and racism from other, usually white, community members. This guarded stance can be a barrier, especially for beginners, to learning the inner dynamic of "letting go" that is central to many meditation practices. Events reserved for people of color can offer the possibility of "letting down one's guard," and enhance learning at different times during or as part of a student of color's path.

3b. A minimum percentage of people of color at mixed events.

EBMC's registration practices, for most retreats and classes open to all, are designed to aim for a minimum percentage (usually 40 percent) of people of color in the room.

Short of the safety of people of color–only events, a minimum percentage of people of color in the room at a mixed-attendance event can help to create a "safe-enough" environment. For example, when there is a critical mass of people of color present, it is more likely that people of color will feel sufficiently safe to name and call out expressions of unconscious bias or racism that they perceive, whether from a teacher or fellow community member. (It would be even preferable, and enhance a sense of safety for people of color, for a white community member to call out expressions of bias and racism. See EBMC Learning #8 below.)

These registration practices, for EBMC, mean that some events are inevitably smaller than they might otherwise be, if the percentage of prospective registrants is more than 60 percent white. Given the commitment to diversity articulated in EBMC's mission, this is an acceptable trade-off.

EBMC LEARNING #4:
IN ORDER TO HAVE A SAFE-ENOUGH ENVIRONMENT FOR PRACTICE, PEOPLE OF COLOR NEED TO SEE THEMSELVES REFLECTED IN THE TEACHING TEAMS.

At EBMC, this has meant that white teachers are typically paired with teachers of color, even if that was not how the white teachers envisioned their program being presented. These pairings also provide opportunities for white teachers to learn how to teach from a perspective of cultural humility and openness to learning

EBMC LEARNING #5:
ECONOMICS IMPACTS DIVERSITY.

5a. Building diversity is "expensive."

One impact of historical oppression present today is the contribution to a grossly uneven distribution of wealth, because much of white wealth was based on the exploitation of black and brown people. Communities of color have, on average, access to fewer resources than white communities. Therefore, don't expect diversity to "pay for itself" in a market economy because so much of the economic wealth of communities of color has been expropriated by a system that has been structured to privilege white people. Expect it to be more expensive to build a truly diverse organization than a predominantly white one.

5b. Eliminate financial barriers.

A corollary of the above is the fact that any financial barriers to participation will negatively impact efforts to build diversity.

EBMC relies on a gift economics model, where all events are offered for no registration fee and financial support comes from a practice of voluntary giving. Community members are invited to give in proportion to their ability. This includes an invitation to those with the greatest means to make voluntary gifts of more than the fee they would be charged at a market-based center for a similar retreat or class, to help balance the gifts of those who can offer less.

5c. Avoid scholarship programs.

By adopting a gift economics model, with no registration fees, EBMC avoids the pitfalls inherent with systems that are fee-based but attempt to increase diversity through scholarship programs. The need to apply for a scholarship in such models adds an additional logistical and emotional barrier for lower-income people, and therefore disproportionately impacts people of color.

5d. Don't make diversity a "program."

At EBMC, diversity, equity, and inclusion are inherently weaved into every aspect of the organization. This avoids the risk of a "silo effect" when an organization considers Diversity to be a program, often with its own separate budget. The most serious commitment to Diversity requires a budgetary commitment throughout the organization, in every program.

EBMC LEARNING #6:
WHEN THE NEEDS OF DIFFERENT COMMUNITIES COLLIDE, STICK WITH YOUR VALUES OF INCLUSIVITY.

Five years after opening its doors, EBMC had outgrown the small storefront space rented in downtown Oakland. Many events, including the weekly sitting group for people of color, were over capacity. Nearing the end of its lease, EBMC began the process of progressively moving upstairs into a larger space in the same building. Unfortunately, this process began without close consultation with EBMC's many communities.

In particular, EBMC members with disabilities expressed resistance to moving above the ground floor, which presented a greater evacuation risk in case of fire, earthquake, or other significant emergencies. In addition, the ambient air in the space triggered reactions in some community members with environmental illness.

The Leadership Sangha (that is, the board of directors), faced with no apparent other appropriate spaces for rent in downtown Oakland, grappled with the competing demands of those wanting to move upstairs quickly and those demanding that another space be found.

In the end, the Leadership Sangha chose to discontinue the process of the move upstairs, and committed to finding a space suitable for all EBMC's communities—even if that meant closing the doors for some time after its current lease expired.

Fortunately, with just weeks to spare on the current lease, a new, larger ground floor space was located where the needs of all of EBMC's communities can be met.

EBMC LEARNING #7:
DIVERSITY IS NOT "EXPEDIENT."

Efficiency and speed are dominant-culture values in the United States. Prioritizing them tends to lead to re-create the dominant paradigms and to stifle or shut down diversity. Be willing to take a risk, to hang out in the zone of not-knowing, to hold out for what you really want, rather than settling for what seems easiest to immediately achieve.

In the above example, the expedient choice would have been for EBMC to move upstairs into the larger space in the same building. Choosing to hang out in the zone of not-knowing (for example, not knowing whether we'd need to close down for a time) was frightening, and took longer, but it laid the groundwork for finding a new space that allowed EBMC to remain committed to its values of radical inclusivity.

EBMC LEARNING #8:
SKILLED THIRD-PARTY FACILITATORS,
WHO ARE WELL VERSED IN THE DYNAMICS OF RACISM AND
WHITE PRIVILEGE, ARE NECESSARY AND INVALUABLE.

The process of resolving the difficult issues that arise in diversity efforts at EBMC has sometimes been rocky. A skilled, neutral, third-party facilitator has sometimes been needed to facilitate challenging conversations. It is critical that such individuals are familiar with the dynamics of racism and white privilege, and comfortable with addressing race-based conflict and tension. The organization demonstrates that it places value on the services of such facilitators by budgeting to include their professional fees.

EBMC LEARNING #9:
FOR PEOPLE OF COLOR TO MOVE INTO POSITIONS OF POWER, WHITE ORGANIZATIONS AND WHITE PEOPLE NEED TO MOVE BACKWARD, INTO SUPPORTIVE ROLES.

At EBMC, this principle is not limited to interpersonal and communication dynamics. It speaks to a commitment to create organizational structures, policies, and practices that allow people of color and other marginalized communities to assume power, by leveling the organizational playing field that has traditionally been tilted in favor of those in the dominant culture with white privilege and other forms of unearned privilege.

EBMC LEARNING #10:
DON'T ASK PEOPLE OF COLOR TO DO THE "HEAVY LIFTING" OF EDUCATING WHITE FOLKS.

Like fish presumably unaware that they are swimming in water, white folks are usually unaware of the unconscious bias and racism that is around and within them. Not so for people of color. It is sometimes said that "The slave had to know the master better than the master knew the master, because his life depended on it." People of color usually see white folks' racism even when the white folks are unaware of it.

In diversity efforts, this can lead to white folks expecting to be educated about their unconscious racism by the people of color. But such an "education process" is usually emotionally draining at best, and traumatizing at worst, for the people of color involved.

At EBMC, this has meant that, as often as possible, we have asked white sangha members to engage with other white folks who are uncomfortable with, or are challenging, EBMC's diversity policies and procedures. EBMC also offers an initial class of four to six sessions and a longer intensive program, "White and Awakening in Sangha." Each class is specifically for white individuals. Both programs are led by white people and designed to help participants develop the skills and awareness to support each other's learning and ability to participate in a broadly inclusive sangha.

EBMC Learning #11:
This is hard work for white folks!

Diversity efforts that go beyond "tokenism" to build a truly multicultural community require white practitioners to face the pain of their unconscious bias and racist conditioning. While many know or discover that there is a lot of freedom to be gained through this effort, it can be frightening for some people. Some white folks, to borrow a concept from Buddhist teachings, have "too much dust in their eyes," and may be unwilling to do the sometimes painful work to loosen that conditioning. They may choose to leave, or decline to engage in the first place, rather than change.

Ironically, if no white people are disengaging or expressing distress, the diversity efforts are probably not transformative enough to create a truly multicultural organization, in the eyes of many people of color.

EBMC Learning #12:
Many white people seeking the Dharma are drawn to an authentic multicultural community.

Some have been surprised, despite EBMC's explicit mission to serve communities of color and other underserved communities (see EBMC Learning #2), by the number of white folks who are drawn to the EBMC community. Most of the waiting lists for events that are open to all are predominantly populated by white folks.

These observations lead to the conclusion that EBMC's rapid growth in its first decade has been, in part, because white folks who are exploring the Dharma are very much drawn to multicultural communities.

Appendix 3

East Bay Meditation Center's Agreements for Multicultural Interactions

(Adapted from Visions Inc., "Guidelines for Productive Work Sessions.")

Try It On: Be willing to "try on" new ideas, or ways of doing things that might not be what you prefer or are familiar with.

Practice Self-Focus: Attend to and speak about your own experiences and responses. Do not speak for a whole group or express assumptions about the experience of others.

Understand the Difference between Intent and Impact: Try to understand and acknowledge impact. Denying the impact of something said by focusing on intent is often more destructive than the initial interaction.

Practice "Both/And": When speaking, substitute "and" for "but." This practice acknowledges and honors multiple realities.

Refrain from Blaming or Shaming Self and Others: Practice giving skillful feedback.

Move Up / Move Back: Encourage full participation by all present. Take note of who is speaking and who is not. If you tend to speak often, consider "moving back" and vice versa.

Practice Mindful Listening: Try to avoid planning what you'll say as you listen to others. Be willing to be surprised, to learn something new. Listen with your whole self.

Confidentiality: Take home learnings but don't identify anyone other than yourself, now or later. If you want to follow up with anyone regarding something they said in this session, ask first and respect their wishes.

Right to Pass: You can say "I pass" if you don't wish to speak.

Appendix Four

History of Diversity-Related Events in the Western Insight Meditation Community

AWARENESS OF HISTORY is itself an important mindfulness practice. Here are some of the highlights of the history of diversity and race within the Western Insight Meditation community. (This is not a comprehensive listing.)

Early 1990s   First Insight Meditation daylongs are held for people of color (PoC).

Mid-1990s   Interracial Buddhist Council forms.

Late 1990s   First Insight Meditation residential retreat for PoC is held in New Mexico.
                First Insight Meditation weekly sitting groups are held for women of color, PoC, and their allies.
                First Spirit Rock Diversity Council forms.

1997   New York Insight Meditation Center is established.

1999   First PoC residential retreat is at Spirit Rock.
                Spirit Rock PoC Scholarship program is founded.
                First diversity training is held at Spirit Rock.
                First three Dharma leaders of color graduate from Spirit Rock's Community Dharma Leaders training program.

2000   *Making the Invisible Visible*, the first collection of PoC stories in the Dharma, is published for the international Buddhist teachers conference (http://www.spiritrock .org/document.doc?id=9).

First PoC serves on Spirit Rock board of directors.
Efforts begin to create an East Bay Dharma center in the Bay Area.

2001   Diversity initiative is ratified by Spirit Rock teachers and board.

2002   African American Dharma retreat and conference is held at Spirit Rock.
First multicultural community daylong (with PoCs and allies) is held at Spirit Rock.

2003   First East Coast PoC retreat is sponsored by Insight Meditation Society and New York Insight at Garrison, New York.

2004   Asian American Dharma retreat and conference is held at Spirit Rock.
First meetings are held for Dharma teachers of color in the Bay Area.
Second Community Dharma Leaders program graduates six Dharma leaders of color.

2005   East Coast PoC residential retreat moves to Insight Meditation Society.
First diversity trainings are held for Spirit Rock staff.

2006   Spirit Rock PoC retreat shifts to an all-*dana* retreat for greater accessibility.

2007   East Bay Meditation Center (EBMC) opens in downtown Oakland.
Spirit Rock forms second generation of Diversity Council.

2008   First joint Spirit Rock and San Francisco Zen Center diversity training is held.

2009   EBMC begins its dedicated year-long Dharma study program, *Commit2Dharma,* with demographics of 75 percent PoC and 75 percent LGBTIQ communities.

2010   Spirit Rock and IMS residential retreat teacher training program graduates four Dharma teachers of color.
First residential retreat for multicultural communities is held at Spirit Rock during Dr. Martin Luther King Jr. weekend.
Fourth iteration of Spirit Rock's Community Dharma Leader's training program begins with 40 percent participation from communities of color.

2011   Spirit Rock Teachers Council invites first three teachers of color into membership.

2012   Development begins on teacher training program to increase numbers of Dharma teachers of color in Western Vipassana communities.

2013   International Vipassana teachers conference has its first diversity training.

2015   Theme of International Buddhist teachers conference is race and diversity.
Fifth iteration of Spirit Rock's Community Dharma Leader training program begins with 38 percent participation from communities of color.
"Sacred Tenderness," a ten-day residential retreat, is held with 40 percent PoC, the most diverse demographic of any previous mainstream retreat.
First ten-day silent residential retreat is held for communities of color at the Mountain Hermitage, New Mexico.

2016   Spirit Rock governance groups pass organization-wide diversity equity and inclusion plan.

Spirit Rock conducts three anti-racism trainings including all internal organizational members and invited community members.

Spirit Rock approves and implements a teacher training program with 85 percent participation from communities of color.

IMS approves and implements a teacher training program with majority participation from communities of color.

2017   Teacher training programs begin at Spirit Rock and at IMS, of four years in length, focused upon empowering teachers of color.

East Bay Meditation Center celebrates its tenth anniversary of opening.

First mainstream residential retreat for general public is led and taught by a full team of teachers of color at Spirit Rock.

2018   Twentieth anniversary of the PoC residential retreat is celebrated at Spirit Rock.

Index

About the Author

LARRY YANG, LCSW, MSW, MFA

LARRY YANG teaches meditation retreats nationally and has a special interest in creating access to the Dharma for diverse multicultural communities. Larry has practiced meditation for almost thirty years, with extensive time in Burma and Thailand and a six-month period of ordination as a Buddhist monk under the guidance of Ajahn Tong. Larry is on the Teacher's Council of Spirit Rock Meditation Center and one of the core teachers of both East Bay Meditation Center (Oakland, California) and Insight Community of the Desert (Palm Springs, California). For seven years, he has been part of the coordinating teaching team developing future community meditation teachers in Spirit Rock's Community Dharma Leadership Program. He is on the core training team of Spirit Rock's current Dharma Teacher Training Program. Because of his work in diversifying and creating access to spiritual communities, he was honored by the public in being voted one of the Community Grand Marshals of the 2016 San Francisco LGBTIQ Pride Parade, whose theme that year was "For Racial and Economic Justice."

Larry's article "Directing the Mind towards Practices in Diversity" was included in *Friends on the Path: Living Spiritual Communities*, by Thich Nhat Hanh. His essay "Family Tree Practice" addresses how meditation and contemplative practice have directly influenced his experiences with racism, heterosexism, and oppression; it is part of *Will Yoga and Meditation Really Change My Life?* edited by Stephen Cope. Larry is a coeditor of *Making the Invisible Visible: Healing Racism in Our Buddhist Communities*, a booklet developed for building inclusive communities within spiritual practice. He has contributed to the groundbreaking anthology *Dharma, Color, and Culture,* edited by Hilda Gutiérrez Baldoquín—a volume that provides a unique perspective from practitioners of color across the spectrum of Buddhist traditions.

In addition, Larry is trained as a psychotherapist and a consultant in cultural competency and organizational awareness—giving workshops and presentations in mindfulness and diversity issues. Organizations for which he has provided training and consultation include Spirit Rock Meditation Center; Insight Meditation Society; Insight Community of the Desert; Insight LA; Insight San Diego; UCLA Mindful Awareness Research Center—Certification in Mindfulness Facilitation Program; Mindfulness Institute Professional Teacher Training; San Francisco Zen Center; CompassPoint Nonprofit Services; Sutter County Department of Health Services; Yuba County Department of Health Services; SF HIV CARE Planning Council; San Francisco State University; California Pacific Medical Center; Youth and Family Services—Solano County, California; University of California Davis; California Adult Protective Services; Chinatown Child Development Center; CIIS Center for Somatic Psychotherapy; Maitri Compassionate Care; Public School District 622 of St. Paul, Minnesota; Loyola Marymount University; and San Francisco General Hospital.

What to Read Next from Wisdom Publications

The Buddha's Teaching on Social and Communal Harmony
An Anthology of Discourses from the Pali Canon
Bhikkhu Bodhi
Foreword by His Holiness the Dalai Lama

"Through scholarship and wise discernment, Bhikkhu Bodhi has chosen a set of discourses that uncover and make clear the Buddha's approach to social affairs. A timely and powerful resource for all varieties of peace work, *The Buddha's Teachings on Social and Communal Harmony* provides a direct way to refer to the Buddha's teachings around developing civil society. This is a fantastic support and inspiration for all of us who value and wish to foster a more harmonious world."—Sharon Salzberg, author of *Lovingkindness* and *Real Happiness*

A New Buddhist Path
Enlightenment, Evolution, and Ethics in the Modern World
David R. Loy

"This gripping, important, and ultimately heartening book by David Loy is a wake-up call for Buddhists and everyone else on how to respond to the current multiple crises."—Lila Kate Wheeler, author of *When Mountains Walked*

The Hidden Lamp
Stories from Twenty-Five Centuries of Awakened Women
Edited by Zenshin Florence Caplow and Reigetsu Susan Moon
Foreword by Zoketsu Norman Fischer

"An amazing collection. This book gives the wonderful feel of the sincerity, the great range, and the nobility of the spiritual work that women are doing and have been doing, unacknowledged, for a very long time. An essential and delightful book."—John Tarrant, author of *The Light Inside the Dark: Zen, Soul, and the Spiritual Life*

The Way of Tenderness
Awakening through Race, Sexuality, and Gender
Zenju Earthlyn Manuel
Foreword by Dr. Charles Johnson

"Manuel's teaching is a thought-provoking, much-needed addition to contemporary Buddhist literature."—*Publishers Weekly*

Interconnected
Embracing Life in Our Global Society
The Karmapa, Ogyen Trinley Dorje

"We are now so interdependent that it is in our own interest to take the whole of humanity into account. Hope lies with the generation who belong to the twenty-first century. If they can learn from the past and shape a different future, later this century the world could be a happier, more peaceful, and more environmentally stable place. I am very happy to see in this book the Karmapa Rinpoche taking a lead and advising practical ways to reach this goal."—His Holiness the Dalai Lama

About Wisdom Publications

Wisdom Publications is the leading publisher of classic and contemporary Buddhist books and practical works on mindfulness. To learn more about us or to explore our other books, please visit our website at wisdomexperience.org or contact us at the address below.

Wisdom Publications
132 Perry Street
New York, NY 10014 USA

We are a 501(c)(3) organization, and donations in support of our mission are tax deductible.

Wisdom Publications is affiliated with the Foundation for the Preservation of the Mahayana Tradition (FPMT).